Husn Ara

Table of Contents

Chapter 1: Introduction to Computer Vision....................4

Overview of Computer Vision.......................4

Historical Context and Evolution in Computer Vision ..6

Applications of Computer Vision 11

Autonomous Vehicles in Computer Vision 15

Surveillance Systems in Computer Vision.................20

Augmented Reality (AR) and Virtual Reality (VR) in Computer Vision 24

Chapter 2: Mathematical Foundations...........................32

Linear Algebra in Computer Vision 32

Calculus in Image Processing....................................45

Probability and Statistics..61

Bayesian Inference 63

Markov Random Field...66

Chapter 3: Image Processing Fundamentals................70

Digital Image Representation......................................70

Image Filtering and Enhancement 90

1. Convolution 90

2. Correlation..93

Edge Detection Techniques (Sobel, Canny) 101

1. Sobel Edge Detection......................................101

2. Canny Edge Detection 104

Image Transformation Techniques 107

Fourier Transform 107

Wavelet Transform...114

Chapter 4: Feature Detection and Description............121

Keypoint Detection..121

Feature Descriptors 128

1

Computer Vision:Tools & Algorithms for Analyzing Images
Feature Matching and Correspondence 137

Chapter 5: Image Segmentation 146

Thresholding Techniques 146

Region-Based Segmentation................................. 152

Edge-Based Segmentation.................................... 160

Active Contour Models (Snakes)....................... 167

Semantic and Instance Segmentation 174

Chapter 6: Object Detection and Recognition 181

Traditional Object Detection Methods.................... 181

Deep Learning for Object Detection...................... 186

Object Recognition Techniques 194

Chapter 7: 3D Computer Vision 205

3D Reconstruction from Images 205

Depth Estimation Techniques................................ 213

3D Object Detection and Tracking......................... 232

Chapter 8: Deep Learning in Computer Vision 240

Convolutional Neural Networks (CNNs)................. 240

1. Architecture and Layers of CNNs 240

Advanced Architectures.. 249

Attention Mechanisms and Transformers 257

1. Self-Attention in Vision 257

Generative Models in Computer Vision.................. 266

Chapter 9: Video Analysis and Action Recognition..... 274

Motion Estimation... 274

Video Object Detection and Tracking 283

Action and Activity Recognition............................. 291

Chapter 10: Advanced Topics in Computer Vision 298

Multi-Task Learning in Vision................................ 298

Domain Adaptation and Transfer Learning 306

Explainable AI in Computer Vision......................... 314

Robustness and Adversarial Attacks........................322

Chapter 11: Computer Vision in Industry....................331

Real-Time Computer Vision Systems 331

Autonomous Systems and Robotics 338

Medical Image Analysis 346

Ethical Considerations and Bias in Computer Vision
....354

Chapter 12: Tools and Frameworks 360

OpenCV (Open Source Computer Vision Library)...360

TensorFlow and Keras..362

PyTorch for Computer Vision....................................364

Datasets and Benchmarks..368

Chapter 13: Future Trends and Research Directions..373

AI in Augmented Reality and Virtual Reality............373

Quantum Computing for Computer Vision 376

Continual Learning in Vision 380

Vision for Autonomous Drones 383

The Future of Vision Transformers 391

Chapter 1: Introduction to Computer Vision

Overview of Computer Vision

Computer Vision is a field of artificial intelligence (AI) that enables computers to interpret and make decisions based on visual data from the world, such as images and videos. It is a multidisciplinary domain combining elements of machine learning, image processing, pattern recognition, and computer graphics. The primary goal of computer vision is to replicate the complex capabilities of human vision and apply them to tasks like object detection, image recognition, and video analysis.

Key Objectives of Computer Vision:

1. **Understanding Visual Data**: Extracting meaningful information from images or videos to understand their content.
2. **Object Detection and Recognition**: Identifying and classifying objects within an image or video.
3. **Image Segmentation**: Dividing an image into regions or segments to simplify its analysis.
4. **3D Reconstruction**: Building three-dimensional models from two-dimensional images.
5. **Motion Analysis**: Understanding the movement of objects in a sequence of images or video frames.

6. **Scene Understanding**: Comprehending the broader context of an image, such as recognizing activities or events.

Historical Context and Evolution:

Computer vision has evolved from simple image processing tasks to complex deep learning-based techniques. Early work in the 1960s and 1970s focused on basic image processing algorithms. With advancements in machine learning and neural networks, computer vision has expanded its capabilities to include sophisticated tasks like facial recognition, autonomous driving, and augmented reality.

Applications of Computer Vision:

- **Medical Imaging**: Assisting in diagnostics by analysing medical images (e.g., X-rays, MRIs).
- **Autonomous Vehicles**: Enabling self-driving cars to navigate by recognizing objects and understanding road conditions.
- **Surveillance**: Monitoring security cameras to detect suspicious activities automatically.
- **Retail**: Enhancing customer experience through virtual try-ons, inventory management, and customer behaviour analysis.
- **Agriculture**: Analysing crops for health, yield prediction, and automated harvesting.
- **Augmented Reality (AR) and Virtual Reality (VR)**: Enhancing real-world environments or creating immersive virtual experiences.

Challenges in Computer Vision:

- **Variability**: Handling changes in lighting, perspective, and occlusion that can affect visual data.
- **Scalability**: Processing large amounts of high-resolution data in real-time.
- **Interpretability**: Making AI decisions in computer vision explainable and transparent.

- **Generalization**: Ensuring that models trained on specific datasets perform well in varied real-world conditions.

Future Directions:

The future of computer vision is likely to involve further integration with deep learning, leading to more accurate and efficient models. Emerging technologies such as quantum computing, federated learning, and explainable AI are expected to push the boundaries of what computer vision systems can achieve. Additionally, ethical considerations, including bias reduction and privacy protection, will play a crucial role in the responsible development and deployment of computer vision applications.

Historical Context and Evolution in Computer Vision

Computer Vision has undergone significant transformation since its inception, evolving from simple image processing techniques to complex deep learning models capable of performing sophisticated visual recognition tasks. The journey of computer vision is marked by several key milestones that have shaped the field into what it is today.

1960s - 1970s: The Early Days

- **Foundations of Image Processing**: The origins of computer vision can be traced back to the 1960s, when researchers began exploring the idea of enabling machines to interpret visual data. Initial efforts focused on basic image processing techniques, such as edge detection, image

6

segmentation, and binary image processing. These early algorithms were inspired by human visual perception and were aimed at extracting simple features from images.

- **Roberts' Operator and Edge Detection**: One of the earliest significant developments was the introduction of the Roberts' Cross operator in 1963 by Lawrence Roberts. This operator was one of the first algorithms designed to detect edges in images, laying the groundwork for more advanced feature detection methods.

1980s: The Rise of Computer Vision as a Field

- **Introduction of Feature Extraction**: During the 1980s, computer vision began to emerge as a distinct field of research. The focus shifted from basic image processing to feature extraction and pattern recognition. Researchers developed techniques like the Hough Transform (for detecting lines and shapes) and the Canny edge detector, which became foundational tools in image analysis.

- **Artificial Intelligence and Vision**: The integration of AI concepts into computer vision began to take shape. Researchers started exploring the idea of using AI to interpret visual data, leading to the development of early object recognition systems. The field also saw the introduction of the first vision-based robotic systems, which could perform tasks such as object manipulation based on visual input.

1990s: Statistical Methods and Machine Learning

- **Adoption of Statistical Methods**: The 1990s marked a shift towards statistical methods in computer vision. Techniques like Principal Component Analysis (PCA) were used for dimensionality reduction and face recognition, while Hidden Markov Models (HMMs) found applications in motion tracking and gesture recognition.

- **Emergence of Machine Learning**: The rise of machine learning during this decade had a profound impact on computer vision. Algorithms such as Support Vector Machines (SVMs) and k-Nearest Neighbours (k-NN) were applied to visual recognition tasks, improving the accuracy and generalization of computer vision systems. This period also saw the development of the first large-scale image databases, which provided the data needed to train and test these algorithms.

2000s: The Era of Feature-Based Vision

- **SIFT and SURF**: The early 2000s witnessed the introduction of robust feature detection and description algorithms, such as Scale-Invariant Feature Transform (SIFT) and Speeded-Up Robust Features (SURF). These methods enabled the extraction of distinctive and invariant features from images, which could be used for tasks like object recognition, image stitching, and 3D reconstruction.

- **Viola-Jones Face Detector**: In 2001, Paul Viola and Michael Jones introduced a real-time face detection framework that became one of the most widely used algorithms in computer vision. The Viola-Jones detector was a significant advancement because it combined simple

Husn Ara

features with a cascade classifier to achieve high detection rates at real-time speeds.

2010s: The Deep Learning Revolution

- **Convolutional Neural Networks (CNNs)**: The most significant shift in computer vision occurred with the advent of deep learning, particularly CNNs. Alex Krizhevsky's AlexNet, which won the ImageNet Large Scale Visual Recognition Challenge (ILSVRC) in 2012, demonstrated the power of deep learning in achieving unprecedented accuracy in image classification. This breakthrough led to widespread adoption of CNNs for a variety of computer vision tasks, including object detection, segmentation, and video analysis.

- **Advanced Architectures**: The 2010s saw the development of more sophisticated neural network architectures, such as VGG, ResNet, and Inception, each pushing the boundaries of what could be achieved with deep learning. These architectures were capable of learning hierarchical representations of visual data, leading to significant improvements in performance across a wide range of tasks.

- **Generative Models and Vision**: The introduction of Generative Adversarial Networks (GANs) in 2014 by Ian Goodfellow opened new possibilities in computer vision, particularly in image synthesis, style transfer, and data augmentation. GANs allowed machines to generate realistic images, further expanding the capabilities of AI in creative and artistic domains.

2020s and Beyond: The Future of Computer Vision

- **Vision Transformers and Attention Mechanisms**: The 2020s are witnessing the rise of Vision Transformers (ViTs) and attention-based mechanisms in computer vision. These models, originally designed for natural language processing, have shown remarkable performance in vision tasks by capturing long-range dependencies in images.

- **AI in Edge and Real-Time Systems**: With the increasing demand for real-time vision applications, such as autonomous driving and AR/VR, there is a growing focus on deploying computer vision models on edge devices. Techniques for model compression, quantization, and efficient inference are becoming crucial for enabling AI-driven vision in resource-constrained environments.

- **Ethics and Bias in Vision Systems**: As computer vision systems become more integrated into society, there is a growing emphasis on addressing ethical concerns, including bias, fairness, and privacy. Researchers and practitioners are actively working on developing methodologies to ensure that AI vision systems are transparent, accountable, and equitable.

- **Continual and Lifelong Learning**: The future of computer vision may involve systems that can learn continuously from new data, adapt to changing environments, and retain previously learned knowledge. This approach, known as continual or lifelong learning, aims to create more resilient and flexible vision models that can operate in dynamic real-world scenarios.

Conclusion

The evolution of computer vision has been marked by significant technological advancements, from early image processing techniques to the powerful deep learning models of today. As the field continues to evolve, it holds immense potential for transforming industries and improving human life through applications that were once considered science fiction. The future of computer vision is poised to bring even more innovative solutions, driven by AI and increasingly sophisticated algorithms.

Applications of Computer Vision

Medical Imaging in Computer Vision

Medical Imaging is one of the most impactful applications of computer vision, revolutionizing the field of healthcare by enhancing the ability to diagnose, monitor, and treat medical conditions. By leveraging computer vision techniques, medical imaging allows for the analysis and interpretation of complex medical data, leading to more accurate and efficient patient care.

Overview of Medical Imaging in Computer Vision

Medical imaging involves the creation of visual representations of the interior of a body for clinical analysis and medical intervention. Traditional imaging techniques include X-rays, MRI (Magnetic Resonance Imaging), CT (Computed Tomography) scans, ultrasound, and PET (Positron Emission Tomography) scans. Computer vision enhances these methods by automating the analysis of the images, detecting patterns, and providing insights that might not be visible to the human eye.

Key Applications of Computer Vision in Medical Imaging

1. **Image Segmentation**:
   - **Tumour and Lesion Segmentation**: Computer vision algorithms can automatically segment tumours, lesions, and other abnormalities from medical images, aiding in early diagnosis and treatment planning. For instance, deep learning-based models like U-Net are widely used for segmenting brain tumours in MRI scans.
   - **Organ and Tissue Segmentation**: Segmentation of organs (e.g., lungs, liver, heart) from CT or MRI images is critical for surgical planning, radiotherapy, and disease monitoring.
2. **Image Classification**:
   - **Disease Detection**: Computer vision models are trained to classify images based on the presence of diseases, such as classifying chest X-rays to detect pneumonia, tuberculosis, or COVID-19. Convolutional Neural Networks (CNNs) are commonly used for these classification tasks.
   - **Histopathology**: In digital pathology, computer vision is used to analyze tissue samples, identifying cancerous cells and grading tumors based on their appearance.
3. **Object Detection**:
   - **Polyp Detection in Endoscopy**: Computer vision algorithms detect polyps in endoscopic images, which are essential for preventing and diagnosing colorectal cancer.
   - **Nodule Detection in Lung CT Scans**: Automated detection of lung nodules in CT

scans helps in the early diagnosis of lung cancer, improving patient outcomes.

4. **Image Reconstruction**:
   - **3D Reconstruction of Organs**: Computer vision techniques reconstruct 3D models of organs from 2D medical images, providing a more comprehensive view for diagnosis and treatment. For example, 3D models of the heart from echocardiograms can assist in planning complex surgeries.
   - **Improving Image Quality**: Algorithms are used to enhance the quality of medical images, such as reducing noise in MRI scans or reconstructing high-resolution images from low-resolution data.

5. **Image Registration**:
   - **Aligning Multimodal Images**: Image registration involves aligning images from different modalities (e.g., MRI and PET) or time points to provide a coherent view of the patient's anatomy or disease progression. This is crucial for comparing images in longitudinal studies or integrating information from different imaging techniques.
   - **Deformable Registration**: Deformable image registration adjusts for changes in organ shape or patient positioning between scans, ensuring accurate alignment and comparison.

6. **Quantitative Analysis**:
   - **Volume Measurement**: Computer vision allows for the accurate measurement of organ volumes, tumour sizes, and other anatomical features, which are essential for treatment planning and monitoring disease progression.
   - **Texture Analysis**: Analysing the texture of tissues in medical images can provide insights into disease states, such as distinguishing between benign and malignant tumours based on their texture patterns.

13

Challenges and Considerations

- **Data Quality and Variability**: Medical imaging data often varies in quality due to differences in imaging devices, patient movement, and other factors. Computer vision models need to be robust to these variations.
- **Interpretability**: Ensuring that the decisions made by computer vision models are interpretable by medical professionals is crucial for gaining trust and ensuring the models' clinical applicability.
- **Regulatory and Ethical Issues**: The deployment of computer vision in medical imaging requires adherence to strict regulatory standards to ensure patient safety. Additionally, ethical considerations around data privacy and the potential for bias in AI models must be addressed.

Future Directions

The future of computer vision in medical imaging is likely to involve more personalized and precise approaches to diagnosis and treatment. This includes:

- **Integrating Genomic Data**: Combining imaging data with genomic information to provide personalized treatment plans.
- **Real-Time Analysis**: Developing models that can provide real-time analysis of medical images during procedures, such as guiding surgeons during complex surgeries.
- **AI-Augmented Radiologists**: Instead of replacing radiologists, AI tools will increasingly augment their capabilities, allowing them to focus on more complex cases and make more informed decisions.

Conclusion

Computer vision in medical imaging is transforming healthcare by providing powerful tools for diagnosis, treatment planning, and disease monitoring. As the technology continues to advance, it will play an increasingly central role in delivering high-quality, personalized medical care.

Autonomous Vehicles in Computer Vision

Autonomous vehicles, also known as self-driving cars, represent one of the most advanced and transformative applications of computer vision. By leveraging sophisticated computer vision algorithms, autonomous vehicles can perceive, understand, and navigate complex environments with minimal or no human intervention. This technology is crucial for enabling vehicles to operate safely and efficiently in real-world conditions.

Overview of Computer Vision in Autonomous Vehicles

Computer vision in autonomous vehicles involves the use of cameras, sensors, and AI algorithms to interpret visual data from the vehicle's surroundings. This data is processed to perform tasks such as detecting and recognizing objects (e.g., pedestrians, other vehicles, traffic signs), estimating distances, tracking objects, and making decisions based on the environment.

Key Components of Computer Vision in Autonomous Vehicles

1. **Object Detection and Recognition**:
   - **Pedestrian Detection**: Identifying pedestrians on or near the road is critical for ensuring the safety of autonomous vehicles. Computer vision models, often based on Convolutional Neural Networks (CNNs), are trained to detect pedestrians in various conditions, including day and

night, different weather conditions, and varying postures.

- ○ **Vehicle Detection**: Recognizing other vehicles on the road, including cars, trucks, motorcycles, and bicycles, is essential for collision avoidance and navigation. Advanced models can detect and classify vehicles in different lanes and predict their trajectories.
- ○ **Traffic Sign Recognition**: Autonomous vehicles must recognize and interpret traffic signs (e.g., stop signs, speed limits, yield signs) to adhere to road regulations. Computer vision systems are trained on large datasets of traffic signs to ensure accurate recognition in diverse environments.

2. **Lane Detection and Road Segmentation**:
   - ○ **Lane Marking Detection**: Lane detection involves identifying the boundaries of the road and the lanes within it. This is achieved using computer vision techniques that analyze the road's texture, color, and geometry. Lane detection is crucial for lane-keeping assistance and autonomous lane changes.
   - ○ **Road Segmentation**: Road segmentation involves dividing the road surface from other elements like sidewalks, curbs, and obstacles. Semantic segmentation algorithms, which assign a class label to each pixel in the image, are commonly used to achieve this. This helps the vehicle understand the drivable area and avoid off-road driving.

3. **Object Tracking**:
   - ○ **Dynamic Object Tracking**: In real-time, autonomous vehicles need to track the movement of various objects, such as other vehicles, pedestrians, and cyclists. Object tracking algorithms, often based on Kalman filters or deep learning techniques, predict the future position of these objects,

enabling the vehicle to make informed decisions about speed and direction.

- o **Multi-Object Tracking**: Autonomous vehicles operate in environments with multiple moving objects. Multi-object tracking systems are designed to handle the complexity of tracking numerous entities simultaneously, ensuring that the vehicle can navigate safely in traffic.

4. **Depth Estimation and 3D Perception**:
   - o **Stereo Vision and LIDAR**: Depth estimation is crucial for understanding the spatial relationships between objects and the vehicle. Stereo vision systems use two cameras to capture images from slightly different angles, allowing the vehicle to estimate depth. LIDAR (Light Detection and Ranging) sensors provide accurate 3D maps of the environment by emitting laser pulses and measuring the reflected light.
   - o **3D Object Detection**: Combining depth information with 2D image data, 3D object detection algorithms identify objects and their positions in three-dimensional space. This enables the vehicle to accurately gauge distances and plan maneuvers accordingly.

5. **Sensor Fusion**:
   - o **Combining Multiple Sensors**: Autonomous vehicles rely on multiple sensors, including cameras, LIDAR, radar, and ultrasonic sensors, to gather comprehensive information about their surroundings. Sensor fusion techniques combine data from these different sources to create a more accurate and reliable representation of the environment. This redundancy improves safety and robustness, especially in challenging conditions like low light or adverse weather.
   - o **Improved Decision-Making**: By integrating data from various sensors, the

vehicle can make better decisions, such as when to change lanes, stop for pedestrians, or adjust speed based on traffic conditions.

6. **Scene Understanding and Semantic Segmentation**:
   - ○ **Comprehensive Environment Analysis**: Scene understanding involves analyzing the entire driving environment, including roads, vehicles, pedestrians, and traffic signals. Semantic segmentation plays a key role by classifying each part of the scene (e.g., road, sidewalk, vehicles) to provide context-aware navigation.
   - ○ **Complex Scenarios**: Autonomous vehicles must navigate complex scenarios, such as intersections, roundabouts, and construction zones. Advanced computer vision algorithms are designed to understand these situations and make real-time decisions.

Challenges in Computer Vision for Autonomous Vehicles

- **Variability in Driving Conditions**: Autonomous vehicles must operate in diverse conditions, including different weather, lighting, and traffic situations. Ensuring that computer vision systems perform reliably in all these scenarios is a significant challenge.
- **Real-Time Processing**: Autonomous vehicles require real-time processing of vast amounts of data from sensors and cameras to make immediate decisions. Achieving low-latency, high-accuracy processing is crucial for safety.
- **Edge Cases and Unpredictable Events**: Handling rare and unpredictable events, such as a pedestrian suddenly crossing the road or an animal appearing on the highway, is difficult for computer vision systems. These "edge cases" require the system to be robust and adaptable.

Future Directions

- **Advancements in AI and Deep Learning**: Continued advancements in AI and deep learning will lead to more sophisticated models capable of understanding complex driving environments with greater accuracy and reliability.
- **Improved Sensor Technologies**: Innovations in sensor technology, such as higher-resolution cameras, more precise LIDAR systems, and advanced radar, will enhance the perception capabilities of autonomous vehicles.
- **Regulation and Standardization**: As autonomous vehicles become more widespread, there will be a growing need for regulatory frameworks and standards to ensure safety, interoperability, and public trust.
- **Collaboration with Infrastructure**: Future autonomous vehicles may communicate with smart infrastructure (e.g., traffic lights, road signs) to improve navigation and safety through shared information.

Conclusion

Computer vision is at the heart of autonomous vehicle technology, enabling self-driving cars to perceive, understand, and interact with the world around them. As research and development continue to advance, computer vision will play an increasingly critical role in making autonomous driving a reality, with the potential to transform transportation, reduce accidents, and improve overall mobility.

Surveillance Systems in Computer Vision

Surveillance systems are among the most prominent applications of computer vision, providing enhanced security, monitoring, and analysis capabilities across various domains, including public safety, industrial settings, and residential environments. By leveraging computer vision, surveillance systems can automatically analyze video feeds, detect unusual activities, and provide real-time alerts, thereby improving the efficiency and effectiveness of security operations.

Overview of Computer Vision in Surveillance Systems

Surveillance systems traditionally rely on cameras to capture video footage, which is then monitored by security personnel. Computer vision automates this process by analysing video data to detect, classify, and track objects, recognize faces, and identify suspicious activities without requiring constant human oversight. This reduces the burden on security teams and increases the likelihood of timely responses to security threats.

Key Components of Computer Vision in Surveillance Systems

1. **Object Detection and Tracking**:
    - **Intrusion Detection**: Computer vision algorithms are used to detect unauthorized entries into restricted areas. These systems can distinguish between different types of objects, such as humans, animals, or vehicles, and trigger alerts when an intrusion is detected.
    - **Object Tracking**: After detecting an object, computer vision systems can track

20

its movement across multiple camera feeds. This is essential for following a person's or vehicle's path through a monitored area, providing valuable information for security personnel.

2. **Facial Recognition**:
   - **Identity Verification**: Facial recognition systems can identify individuals by comparing real-time video feeds with a database of known faces. This is used in access control, identifying persons of interest, and detecting known criminals in public spaces.
   - **Crowd Surveillance**: In large public events or gatherings, facial recognition can be employed to monitor crowds for persons of interest, enhancing security by quickly identifying and locating individuals in a crowd.

3. **Behavioural Analysis**:
   - **Anomaly Detection**: Computer vision systems can learn normal patterns of behaviour in a monitored area and detect deviations from these patterns. For example, loitering, running in a normally calm area, or leaving an unattended bag might be flagged as suspicious behaviour.
   - **Violence Detection**: Advanced algorithms can analyse body movements and interactions to detect signs of violent behaviour, such as fights or assaults, and send immediate alerts to security personnel.

4. **License Plate Recognition (LPR)**:
   - **Vehicle Monitoring**: License Plate Recognition systems use computer vision to read vehicle license plates from video feeds. This technology is commonly used for monitoring parking lots, toll booths, and roadways to identify vehicles, enforce regulations, and track vehicles of interest.
   - **Traffic Management**: In addition to security, LPR can be used in traffic

management systems to monitor vehicle flow, identify stolen vehicles, and automate toll collection.

5. **Crowd Counting and Density Estimation**:
   - **Event Monitoring**: Surveillance systems can estimate the number of people in a particular area, which is crucial for managing large events, preventing overcrowding, and ensuring public safety.
   - **Emergency Response**: During emergencies, understanding crowd density can help in planning evacuation routes and deploying resources more effectively.

6. **Integration with IoT and Smart Infrastructure**:
   - **Smart City Applications**: Surveillance systems can be integrated with IoT devices and smart city infrastructure to provide real-time monitoring and control over various urban systems, such as street lighting, traffic signals, and public transportation.
   - **Automated Responses**: Integration with other systems allows for automated responses, such as locking doors, turning on lights, or directing police to a specific location based on detected events.

Challenges in Computer Vision for Surveillance Systems

- **Privacy Concerns**: The widespread use of surveillance systems, especially those involving facial recognition, raises significant privacy issues. Balancing security with individual privacy rights is a major challenge.
- **Data Management**: Surveillance systems generate massive amounts of video data, which must be stored, processed, and analysed efficiently. Managing and securing this data, especially in real-time, is a complex task.
- **Accuracy and Bias**: Ensuring the accuracy of detection and recognition algorithms is crucial,

especially in high-stakes environments. Bias in algorithms, particularly in facial recognition, can lead to false positives or negatives, with serious consequences.

Future Directions

- **AI-Powered Analytics**: Future surveillance systems will increasingly rely on AI to provide more advanced analytics, such as predicting potential security threats based on patterns in behavior or movement.
- **Edge Computing**: To reduce latency and improve real-time processing, surveillance systems will increasingly adopt edge computing, where data is processed closer to the source (e.g., on the camera itself), rather than being sent to a central server.
- **Enhanced Privacy Protections**: As concerns over privacy grow, new techniques such as differential privacy and anonymization of video data will be developed to protect individuals while still providing effective surveillance.
- **Autonomous Surveillance**: Drones and autonomous robots equipped with computer vision could become standard tools in surveillance, capable of monitoring large areas, responding to incidents, and collecting data in situations where it would be unsafe for humans.

Conclusion

Computer vision has significantly advanced the capabilities of surveillance systems, providing automated, intelligent monitoring and analysis that enhances security across various environments. As technology continues to evolve, these systems will become more sophisticated, with improved accuracy, real-time processing, and integration with other smart technologies, while also addressing the ethical and privacy concerns associated with surveillance.

Augmented Reality (AR) and Virtual Reality (VR) in Computer Vision

Augmented Reality (AR) and **Virtual Reality (VR)** are immersive technologies that blend the physical and digital worlds, offering new ways to interact with information, environments, and each other. Computer vision plays a pivotal role in enabling these technologies by providing the ability to interpret and manipulate visual data in real time.

Overview of AR and VR in Computer Vision

- **Augmented Reality (AR)** overlays digital information onto the physical world, enhancing the user's perception and interaction with their environment. Examples include AR apps that display virtual objects in a real-world setting, such as furniture placement tools or AR games like Pokémon GO.
- **Virtual Reality (VR)** creates entirely simulated environments that users can interact with using specialized devices like VR headsets. In VR, users are fully immersed in a digital world, which can range from realistic simulations to fantastical virtual spaces.

Key Components of Computer Vision in AR and VR

1. **Object Recognition and Tracking**:
    - **Marker-Based AR**: In marker-based AR, specific visual markers (e.g., QR codes or images) are recognized by the camera,

and digital content is overlaid on top of these markers. Computer vision algorithms detect and track these markers in real time, ensuring that the digital content stays aligned with the physical world.

- o **Markerless AR**: Markerless AR does not rely on predefined markers but uses features of the environment (e.g., walls, floors, objects) to place and anchor digital content. Advanced computer vision techniques, including SLAM (Simultaneous Localization and Mapping), are used to map the environment and track the user's position within it.

2. **Environment Understanding**:
   - o **Scene Reconstruction**: In both AR and VR, understanding the 3D structure of the environment is crucial. Computer vision techniques such as depth sensing, stereo vision, and photogrammetry are used to create detailed 3D maps of the environment, allowing for accurate placement and interaction with virtual objects.
   - o **Semantic Understanding**: Beyond just mapping the environment, AR systems can use computer vision to recognize and classify objects within the scene (e.g., recognizing a table or chair). This enables more intelligent interactions, such as placing a virtual object on a table or avoiding obstacles in VR.

3. **User Interaction**:
   - o **Gesture Recognition**: In AR and VR, users often interact with digital content using gestures, such as hand movements. Computer vision algorithms analyse video feeds to recognize and interpret these gestures, enabling natural and intuitive control over virtual objects and interfaces.
   - o **Eye Tracking**: Eye-tracking technology is increasingly used in VR to monitor where the user is looking. This allows for foveated

rendering, where only the part of the scene that the user is directly looking at is rendered in high detail, optimizing performance and providing a more immersive experience.

4. **Pose Estimation and Body Tracking**:
   o **Head and Body Tracking in VR**: Accurate tracking of the user's head and body is essential for creating a convincing VR experience. Computer vision algorithms track the position and orientation of the user's head and body in real-time, ensuring that the virtual environment responds correctly to their movements.
   o **Full-Body AR**: In some AR applications, full-body tracking is used to integrate the user's entire body into the AR environment. This can be used for fitness apps, virtual try-ons, or immersive gaming experiences.

5. **Spatial Anchoring and Mapping**:
   o **Anchoring Virtual Objects**: In AR, virtual objects need to remain fixed in the real world as the user moves around. Computer vision techniques are used to create anchors within the physical space, ensuring that digital content remains stable and accurately positioned.
   o **SLAM (Simultaneous Localization and Mapping)**: SLAM is a critical technology in AR, allowing devices to simultaneously map their environment and track their position within it. This enables AR experiences to be more immersive and responsive to the user's movements.

6. **Rendering and Real-Time Graphics**:
   o **Realistic Rendering in AR and VR**: The quality of visual rendering is crucial for immersion. Computer vision techniques are used to ensure that virtual objects are rendered with the correct lighting, shadows, and occlusions, making them appear as natural parts of the environment.

Husn Ara

- ○ **Latency Reduction**: In both AR and VR, minimizing latency is essential for maintaining a seamless experience. Computer vision helps optimize rendering processes and ensures that the virtual content responds instantly to user movements.

Challenges in AR and VR Computer Vision

- **Real-Time Processing**: Both AR and VR require high-speed processing to analyse visual data and render graphics in real-time. Ensuring low latency while maintaining high visual fidelity is a significant challenge.
- **Environmental Variability**: AR systems must operate reliably in diverse and dynamic environments, which can vary in lighting, texture, and layout. Adapting to these changes in real-time is complex.
- **User Comfort**: In VR, issues like motion sickness can arise if the system's tracking or rendering is not perfectly aligned with the user's movements. Ensuring a comfortable experience requires precise and responsive computer vision algorithms.

Future Directions

- **AI-Driven AR/VR**: The integration of AI with AR and VR will enable more intelligent and adaptive systems, capable of understanding complex scenes, predicting user intentions, and providing more personalized experiences.
- **Enhanced Interaction**: Future advancements in computer vision will allow for more natural and immersive interactions in AR and VR, such as more precise gesture recognition, real-time emotion analysis, and more realistic avatars.
- **Mixed Reality (MR)**: The convergence of AR and VR into mixed reality (MR) will create even more Immersive experiences, blending physical and

27

digital worlds seamlessly. Computer vision will be key in achieving this level of integration.

Conclusion

Augmented Reality and Virtual Reality are transforming how we interact with digital content and the world around us. Through advanced computer vision techniques, AR and VR are becoming more immersive, responsive, and accessible, opening up new possibilities in gaming, education, healthcare, and beyond. As these technologies continue to evolve, the role of computer vision will only grow, driving innovation and shaping the future of how we experience both virtual and augmented worlds.

Key Challenges in Computer Vision

Computer vision, the field of study focused on enabling machines to interpret and understand visual information from the world, has made tremendous strides over the past few decades. However, despite significant advancements, several key challenges remain in developing robust and accurate computer vision systems.

1. Data Quality and Quantity

- **Insufficient Data**: High-quality labelled data is essential for training computer vision models, especially for deep learning algorithms. However, in many domains, such as medical imaging or autonomous driving, collecting and labelling large datasets can be costly, time-consuming, and sometimes impractical.
- **Imbalanced Data**: In many real-world applications, datasets are often imbalanced, meaning that certain classes are underrepresented. This can lead to biased models that perform poorly on rare but important cases.
- **Noisy Data**: The presence of noisy or incorrectly labelled data can degrade model performance. Handling noisy data and improving data quality remains a challenge.

2. Generalization and Robustness

- **Domain Shift**: Computer vision models often struggle to generalize well across different environments or conditions not seen during training. For example, a model trained on images captured in daylight may perform poorly on images taken at night or in different weather conditions.
- **Adversarial Attacks**: Computer vision models, especially deep learning-based ones, are vulnerable to adversarial attacks, where small perturbations in the input image can cause the model to make incorrect predictions. Ensuring robustness against such attacks is an ongoing challenge.
- **Overfitting**: Overfitting occurs when a model performs well on training data but fails to generalize to new, unseen data. This is particularly a problem in complex models with large numbers of parameters.

3. Real-Time Processing

- **Computational Complexity**: Many computer vision algorithms, particularly deep learning models, require significant computational resources, making real-time processing challenging. This is a critical issue for applications like autonomous vehicles, where decisions must be made in milliseconds.
- **Latency**: Reducing latency in processing visual data is crucial for real-time applications such as augmented reality (AR), virtual reality (VR), and robotics. Ensuring low-latency processing while maintaining high accuracy is difficult.

4. Interpretability and Explainability

- **Black Box Models**: Many state-of-the-art computer vision models, particularly deep neural networks, operate as "black boxes," making it difficult to understand how they arrive at their decisions. This lack of interpretability can be problematic in critical applications like healthcare or autonomous driving, where understanding the decision-making process is essential.

- **Explainable AI (XAI)**: Developing methods to make computer vision models more interpretable and explainable is an ongoing challenge. Researchers are working on techniques to visualize and explain the features and decisions made by complex models.

5. Scalability and Deployment

- **Scalability**: Scaling computer vision systems to handle large volumes of data in real-world applications is challenging. This includes processing vast amounts of video data in surveillance, social media, and other industries.
- **Deployment in Resource-Constrained Environments**: Deploying computer vision models in resource-constrained environments, such as mobile devices, drones, or embedded systems, requires models that are both efficient in terms of memory and power consumption.

6. Ethical and Privacy Concerns

- **Bias and Fairness**: Computer vision systems can inherit biases present in the training data, leading to unfair or discriminatory outcomes. Addressing and mitigating bias in computer vision models is critical for ensuring fairness and equity.
- **Privacy**: The use of computer vision in surveillance, facial recognition, and other applications raises significant privacy concerns. Balancing the benefits of computer vision technologies with individuals' rights to privacy is a key ethical challenge.

7. Understanding Complex Scenes

- **Contextual Understanding**: While current models can perform object detection and recognition, understanding complex scenes

30

involving multiple objects, interactions, and contextual information remains challenging. For example, accurately interpreting the interactions between pedestrians and vehicles in a crowded urban environment is difficult.

- **3D Scene Understanding**: Understanding and reconstructing 3D scenes from 2D images is still a major challenge. Accurately estimating depth, understanding object shapes, and recognizing objects from different viewpoints are complex tasks.

8. Integration with Other Modalities

- **Multimodal Fusion**: Integrating visual data with other types of data, such as audio, text, or sensor information, to create more comprehensive and accurate models is challenging. This requires effective multimodal fusion techniques that can combine information from different sources in a meaningful way.

Conclusion

While computer vision has made significant progress, many challenges remain in developing systems that are accurate, robust, interpretable, and scalable. Addressing these challenges requires ongoing research and innovation, particularly in areas such as data quality, generalization, real-time processing, and ethical considerations. As these challenges are overcome, the potential applications of computer vision will continue to expand, transforming industries and improving lives.

Chapter 2: Mathematical Foundations

Linear Algebra in Computer Vision

Matrices and Vectors in Computer Vision

Matrices and vectors are fundamental in computer vision for representing and manipulating images, performing transformations, and solving various vision-related tasks. Below, we explore how vectors and matrices are used in computer vision, including code examples to illustrate their applications.

Vectors

Definition: A vector is a one-dimensional array of numbers. In computer vision, vectors can represent pixel values, feature descriptors, or coordinates.

Applications:

- **Image Representation**: Flattening an image matrix into a vector for processing.
- **Feature Vectors**: Representing features extracted from images for tasks like classification or clustering.

Example Code:

```
import numpy as np


# Create a vector representing pixel intensities

vector = np.array([0, 255, 128, 64])


# Operations on vectors

vector_sum = vector + 10   # Increase all pixel values by 10

vector_normalized = vector / 255  # Normalize pixel values


print("Original Vector:", vector)

print("Vector After Addition:", vector_sum)

print("Normalized Vector:", vector_normalized)
```

Matrices

Definition: A matrix is a two-dimensional array of numbers arranged in rows and columns. In computer vision, matrices are commonly used to represent images and perform various transformations.

Applications:

- **Image Representation**: Images are naturally represented as matrices where each element corresponds to a pixel value.
- **Image Transformations**: Applying operations like rotation, scaling, and translation using matrix multiplications.
- **Convolution Operations**: Applying filters to images using convolution matrices.

Example Code:

```python
import numpy as np


# Create a 3x3 matrix representing a grayscale image

image_matrix = np.array([

    [0, 128, 255],

    [64, 192, 128],

    [255, 0, 64]

])


# Apply a transformation (e.g., adding a constant value to all pixels)

transformed_matrix = image_matrix + 50


# Transpose the matrix

transposed_matrix = np.transpose(image_matrix)


print("Original Image Matrix:\n", image_matrix)

print("Transformed Image Matrix:\n", transformed_matrix)

print("Transposed Image Matrix:\n", transposed_matrix)
```

Convolution Operation

Convolution is a key operation in computer vision for filtering images. It involves applying a filter (or kernel) matrix to an image matrix to extract features or perform operations like blurring or edge detection.

Example Code:

```python
from scipy.signal import convolve2d

import numpy as np


# Define a 3x3 image matrix

image_matrix = np.array([

    [1, 2, 3],

    [4, 5, 6],

    [7, 8, 9]

])


# Define a 3x3 filter matrix (e.g., edge detection filter)

filter_matrix = np.array([

    [-1, 0, 1],

    [-1, 0, 1],

    [-1, 0, 1]

])


# Apply convolution
```

```
convolved_matrix       =       convolve2d(image_matrix,
filter_matrix, mode='same')
```

```
print("Image Matrix:\n", image_matrix)
```

```
print("Filter Matrix:\n", filter_matrix)
```

```
print("Convolved Matrix:\n", convolved_matrix)
```

Affine Transformation

Affine transformations (such as rotation, scaling, and translation) are performed using transformation matrices. Here's an example of applying a scaling transformation:

Example Code:

```
import numpy as np
```

```
# Define a 2D point
```

```
point = np.array([1, 2])
```

```
# Define a scaling matrix (scaling by a factor of 2)
```

```
scaling_matrix = np.array([

    [2, 0],

    [0, 2]

])
```

```
# Apply the scaling transformation

scaled_point = np.dot(scaling_matrix, point)


print("Original Point:", point)

print("Scaled Point:", scaled_point)
```

Principal Component Analysis (PCA)

PCA is a dimensionality reduction technique that uses eigenvalues and eigenvectors of the covariance matrix. Here's an example of performing PCA:

Example Code:

```
from sklearn.decomposition import PCA

import numpy as np


# Sample data: 2D points

data = np.array([

    [1, 2],

    [3, 4],

    [5, 6],

    [7, 8]

])


# Perform PCA to reduce to 1D
```

```
pca = PCA(n_components=1)

transformed_data = pca.fit_transform(data)


print("Original Data:\n", data)

print("Transformed Data:\n", transformed_data)

print("PCA Components:\n", pca.components_)

print("Explained Variance Ratio:\n", pca.explained_variance_ratio_)
```

Summary

Matrices and vectors are essential in computer vision for various tasks, including image representation, transformation, and feature extraction. Understanding how to manipulate and apply these mathematical constructs is crucial for developing effective computer vision solutions. The provided code examples illustrate basic operations and applications of matrices and vectors in the context of computer vision.

Eigenvalues and Eigenvectors

Eigenvalues and **eigenvectors** are fundamental concepts in linear algebra with wide-ranging applications in computer vision, machine learning, and data analysis. They provide insight into the structure and behaviour of linear transformations and are used in techniques such as Principal Component Analysis (PCA) and dimensionality reduction.

Definitions

- Eigenvalue: For a square matrix A, an eigenvalue λ is a scalar such that there exists a non-zero vector v (called an eigenvector) for which the matrix equation $Av = \lambda v$ holds. In other words, the action of matrix A on eigenvector v only scales v by λ, without changing its direction.

- Eigenvector: An eigenvector v of a square matrix A is a non-zero vector that satisfies the equation $Av = \lambda v$, where λ is the corresponding eigenvalue. Eigenvectors point in the direction along which the linear transformation acts by stretching or compressing.

38

Mathematical Formulation

Given a square matrix A, the eigenvalue equation is:

$$Av = \lambda v$$

where:

- A is the matrix.
- v is the eigenvector.
- λ is the eigenvalue.

Rearranging the equation, we get:

$$(A - \lambda I)v = 0$$

where I is the identity matrix. To find eigenvalues and eigenvectors, we solve the characteristic polynomial:

$$\det(A - \lambda I) = 0$$

Example Code

Here's how you can compute eigenvalues and eigenvectors using Python with NumPy:

import numpy as np

Define a square matrix

A = np.array([

   [4, 1],

   [2, 3]

])

Compute eigenvalues and eigenvectors

eigenvalues, eigenvectors = np.linalg.eig(A)

```
print("Matrix A:\n", A)

print("Eigenvalues:", eigenvalues)

print("Eigenvectors:\n", eigenvectors)



# Verify the result: A * v should be equal to lambda * v for
each eigenvalue/eigenvector pair

for i in range(len(eigenvalues)):

    eigenvalue = eigenvalues[i]

    eigenvector = eigenvectors[:, i]

    Av = np.dot(A, eigenvector)

    lambda_v = eigenvalue * eigenvector

    print(f"\nEigenvalue: {eigenvalue}")

    print("A * v:\n", Av)

    print("Lambda * v:\n", lambda_v)

    print("Difference:", np.allclose(Av, lambda_v))
```

Explanation

1. **Matrix Definition**: Define a square matrix AAA.
2. **Compute Eigenvalues and Eigenvectors**: Use NumPy's np.linalg.eig function to compute the eigenvalues and eigenvectors.
3. **Verification**: For each eigenvalue and eigenvector pair, verify the eigenvalue equation $Av=\lambda vAv = \lambda vAv=\lambda v$.

Applications in Computer Vision

40

1. **Principal Component Analysis (PCA)**:
    - PCA uses eigenvalues and eigenvectors to reduce the dimensionality of data by projecting it onto the directions (principal components) with the highest variance. The eigenvectors correspond to these principal components, and the eigenvalues indicate the amount of variance captured.
2. **Image Compression**:
    - Techniques such as Singular Value Decomposition (SVD) for image compression involve eigenvalues and eigenvectors to approximate images with fewer components, reducing storage requirements while preserving important features.
3. **Face Recognition**:
    - Eigenfaces is a method for face recognition that uses PCA to find eigenvectors (eigenfaces) of face images. These eigenfaces capture the most significant features of faces and can be used to recognize individuals.
4. **Dimensionality Reduction**:
    - In various computer vision tasks, dimensionality reduction techniques rely on eigenvalues and eigenvectors to simplify data while preserving essential information, improving computational efficiency and performance.

Conclusion

Eigenvalues and eigenvectors are essential in understanding and applying linear transformations in computer vision and data analysis. They provide valuable insights into the structure of matrices and are used in various algorithms for dimensionality reduction, image compression, and feature extraction. The provided code demonstrates how to compute and verify eigenvalues and eigenvectors using Python, offering a practical approach to applying these concepts in real-world scenarios.

Singular Value Decomposition (SVD)

Singular Value Decomposition (SVD) is a powerful matrix factorization technique used in various fields such as image processing, data compression, and machine learning. It decomposes a matrix into three other matrices, revealing important properties of the original matrix.

Definition

For a given matrix A of size $m \times n$, SVD decomposes it into three matrices:

$$A = U\Sigma V^T$$

where:

- U: An $m \times m$ orthogonal matrix containing the left singular vectors.
- Σ: An $m \times n$ diagonal matrix containing the singular values.
- V^T: An $n \times n$ orthogonal matrix containing the right singular vectors (transposed).

Mathematical Formulation

1. Left Singular Vectors (U): Columns of U are orthonormal eigenvectors of AA^T.
2. Singular Values (Σ): Diagonal entries of Σ are the square roots of the eigenvalues of $A^T A$ (they represent the "strength" of the corresponding singular vectors).
3. Right Singular Vectors (V): Columns of V are orthonormal eigenvectors of $A^T A$.

Applications

1. **Dimensionality Reduction**: SVD is used in techniques like Principal Component Analysis (PCA) to reduce the dimensionality of data while retaining important features.
2. **Image Compression**: By keeping only the largest singular values, SVD can approximate the original image with fewer components, achieving compression.
3. **Noise Reduction**: In image processing, SVD helps to filter out noise by reconstructing an approximation of the image with significant singular values only.

Example Code

Here's how to perform SVD in Python using NumPy:

```python
import numpy as np


# Define a matrix A

A = np.array([

    [1, 2, 3],

    [4, 5, 6],

    [7, 8, 9]

])


# Perform Singular Value Decomposition

U, Sigma, VT = np.linalg.svd(A)


# Convert Sigma to a diagonal matrix

Sigma_matrix = np.zeros((A.shape[0], A.shape[1]))

Sigma_matrix[:len(Sigma), :len(Sigma)] = np.diag(Sigma)


print("Original Matrix A:\n", A)

print("Left Singular Vectors (U):\n", U)

print("Singular Values (Sigma):\n", Sigma)

print("Right Singular Vectors Transposed (VT):\n", VT)
```

print("Reconstructed Matrix A using SVD:\n", np.dot(U, np.dot(Sigma_matrix, VT)))

Explanation

1. Matrix Definition: Define a matrix A to decompose.

2. Compute SVD: Use NumPy's `np.linalg.svd` function to compute U, Σ, and V^T.

3. Reconstruct Matrix: Verify the decomposition by reconstructing the original matrix from U, Σ, and V^T.

Applications in Computer Vision

1. **Image Compression**: By approximating an image matrix using only the largest singular values, SVD reduces the image's storage requirements while preserving essential features. This technique is widely used for compressing and storing images efficiently.

2. **Noise Reduction**: In image processing, SVD helps to remove noise by reconstructing images from the dominant singular values and vectors, filtering out the less significant components that may represent noise.

3. **Feature Extraction**: In machine learning and computer vision, SVD helps in feature extraction by identifying the most significant components in the data, which can be used for further analysis or model training.

4. **Dimensionality Reduction**: SVD is used in dimensionality reduction techniques, where the goal is to reduce the number of features while retaining as much variance as possible. This is useful in tasks like face recognition, where reducing the dimensionality of face images can improve computational efficiency and performance.

Conclusion

Singular Value Decomposition (SVD) is a versatile matrix factorization technique with a wide range of applications in computer vision, data analysis, and machine learning. It provides insights into the structure of matrices and allows for dimensionality reduction, image compression, and noise reduction. The provided code demonstrates how to perform and verify SVD in Python, offering a practical approach to leveraging this powerful tool in various applications.

Calculus in Image Processing

Gradients and Edge Detection

Gradients and **edge detection** are fundamental concepts in image processing and computer vision. They are used to detect changes in intensity and highlight boundaries within images. These techniques are crucial for various tasks such as object detection, image segmentation, and feature extraction.

Gradients

Definition:

In the context of images, the gradient represents the rate of change in intensity at each point in the image. The gradient vector points in the direction of the steepest ascent in intensity, and its magnitude indicates the rate of change.

- **Gradient**: A vector that points in the direction of the greatest rate of increase of intensity in an image. It is often calculated using the first derivatives of the image intensity function.

Applications:

- **Edge Detection**: Gradients are used to identify edges where there is a significant change in intensity.
- **Image Segmentation**: Helps in separating objects from the background by detecting boundaries.

Example Code:

```
import numpy as np

import matplotlib.pyplot as plt

from scipy.ndimage import sobel


# Load or create an example image (grayscale)

image = np.array([

    [10, 20, 30, 40],

    [50, 60, 70, 80],

    [90, 100, 110, 120],

    [130, 140, 150, 160]

], dtype=float)


# Compute gradients using Sobel operator

gradient_x = sobel(image, axis=0)   # Gradient in x
direction

gradient_y = sobel(image, axis=1)   # Gradient in y
direction


# Compute magnitude and direction of the gradient

gradient_magnitude   =   np.sqrt(gradient_x**2   +
gradient_y**2)
```

```
gradient_direction = np.arctan2(gradient_y, gradient_x) #
Direction of the gradient


print("Gradient in X direction:\n", gradient_x)

print("Gradient in Y direction:\n", gradient_y)

print("Gradient Magnitude:\n", gradient_magnitude)

print("Gradient Direction:\n", gradient_direction)


# Plot results

fig, axes = plt.subplots(1, 4, figsize=(15, 5))

axes[0].imshow(image, cmap='gray')

axes[0].set_title('Original Image')

axes[1].imshow(gradient_x, cmap='gray')

axes[1].set_title('Gradient X')

axes[2].imshow(gradient_y, cmap='gray')

axes[2].set_title('Gradient Y')

axes[3].imshow(gradient_magnitude, cmap='gray')

axes[3].set_title('Gradient Magnitude')


for ax in axes:

    ax.axis('off')


plt.tight_layout()

plt.show()
```

Edge Detection

Definition:

Computer Vision:Tools & Algorithms for Analyzing Images
Edge detection is a technique used to identify the boundaries of objects within an image. It relies on finding points where the image intensity changes significantly, which typically correspond to edges.

- **Edge**: A significant change in intensity or color that defines the boundary of an object.

Common Edge Detection Operators:

1. **Sobel Operator**: Computes the gradient of the image intensity at each pixel, emphasizing edges in both the horizontal and vertical directions.
2. **Canny Edge Detector**: A multi-stage algorithm that detects edges by finding areas of the image with rapid intensity changes and suppressing noise.

Example Code Using Sobel Operator:

```
import numpy as np

import matplotlib.pyplot as plt

from scipy.ndimage import sobel


# Load or create an example image (grayscale)

image = np.array([

    [10, 20, 30, 40],

    [50, 60, 70, 80],

    [90, 100, 110, 120],

    [130, 140, 150, 160]

], dtype=float)
```

```python
# Compute gradients using Sobel operator

gradient_x = sobel(image, axis=0)   # Gradient in x
direction

gradient_y = sobel(image, axis=1)   # Gradient in y
direction


# Compute magnitude of the gradient

gradient_magnitude    =    np.sqrt(gradient_x**2    +
gradient_y**2)


# Plot results

fig, axes = plt.subplots(1, 3, figsize=(15, 5))

axes[0].imshow(image, cmap='gray')

axes[0].set_title('Original Image')

axes[1].imshow(gradient_x, cmap='gray')

axes[1].set_title('Gradient X')

axes[2].imshow(gradient_y, cmap='gray')

axes[2].set_title('Gradient Y')


plt.tight_layout()

plt.show()
```

```
# Display the gradient magnitude as edge detection result

plt.imshow(gradient_magnitude, cmap='gray')

plt.title('Edge Detection using Sobel Operator')

plt.axis('off')

plt.show()
```

Example Code Using Canny Edge Detector:

```
from skimage import feature
import numpy as np
import matplotlib.pyplot as plt

# Load or create an example image (grayscale)
image = np.array([
    [10, 20, 30, 40],
    [50, 60, 70, 80],
    [90, 100, 110, 120],
    [130, 140, 150, 160]
], dtype=float)

# Compute edges using the Canny edge detector
edges = feature.canny(image)

# Plot results
plt.figure(figsize=(8, 8))
```

```
plt.subplot(1, 2, 1)

plt.imshow(image, cmap='gray')

plt.title('Original Image')

plt.axis('off')


plt.subplot(1, 2, 2)

plt.imshow(edges, cmap='gray')

plt.title('Edges using Canny')

plt.axis('off')


plt.show()
```

Explanation

1. **Gradient Calculation**: Compute gradients in the x and y directions using the Sobel operator, which highlights edges by detecting changes in intensity.
2. **Edge Detection**: Use the gradient magnitude to identify edges in the image, or apply the Canny edge detector for more sophisticated edge detection.
3. **Visualization**: Plot the original image, gradients, and edge detection results to visualize the effects of these techniques.

Applications in Computer Vision

1. **Object Detection**: Edge detection helps in identifying object boundaries, which is crucial for object recognition and tracking.
2. **Image Segmentation**: Detecting edges is often the first step in segmenting different regions of an image, such as separating objects from the background.
3. **Feature Extraction**: Edges are used to extract features that are important for various computer

vision tasks, including image classification and object detection.

Conclusion

Gradients and edge detection are essential techniques in image processing and computer vision. Gradients provide information about changes in intensity, while edge detection identifies boundaries within images. These methods are used in a wide range of applications, from object recognition to image segmentation, and are fundamental tools in the computer vision toolkit. The provided code examples demonstrate how to compute and visualize gradients and perform edge detection using both the Sobel operator and the Canny edge detector.

Optimization Techniques

Optimization techniques are essential for improving the performance of machine learning models by minimizing or maximizing objective functions. They are used to find the best parameters for models, improve accuracy, and enhance efficiency. Here, we cover several common optimization techniques used in machine learning and provide example code for each.

1. Gradient Descent

Definition: Gradient Descent is an iterative optimization algorithm used to minimize a loss function by updating the parameters in the direction of the negative gradient. It's commonly used in training machine learning models.

Mathematical Formulation:

Given a loss function $J(\theta)$ with parameters θ, the update rule for gradient descent is:

$$\theta = \theta - \alpha \nabla J(\theta)$$

where:

- α is the learning rate.
- $\nabla J(\theta)$ is the gradient of the loss function with respect to θ.

Example Code:

```python
import numpy as np


# Define the loss function and its gradient

def loss_function(x):

    return (x - 2)**2


def gradient(x):

    return 2 * (x - 2)


# Gradient Descent parameters

learning_rate = 0.1

iterations = 100

x = 0  # Initial guess


# Gradient Descent algorithm

for i in range(iterations):

    grad = gradient(x)

    x = x - learning_rate * grad

    if i % 10 == 0:

        print(f"Iteration {i}: x = {x}, loss = {loss_function(x)}")
```

```
print(f"Optimal value: x = {x}, loss = {loss_function(x)}")
```

2. Stochastic Gradient Descent (SGD)

Definition: Stochastic Gradient Descent is a variant of gradient descent where the update is performed using a single or a few training examples at a time, rather than the entire dataset.

Mathematical Formulation:

For a single training example (x_i, y_i), the update rule is:

$$\theta = \theta - \alpha \nabla J(\theta; x_i, y_i)$$

Example Code:

```
import numpy as np
```

```
# Define the loss function and its gradient
```

```
def loss_function(x):
    return (x - 2)**2
```

```
def gradient(x):
    return 2 * (x - 2)
```

```
# Stochastic Gradient Descent parameters
```

```
learning_rate = 0.1
```

iterations = 100

x = 0 # Initial guess

Stochastic Gradient Descent algorithm

for i in range(iterations):

  # Simulate using one training example

  grad = gradient(x)

  x = x - learning_rate * grad

  if i % 10 == 0:

    print(f"Iteration {i}: x = {x}, loss = {loss_function(x)}")

print(f"Optimal value: x = {x}, loss = {loss_function(x)}")

3. Momentum

Definition: Momentum is an optimization technique that helps accelerate gradient descent by using a moving average of gradients. It helps to navigate along the relevant direction and dampen oscillations.

Mathematical Formulation:

The update rule with momentum is:

$$v = \beta v + \alpha \nabla J(\theta)$$
$$\theta = \theta - v$$

where v is the velocity, β is the momentum term, and α is the learning rate.

Example Code:

```python
import numpy as np


# Define the loss function and its gradient

def loss_function(x):

    return (x - 2)**2


def gradient(x):

    return 2 * (x - 2)


# Momentum parameters

learning_rate = 0.1

beta = 0.9

iterations = 100

x = 0  # Initial guess

v = 0  # Initial velocity


# Momentum algorithm

for i in range(iterations):

    grad = gradient(x)

    v = beta * v + learning_rate * grad

    x = x - v
```

```
if i % 10 == 0:

    print(f"Iteration {i}: x = {x}, loss = {loss_function(x)}")
```

```
print(f"Optimal value: x = {x}, loss = {loss_function(x)}")
```

4. Adam Optimization

Definition: Adam (Adaptive Moment Estimation) is an advanced optimization algorithm that combines the advantages of two other extensions of gradient descent: AdaGrad and RMSProp. It adapts the learning rate for each parameter based on estimates of first and second moments of gradients.

Mathematical Formulation:

Adam updates parameters as follows:

$$m_t = \beta_1 m_{t-1} + (1 - \beta_1)\nabla J(\theta)$$
$$v_t = \beta_2 v_{t-1} + (1 - \beta_2)(\nabla J(\theta))^2$$
$$\hat{m}_t = \frac{m_t}{1-\beta_1^t}$$
$$\hat{v}_t = \frac{v_t}{1-\beta_2^t}$$
$$\theta = \theta - \alpha\frac{\hat{m}_t}{\sqrt{\hat{v}_t}+\epsilon}$$

where m_t and v_t are the first and second moment estimates. β_1 and β_2 are decay rates, and ϵ is a small constant to prevent division by zero.

Example Code:

```python
import numpy as np


# Define the loss function and its gradient
def loss_function(x):
    return (x - 2)**2


def gradient(x):
```

```
    return 2 * (x - 2)


# Adam parameters
learning_rate = 0.1
beta1 = 0.9
beta2 = 0.999
epsilon = 1e-8
iterations = 100
x = 0  # Initial guess
m = 0  # Initial first moment
v = 0  # Initial second moment
m_hat = 0  # Bias-corrected first moment
v_hat = 0  # Bias-corrected second moment


# Adam algorithm
for t in range(1, iterations + 1):
    grad = gradient(x)
    m = beta1 * m + (1 - beta1) * grad
    v = beta2 * v + (1 - beta2) * grad**2
    m_hat = m / (1 - beta1**t)
    v_hat = v / (1 - beta2**t)
    x = x - learning_rate * m_hat / (np.sqrt(v_hat) + epsilon)
    if t % 10 == 0:
        print(f"Iteration {t}: x = {x}, loss = {loss_function(x)}")


print(f"Optimal value: x = {x}, loss = {loss_function(x)}")
```

5. Newton's Method

Definition: Newton's Method is a second-order optimization technique that uses the Hessian matrix (second derivatives) to find the root of the function. It can converge faster than first-order methods if the function is well-behaved.

Mathematical Formulation:

The update rule is:

$$\theta = \theta - H^{-1}\nabla J(\theta)$$

where H is the Hessian matrix.

Example Code:

```python
import numpy as np


# Define the loss function, its gradient, and Hessian matrix
def loss_function(x):
    return (x - 2)**2


def gradient(x):
    return 2 * (x - 2)


def hessian(x):
    return np.array([[2]])


# Newton's Method parameters
iterations = 10
```

```
x = 0  # Initial guess


# Newton's Method algorithm

for i in range(iterations):

    grad = gradient(x)

    H = hessian(x)

    x = x - np.linalg.inv(H) @ grad

    if i % 1 == 0:

        print(f"Iteration {i}: x = {x}, loss = {loss_function(x)}")


print(f"Optimal value: x = {x}, loss = {loss_function(x)}")
```

Summary

- **Gradient Descent**: Updates parameters in the direction of the negative gradient to minimize the loss function.
- **Stochastic Gradient Descent (SGD)**: Uses individual training examples for updates, making it suitable for large datasets.
- **Momentum**: Accelerates gradient descent by considering past gradients, which helps in navigating along the relevant direction.
- **Adam Optimization**: Combines the benefits of AdaGrad and RMSProp, adapting learning rates based on first and second moments of gradients.
- **Newton's Method**: Utilizes second-order derivatives (Hessian matrix) to find parameter updates, potentially achieving faster convergence.

These optimization techniques are crucial for training machine learning models effectively, each offering different advantages depending on the problem and dataset.

Husn Ara
Probability and Statistics

Probability and Statistics is a branch of mathematics that deals with the analysis of random events and data. It provides tools to quantify uncertainty, model randomness, and make inferences based on data. Here's a brief overview of both areas:

1. Probability:

Probability deals with the likelihood of events occurring. It provides a framework for quantifying how likely or unlikely events are.

- **Basic Concepts:**
    - **Experiment:** A process that leads to an outcome (e.g., rolling a die).
    - **Sample Space (S):** The set of all possible outcomes of an experiment (e.g., {1, 2, 3, 4, 5, 6} for a die).
    - **Event (E):** A subset of the sample space, i.e., one or more outcomes (e.g., getting an even number).

- **Probability of an Event (P(E)):** A number between 0 and 1 that represents how likely an event is to occur, defined as:

$$P(E) = \frac{\text{Number of favorable outcomes}}{\text{Total number of outcomes}}$$

- **Complementary Events:** The probability of an event not occurring is 1 minus the probability of it occurring.

$$P(\text{not } E) = 1 - P(E)$$

- **Conditional Probability (P(A|B)):** The probability of event A occurring given that event B has occurred.

$$P(A|B) = \frac{P(A \cap B)}{P(B)}$$

- **Independent Events:** Two events are independent if the occurrence of one does not affect the probability of the other. For independent events, $P(A \cap B) = P(A)P(B)$.

- **Probability Distributions:**
  - **Discrete Probability Distributions:** Deals with finite or countable sample spaces (e.g., Binomial, Poisson distributions).
  - **Continuous Probability Distributions:** Deals with continuous sample spaces (e.g., Normal, Exponential distributions).

2. Statistics:

Statistics is the study of collecting, analyzing, interpreting, and presenting data.

- **Descriptive Statistics:**
  - **Measures of Central Tendency:** Mean, median, and mode describe the central point of a data set.
  - **Measures of Dispersion:** Variance, standard deviation, and range show how spread out the data is.
- **Inferential Statistics:**

- o **Population vs. Sample:** A population is the entire set of individuals or items, while a sample is a subset of the population.
- o **Hypothesis Testing:** A method of making decisions based on data, usually by testing whether a certain hypothesis about a population parameter is true.
- o **Confidence Intervals:** A range of values that is likely to contain the population parameter with a certain level of confidence.
- o **p-value:** A measure that helps in hypothesis testing. A small p-value (typically < 0.05) indicates strong evidence against the null hypothesis.
- **Common Distributions:**
  - o **Normal Distribution:** A bell-shaped distribution that is symmetric around the mean.
  - o **t-Distribution:** Used when the sample size is small, and the population standard deviation is unknown.
  - o **Chi-Square Distribution:** Often used in hypothesis testing for categorical data.

These tools from probability and statistics are widely used in fields such as science, engineering, economics, and social sciences to model uncertainty, analyse data, and draw conclusions.

Bayesian Inference

Bayesian Inference is a method of statistical inference in which Bayes' theorem is used to update the probability of a hypothesis as more evidence or data becomes available. It contrasts with frequentist inference, where probabilities are interpreted strictly in terms of long-run frequencies of events.

Key Concepts in Bayesian Inference:

1. **Bayes' Theorem:** The foundation of Bayesian inference is Bayes' theorem, which relates the conditional probability of an event given another event. For a hypothesis H and data D, Bayes' theorem is expressed as:

$$P(H|D) = \frac{P(D|H)P(H)}{P(D)}$$

Where:

- $P(H|D)$ is the **posterior probability**: the probability of the hypothesis H given the data D.

- $P(D|H)$ is the **likelihood**: the probability of the data D given the hypothesis H is true.

- $P(H)$ is the **prior probability**: the initial probability of the hypothesis before considering the data.

- $P(D)$ is the **marginal likelihood** (or evidence): the total probability of the data under all possible hypotheses.

2. **Prior, Likelihood, and Posterior:**

- **Prior:** This reflects our initial belief about the hypothesis before we observe any data. It can be subjective or based on past experience.

- **Likelihood:** This tells us how likely the observed data is, assuming the hypothesis is true.

- **Posterior:** This is the updated belief about the hypothesis after observing the data, computed using Bayes' theorem.

3. **Updating Beliefs:** In Bayesian inference, the prior is updated into the posterior as new data is collected. Each new piece of data modifies the prior belief, refining the hypothesis. The process can be repeated as more data becomes available, making Bayesian inference a dynamic process of learning from data.

4. **Marginal Likelihood:** The denominator $P(D)$, also called the evidence, is computed by integrating over all possible hypotheses. For a set of possible hypotheses $H_1, H_2, \ldots$, the marginal likelihood is:

$$P(D) = \sum P(D|H_i)P(H_i)$$

Example of Bayesian Inference:

Imagine a medical test for a disease that has a 95% accuracy. Let:

- H be the event that a person has the disease.
- D be the event of a positive test result.

The test's sensitivity (true positive rate) is 95%, and the specificity (true negative rate) is 90%. Suppose the prior probability that a randomly chosen person has the disease is 1% (i.e., $P(H) = 0.01$).

Using Bayes' theorem, the posterior probability that a person has the disease given a positive test result is:

$$P(H|D) = \frac{P(D|H)P(H)}{P(D|H)P(H) + P(D|\neg H)P(\neg H)}$$

Here:

- $P(D|H) = 0.95$ (test correctly identifies those with the disease).
- $P(D|\neg H) = 0.10$ (false positive rate).
- $P(H) = 0.01$.
- $P(\neg H) = 0.99$.

After calculation, this would yield the updated probability that the person actually has the disease after receiving a positive test result, which would typically be much lower than expected, highlighting the importance of prior probabilities.

Advantages of Bayesian Inference:

1. **Flexibility with Prior Knowledge:** It incorporates prior information and allows for its formal updating as new data becomes available.
2. **Dynamic Learning:** It naturally accommodates the idea of learning from data and refining beliefs.
3. **Probabilistic Interpretations:** Bayesian inference provides direct probabilistic interpretations for parameters and models, such as credible intervals for parameter estimates.

Disadvantages of Bayesian Inference:

1. **Choice of Prior:** Selecting the prior can sometimes be subjective, which may influence the results.
2. **Computational Complexity:** Bayesian methods, especially for complex models, can be computationally intensive and require

sophisticated numerical methods like Markov Chain Monte Carlo (MCMC).

Bayesian inference is used in various fields like machine learning, medical decision-making, and economics, where prior information can be integrated into the model and updated with new evidence.

Markov Random Field

A **Markov Random Field (MRF)** is a type of probabilistic graphical model that represents the dependencies between random variables using an undirected graph. MRFs are used in various areas, such as computer vision, image processing, natural language processing, and statistical physics, to model the joint distribution of variables that have local dependencies.

Key Concepts of Markov Random Fields:

1. **Undirected Graph:** In a Markov Random Field, the relationships between random variables are represented by an undirected graph. Each node in the graph corresponds to a random variable, and edges between nodes represent direct probabilistic dependencies.

2. **Markov Property:** MRFs satisfy the **Markov property**, which means that each variable is conditionally independent of all other variables given its neighbors in the graph. If a variable X_i is connected only to a set of neighbors $N(X_i)$, then X_i is conditionally independent of all other variables in the graph given $N(X_i)$.

   This property can be mathematically expressed as:

   $$P(X_i|X_{\{j \neq i\}}) = P(X_i|N(X_i))$$

   where $X_{\{j \neq i\}}$ represents all other variables except X_i, and $N(X_i)$ represents the set of neighbors of X_i.

3. **Clique Factorization:** The joint probability distribution of all variables in an MRF can be factorized in terms of cliques, which are fully connected subsets of nodes in the graph. The Hammersley-Clifford theorem states that the joint distribution of an MRF can be represented as a product of **potential functions** (or clique potentials) defined over these cliques:

$$P(X_1, X_2, \ldots, X_n) = \frac{1}{Z} \prod_{C \in \mathcal{C}} \phi_C(X_C)$$

Where:

- $X_1, X_2, \ldots, X_n$ are the random variables.
- $\mathcal{C}$ represents the set of cliques in the graph.
- $\phi_C(X_C)$ is the potential function over clique C, representing the interactions among the variables in that clique.
- Z is the **partition function**, which normalizes the distribution to ensure it sums to 1:

$$Z = \sum_X \prod_{C \in \mathcal{C}} \phi_C(X_C)$$

1. **Local and Global Consistency:** In MRFs, local properties (dependencies among neighbours) extend to global consistency over the entire graph due to the undirected nature of the model. As long as local conditional probabilities are satisfied, the entire joint distribution can be determined.

Types of Markov Random Fields:

There are two common types of Markov Random Fields:

1. **Discrete MRF:** The random variables in the graph take discrete values (e.g., pixel labels in image segmentation).
2. **Continuous MRF:** The random variables take continuous values (e.g., pixel intensities in image processing).

Applications of Markov Random Fields:

MRFs are commonly used in areas where spatial or structural dependencies exist between variables. Some notable applications include:

1. **Image Processing and Computer Vision:**
    - **Image Denoising:** MRFs can model the relationships between neighbouring pixels to smooth out noise while preserving important structures like edges.
    - **Image Segmentation:** MRFs are used to model the spatial dependencies between pixel labels in tasks where pixels need to be grouped based on similarity.
2. **Statistical Physics:** MRFs have their origins in statistical physics, where they are used to model systems of interacting particles, such as in the Ising model (a special type of MRF used to describe ferromagnetism).
3. **Natural Language Processing:** MRFs can be applied in NLP for tasks like part-of-speech tagging, where the probability of a word's tag depends on its neighbours.
4. **Machine Learning:** MRFs are used in machine learning to model dependencies between features in classification or regression problems.

Relation to Other Models:

- **Markov Chains:** A Markov chain is a special case of an MRF, where the graph is a simple chain, and each node depends only on its immediate predecessor and successor.
- **Conditional Random Fields (CRFs):** CRFs are an extension of MRFs where the goal is to model the conditional distribution of output variables given observed input data. They are widely used in structured prediction tasks, like sequence labelling.

Advantages of MRFs:

1. **Modelling Dependencies:** MRFs are effective in modelling systems where variables are locally

dependent but not necessarily dependent on distant variables.

2. **Undirected Graph Structure:** The undirected graph structure allows for more flexibility in modelling symmetric relationships between variables, unlike directed models (e.g., Bayesian Networks).

Challenges of MRFs:

1. **Computational Complexity:** The inference and learning tasks in MRFs, such as calculating the partition function or marginal probabilities, are computationally expensive, especially for large graphs.
2. **Parameter Estimation:** Estimating the potential functions can be difficult, and requires sophisticated methods like Gibbs sampling, Markov Chain Monte Carlo (MCMC), or variational methods.

Markov Random Fields provide a powerful framework for modelling complex dependencies in various fields, especially in domains where spatial or local interactions are important.

Chapter 3: Image Processing Fundamentals

Digital Image Representation

Digital Image Representation refers to how images are stored and processed in digital form, allowing computers and other digital devices to display, manipulate, and analyze them. In digital images, visual information is captured as a grid of tiny, discrete units called **pixels**, each holding a specific value that represents color or intensity.

Key Components of Digital Image Representation:

1. **Pixels:**
   - **Pixel (Picture Element):** The smallest unit in a digital image. Each pixel contains information about the color or intensity of a tiny portion of the image. The number of pixels in an image defines its resolution.
   - **Resolution:** The width and height of an image in terms of pixels (e.g., 1920x1080). Higher resolution means more pixels, resulting in better image detail.
2. **Bit Depth:**

- o **Bit Depth:** Refers to the number of bits used to represent the color of a pixel. It determines the range of colors or shades that can be displayed.
    - **1-bit image:** Can represent two values (black and white).
    - **8-bit image (Grayscale):** Can represent 256 shades of gray.
    - **24-bit image (True color):** Can represent around 16.7 million colors, with 8 bits each for red, green, and blue (RGB channels).

3. **Color Models:** Digital images use color models to represent pixel values. The most common models are:
    - o **RGB (Red, Green, Blue):** A color model used in most digital displays and devices. Each pixel's color is a combination of three primary colors:
        - **Red (R):** Intensity from 0 to 255.
        - **Green (G):** Intensity from 0 to 255.
        - **Blue (B):** Intensity from 0 to 255. By varying these three components, millions of colors can be created.
    - o **CMYK (Cyan, Magenta, Yellow, Black):** Commonly used in printing. This model is subtractive (the more color you add, the closer it gets to black), in contrast to RGB's additive model.
    - o **Grayscale:** Represents images in shades of gray, ranging from black (0) to white (255), with no color information.

4. **Image Resolution and Size:**
    - o **Spatial Resolution:** Refers to the amount of detail in an image, determined by the number of pixels in the horizontal and vertical dimensions (e.g., 1024x768).
    - o **Pixel Density (DPI or PPI):** Measured in dots per inch (DPI) or pixels per inch (PPI).

Higher DPI means more detail and sharpness, especially important for printed images.

5. **Raster vs. Vector Images:**
   - **Raster Images:** Composed of a grid of individual pixels. Each pixel has a specific color, and the image size is fixed. Most common image formats (e.g., JPEG, PNG, GIF) are raster-based. Raster images lose quality when resized because they are resolution-dependent.
   - **Vector Images:** Made of mathematical formulas that define shapes, lines, and curves. Vector images (e.g., SVG, EPS) can be scaled without loss of quality, making them ideal for logos and illustrations.

6. **Image File Formats:** Digital images are stored in different file formats, each with its strengths and weaknesses based on compression, quality, and file size:
   - **JPEG (Joint Photographic Experts Group):** A commonly used format that employs lossy compression to reduce file size. Ideal for photographs, but repeated compression can degrade quality.
   - **PNG (Portable Network Graphics):** Supports lossless compression and transparency (alpha channel), making it ideal for web graphics and images requiring transparency.
   - **GIF (Graphics Interchange Format):** Supports only 256 colors and is used for simple images and animations. It supports transparency but is limited in color depth.
   - **TIFF (Tagged Image File Format):** A high-quality format often used in printing and professional photography, supporting lossless compression and high bit depths.

- o **BMP (Bitmap):** An uncompressed format used in Windows environments, with large file sizes but high quality.

7. **Compression:**
   - o **Lossy Compression:** Reduces file size by permanently removing some image data. It is effective for photographs where small data loss is not noticeable (e.g., JPEG).
   - o **Lossless Compression:** Reduces file size without losing any image data, preserving quality (e.g., PNG, TIFF).

8. **Channels:**
   - o **RGB Channels:** In color images, each pixel can be split into three channels (Red, Green, Blue). Each channel holds the intensity of that particular color at the pixel location.
   - o **Alpha Channel:** An additional channel used for transparency. It specifies how opaque each pixel is, with 0 representing full transparency and 255 representing full opacity.

Digital Image Processing:

Once a digital image is represented in pixel form, it can be processed using various techniques:

1. **Filtering:** Enhances or suppresses certain aspects of the image, such as noise reduction, edge detection, or blurring.
2. **Transformation:** Manipulates the image for resizing, rotating, or warping.
3. **Segmentation:** Divides the image into meaningful parts or objects, often used in image analysis.
4. **Compression:** Reduces file size for storage and transmission, using lossy or lossless techniques.

Application of Digital Image Representation:

- **Photography:** Images captured by digital cameras are represented as a matrix of pixel values.
- **Medical Imaging:** Techniques like MRI and CT scans convert physical data into pixel grids to visualize internal body structures.
- **Remote Sensing:** Satellites capture Earth's images and represent them in digital form for analysis in geography, agriculture, etc.
- **Graphics Design and Web Design:** Designers use digital images for various visual content creation.

Understanding digital image representation is crucial in various fields, from computer graphics to scientific imaging, as it forms the basis for processing, analyzing, and interpreting visual information.

Digital Image Representation Example

To represent and manipulate digital images programmatically, Python is commonly used along with libraries like **Pillow** (for image processing) and **NumPy** (for numerical operations). Below is an example that demonstrates how to load, represent, and manipulate a digital image using Python code.

Steps:

1. Load an image.
2. Represent the image as a matrix of pixel values.
3. Perform basic manipulations (e.g., convert to grayscale, resize, and display).
4. Save the manipulated image.

Code Example:

```
# Importing the necessary libraries

from PIL import Image
```

Husn Ara

```python
import numpy as np

import matplotlib.pyplot as plt


# Step 1: Load an image

image_path = "path_to_your_image.jpg"  # Specify the image path

image = Image.open(image_path)


# Step 2: Represent the image as a matrix of pixel values (NumPy array)

image_array = np.array(image)


# Display the shape of the image array (Height, Width, Color Channels)

print("Image shape (Height, Width, Channels):", image_array.shape)


# Step 3: Display the original image

plt.figure(figsize=(6, 6))

plt.imshow(image)

plt.title("Original Image")

plt.axis("off")  # Hide axes

plt.show()


# Step 4: Convert the image to grayscale

# Convert the image to grayscale using Pillow's convert method
```

75

```python
gray_image = image.convert('L')   # 'L' mode is for grayscale (Luminance)


# Step 5: Represent grayscale image as an array and display it

gray_image_array = np.array(gray_image)


# Display the grayscale image

plt.figure(figsize=(6, 6))

plt.imshow(gray_image, cmap='gray')

plt.title("Grayscale Image")

plt.axis("off")

plt.show()


# Step 6: Resize the grayscale image

resized_image = gray_image.resize((100, 100)) # Resize to 100x100 pixels


# Display the resized image

plt.figure(figsize=(6, 6))

plt.imshow(resized_image, cmap='gray')

plt.title("Resized Image (100x100)")

plt.axis("off")

plt.show()


# Step 7: Save the manipulated image
```

```
resized_image.save("resized_grayscale_image.jpg")    #
Save as a new image file
```

```
# Step 8: Perform a basic pixel manipulation - Invert colors
of grayscale
```

```
inverted_image_array = 255 - gray_image_array # Invert
the pixel values (grayscale)
```

```
# Display the inverted grayscale image
```

```
plt.figure(figsize=(6, 6))
```

```
plt.imshow(inverted_image_array, cmap='gray')
```

```
plt.title("Inverted Grayscale Image")
```

```
plt.axis("off")
```

```
plt.show()
```

```
# Save the inverted image
```

```
inverted_image                              =
Image.fromarray(inverted_image_array)
```

```
inverted_image.save("inverted_grayscale_image.jpg")
```

Explanation:

1. **Loading an Image:**
   - We use the PIL.Image.open() method to load an image from the disk. This image is represented in RGB format by default.
2. **Image as a NumPy Array:**
   - Converting the image into a NumPy array allows easy access to pixel values. Each pixel is represented as a tuple (R, G, B), or a single value for grayscale images.
3. **Displaying the Image:**

- o Using **matplotlib**, the image is displayed, and by converting it to grayscale, we can show how pixel intensities are represented.

4. **Basic Manipulations:**
   - o The image is resized, converted to grayscale, and inverted by simple pixel manipulations.

5. **Saving the Image:**
   - o The modified image is saved to disk using save() from Pillow.

Pixel Value Representation:

- **Original Image:** Represented as an array of shape (height, width, 3), where the 3 represents the Red, Green, and Blue color channels.
- **Grayscale Image:** Converted to a shape of (height, width), where each value represents the brightness of the corresponding pixel.

Sample Output:

- The output includes the original image, the grayscale version, the resized grayscale image, and the inverted grayscale image, displayed using matplotlib.

This code demonstrates the fundamental steps involved in representing and manipulating digital images using code. You can apply various image processing techniques after converting the image to a matrix representation, such as filtering, transformations, and advanced manipulations.

Pixels and Image Formats

Pixels and **image formats** are fundamental concepts in digital image processing. Let's break them down:

1. Pixels

A **pixel** (short for "picture element") is the smallest unit of a digital image. Each pixel represents a single point in the image, and its value determines the color and intensity at that point. Pixels are arranged in a grid, where each pixel holds data about its color.

- **Color Representation:**
  - **Grayscale Images:** In a grayscale image, each pixel holds a single value representing the intensity of light, typically ranging from 0 (black) to 255 (white).
  - **Color Images (RGB):** In an RGB image, each pixel holds three values corresponding to the intensities of red, green, and blue channels. Each value usually ranges from 0 to 255, and combinations of these values produce different colors.

  For example:

  - Black pixel: (0, 0, 0)
  - White pixel: (255, 255, 255)
  - Pure Red: (255, 0, 0)
  - Pure Green: (0, 255, 0)
  - Pure Blue: (0, 0, 255)
- **Image Resolution:** The number of pixels in an image is called the resolution, which is typically described as width × height (e.g., 1920×1080). Higher resolution images contain more pixels and more detail.
- **Pixel Density (DPI/PPI):**
  - **DPI (Dots per Inch):** Commonly used in printing to describe the density of printed pixels.
  - **PPI (Pixels per Inch):** Describes the pixel density on a screen. Higher PPI means a sharper image.

2. Image Formats

Image formats refer to the way images are encoded and stored in digital systems. They define how pixel data is compressed, organized, and saved, and they impact image quality, file size, and compatibility.

Popular Image Formats:

1. **JPEG (Joint Photographic Experts Group):**
   - **File extension:** .jpg or .jpeg
   - **Compression type:** Lossy
   - **Color depth:** 24-bit (16.7 million colors)
   - **Best for:** Photographs and images with gradients.
   - **Characteristics:**
     - Uses lossy compression, meaning some image detail is discarded to reduce file size.
     - Compression artifacts (blocky or blurry areas) may appear if the image is compressed too much.
   - **Use case:** Ideal for web images and photos, where smaller file size is important and slight quality loss is acceptable.

2. **PNG (Portable Network Graphics):**
   - **File extension:** .png
   - **Compression type:** Lossless
   - **Color depth:** Supports 8-bit grayscale, 24-bit RGB, and 32-bit RGBA (RGB + Alpha transparency)
   - **Best for:** Graphics, logos, and images with transparency.
   - **Characteristics:**
     - Lossless compression retains all image data, so there's no quality loss.
     - Supports transparency, which makes it ideal for logos and web graphics with non-rectangular shapes.

Husn Ara

- o **Use case:** Best for images where transparency is needed or for images with sharp edges (e.g., illustrations, screenshots).

3. **GIF (Graphics Interchange Format):**
   - o **File extension:** .gif
   - o **Compression type:** Lossless (LZW compression)
   - o **Color depth:** 8-bit (256 colors)
   - o **Best for:** Simple images, animations, or graphics with limited colors.
   - o **Characteristics:**
     - Limited to 256 colors, making it unsuitable for high-quality photos.
     - Supports animation by storing multiple frames in a single file.
     - Can have transparent areas but no partial transparency (either fully opaque or fully transparent).
   - o **Use case:** Used for simple animations and images with few colors, like icons or web buttons.

4. **BMP (Bitmap Image File):**
   - o **File extension:** .bmp
   - o **Compression type:** None or lossless (can be uncompressed or use RLE compression)
   - o **Color depth:** 1-bit (black/white), 8-bit (256 colors), or 24-bit (16.7 million colors)
   - o **Best for:** Storing raw image data without compression.
   - o **Characteristics:**
     - Typically uncompressed, resulting in large file sizes.
     - Stores pixel-by-pixel information, making it suitable for high-quality imaging without data loss.
   - o **Use case:** Rarely used today due to its large file size. Used in some specialized applications where uncompressed quality is required.

5. **TIFF (Tagged Image File Format):**
   - o **File extension:** .tiff or .tif

- o **Compression type:** Lossless (supports both lossless and lossy compression)
- o **Color depth:** 24-bit or 48-bit (higher color depth than JPEG/PNG)
- o **Best for:** High-quality images, such as in professional photography or printing.
- o **Characteristics:**
  - Can store multiple layers and high-bit-depth images.
  - Often used for high-quality images and scanned documents because it retains all image data.
  - Very large file size.
- o **Use case:** Used in professional photography, printing, and medical imaging where high detail and quality are required.

6. **SVG (Scalable Vector Graphics):**
- o **File extension:** .svg
- o **Compression type:** None (vector-based)
- o **Best for:** Vector images like logos, icons, and illustrations.
- o **Characteristics:**
  - Unlike raster images (JPEG, PNG), SVG is vector-based, meaning it stores instructions on how to draw the image rather than pixel data.
  -

Comparison Between Formats:

Format	Compression	Color Depth	Transparency	Best for
JPEG	Lossy	24-bit	No	Photos, web images
PNG	Lossless	24/32-bit	Yes (supports alpha channel)	Graphics, logos, images with

Format	Compression	Color Depth	Transparency	Best for
				transparency
GIF	Lossless	8-bit	Yes (limited)	Simple animations, icons
BMP	Uncompressed	1-bit to 24-bit	No	Raw image data, rare use
TIFF	Lossless	24/48-bit	Yes	High-quality images, professional photography
SVG	Vector-based	N/A	Yes	Scalable logos, illustrations

Conclusion:

- **Pixels** are the building blocks of digital images, with each pixel holding color or intensity information.
- **Image formats** vary based on compression (lossy or lossless), color depth, and use case. JPEG is best for photos, PNG for graphics with transparency, GIF for simple animations, TIFF for high-quality images, and SVG for scalable vector graphics.

Choosing the right image format depends on the specific needs of the application, such as file size, image quality, and transparency.

Color Spaces (RGB, HSV, YUV)

Color spaces are systems that define how colors are represented in a digital image. Different color spaces are used for different purposes, and they help in understanding how colors are perceived, displayed, and manipulated in various applications.

Here are three common color spaces: **RGB**, **HSV**, and **YUV**.

---

1. RGB (Red, Green, Blue)

Overview:

- **RGB** is the most common color space used in digital devices such as cameras, computer screens, and TVs. It is an **additive color model** where colors are created by combining different intensities of the three primary colors: **Red (R)**, **Green (G)**, and **Blue (B)**.
- When the three colors are mixed at their maximum intensity, they form white. When all are at zero intensity, the result is black.

Representation:

- Each pixel in an RGB image is represented by a tuple of three values (R, G, B), with each value typically ranging from 0 to 255 (for 8-bit images).

  Example:

  o **Black**: (0, 0, 0)

- **White**: (255, 255, 255)
- **Red**: (255, 0, 0)
- **Green**: (0, 255, 0)
- **Blue**: (0, 0, 255)

Use Cases:

- **Computer Displays:** RGB is used because electronic screens generate colors using light (additive mixing).
- **Image Processing:** Most image file formats (JPEG, PNG, BMP) store pixel data in the RGB format.

Pros:

- Widely used in digital applications and devices.
- Matches how computer screens and digital cameras capture and display images.

Cons:

- Not perceptually uniform, meaning changes in RGB values do not correspond to uniform changes in perceived color. This makes tasks like color manipulation or correction more complex.

2. HSV (Hue, Saturation, Value)

Overview:

- **HSV** is a **cylindrical color space** that is often more intuitive for humans to work with, especially when dealing with color adjustments. It separates color into three components:
  - **Hue (H):** Describes the type of color (e.g., red, green, blue). It is represented as an angle on the color wheel (0° - 360°). For example, 0° is red, 120° is green, and 240° is blue.
  - **Saturation (S):** Describes the intensity or purity of the color, with 0 being completely

unsaturated (gray) and 100% being fully saturated (vivid).

- **Value (V):** Describes the brightness or intensity of the color, ranging from 0 (black) to 100% (brightest).

Representation:

- Each pixel in HSV is represented as a tuple (H, S, V), where:
  - **H** ranges from 0 to 360 (angle on the color wheel).
  - **S** and **V** range from 0 to 1 or 0 to 100%.

Example:

- **Red:** (0°, 100%, 100%)
- **Green:** (120°, 100%, 100%)
- **Blue:** (240°, 100%, 100%)
- **Black:** (Any H, 0%, 0%)
- **White:** (Any H, 0%, 100%)

Use Cases:

- **Image Editing:** Easier to adjust color properties like brightness or saturation independently of hue.
- **Computer Vision:** Used in applications such as object tracking, because it separates color information from intensity, making it easier to detect colors under varying lighting conditions.

Pros:

- More intuitive for tasks like adjusting hue, brightness, and saturation.
- Helps in object detection and color-based filtering due to its separation of color information.

Cons:

- Not as widely supported in hardware as RGB.

Husn Ara

- Conversion between RGB and HSV can introduce complexity.

3. YUV (Luminance and Chrominance)

Overview:

- **YUV** is a **color space** that separates an image into **luminance (Y)** and **chrominance (U, V)** components. It is widely used in video compression and broadcast TV systems.
  - ○ **Y (Luminance):** Represents the brightness of the image (grayscale version).
  - ○ **U (Chrominance Blue):** Represents the difference between the blue component and luminance.
  - ○ **V (Chrominance Red):** Represents the difference between the red component and luminance.
- The **YUV** space is designed to take advantage of the fact that the human eye is more sensitive to brightness than to color. By separating luminance (brightness) from chrominance (color), it allows for more efficient compression (e.g., in video formats like MPEG and JPEG).

Representation:

- Each pixel is represented as a tuple (Y, U, V):
  - ○ **Y** ranges from 0 to 1 (or 0 to 255 for 8-bit images).
  - ○ **U** and **V** represent color information, typically within a range of -0.5 to 0.5 (scaled appropriately in digital formats).

Use Cases:

- **Video Compression:** Used in standards like JPEG, MPEG, and broadcast TV systems (NTSC, PAL). By reducing the chrominance information, significant compression can be achieved without a noticeable loss in perceived image quality.
- **Broadcasting:** Television and video signals often use YUV because it allows efficient storage and transmission of color information while preserving the luminance detail that the human eye perceives most strongly.

Pros:

- Efficient for video compression, reducing bandwidth while maintaining image quality.
- Separates luminance from color, making it ideal for grayscale image processing.

Cons:

- Complex to manipulate color directly in this space.
- Requires conversion from RGB for display on most screens.

Comparison of RGB, HSV, and YUV

Color Space	Components	Best for	Strengths	Weaknesses
RGB	Red, Green, Blue	Displays, image processing, web design	Easy for devices to use, directly maps to displays	Not perceptually uniform, complex for color manipulation

Color Space	Components	Best for	Strengths	Weaknesses
HSV	Hue, Saturation, Value	Color editing, computer vision tasks	Intuitive for adjusting color properties	Not as widely supported as RGB
YUV	Luminance (Y), Chrominance (U, V)	Video compression, broadcasting	Efficient for compression, separates luminance for better quality retention	Complex color manipulation, designed for specific use cases

Conclusion

- **RGB** is great for devices and simple color manipulation but lacks perceptual uniformity.
- **HSV** is intuitive for adjusting color and is used in many applications where hue and brightness need to be controlled separately.
- **YUV** is efficient for video compression and transmission, making it crucial for TV, broadcasting, and video formats.

Different color spaces serve different purposes, and the choice of color space often depends on the specific application, such as image processing, computer vision, video compression, or display technology.

Image Filtering and Enhancement

Convolution and Correlation

Convolution and **correlation** are two fundamental operations in image processing, signal processing, and various areas of machine learning, particularly in the context of neural networks (like Convolutional Neural Networks, CNNs). Both involve mathematical operations on two functions or matrices, but they have different interpretations and applications.

Let's explore both in detail:

1. Convolution

In the context of image processing, **convolution** is a mathematical operation that combines an input image with a **kernel** (or filter) to produce a transformed image. The kernel moves over the input image, and at each position, the sum of the product of the kernel values and the overlapping pixel values is computed.

The convolution operation is mathematically defined as:

$$(f * g)(x) = \sum_a f(a) \cdot g(x - a)$$

Where:

- f is the input function (or image).

- g is the kernel (or filter).

- x is the point at which the convolution is being evaluated.

In digital images, this formula is applied as a discrete convolution.

Steps in Image Convolution:

1. Place the kernel/filter over the input image, starting from the top-left corner.
2. Multiply each pixel value of the input image with the corresponding kernel value.
3. Sum the results of these multiplications.
4. Replace the pixel at the center of the kernel with the sum of the products.
5. Move the kernel over the image by a certain stride (usually 1 pixel), and repeat the process until the entire image is covered.

Example:

Let's consider a simple 3x3 kernel and a 5x5 image:

import numpy as np

from scipy.signal import convolve2d

Input image (5x5)

image = np.array([[1, 2, 3, 0, 1],

[4, 5, 6, 1, 0],

```
    [7, 8, 9, 2, 1],

    [1, 0, 2, 3, 4],

    [3, 1, 0, 5, 6]]])


# Kernel (3x3)

kernel = np.array([[0, -1, 0],

    [-1, 5, -1],

    [0, -1, 0]])


# Perform convolution

convolved_image = convolve2d(image, kernel,
mode='valid')  # 'valid' means no zero-padding

print(convolved_image)
```

Applications of Convolution in Image Processing:

- **Edge Detection:** Using kernels like the **Sobel** or **Prewitt** operators.
- **Blurring/Sharpening:** Applying kernels like a **Gaussian blur** or a **sharpening** filter.
- **Feature Extraction in CNNs:** Convolution layers in neural networks automatically learn filters to detect patterns and features.

Key Properties of Convolution:

- **Linearity:** The convolution of a sum of functions is the sum of their convolutions.
- **Shift Invariance:** The convolution operation does not depend on the position of the signal.

- **Associativity:** Convolutions can be combined in a sequence without changing the result.

---

2. Correlation

In contrast, **correlation** measures the similarity between two signals (or images) by sliding one signal (the kernel) over another and calculating how similar they are at each position. The major difference from convolution is the **direction** in which the kernel is applied. In **correlation**, there is no flipping of the kernel, whereas in convolution, the kernel is flipped before being applied.

Mathematically, correlation is defined as:

$$(f \star g)(x) = \sum_{a} f(a) \cdot g(x + a)$$

Where:

- f is the input function (or image).

- g is the kernel.

- x is the point at which the correlation is being evaluated.

Steps in Image Correlation:

1. The kernel is placed over the image at the top-left corner.
2. Multiply the corresponding image and kernel values without flipping the kernel.
3. Sum the products.
4. Slide the kernel across the image, repeating the process.

Example:

The Python code to perform correlation is similar to convolution but without kernel flipping. In practice, most libraries like NumPy or SciPy perform correlation by default when using convolution functions without flipping the kernel manually.

```python
import numpy as np

from scipy.signal import correlate2d


# Input image (5x5)

image = np.array([[1, 2, 3, 0, 1],

                  [4, 5, 6, 1, 0],

                  [7, 8, 9, 2, 1],

                  [1, 0, 2, 3, 4],

                  [3, 1, 0, 5, 6]])


# Kernel (3x3)

kernel = np.array([[0, 1, 0],

                   [1, 5, 1],

                   [0, 1, 0]])


# Perform correlation

correlated_image = correlate2d(image, kernel, mode='valid')
```

```
print(correlated_image)
```

Applications of Correlation in Image Processing:

- **Template Matching:** Correlation is used to find a smaller pattern (template) in a larger image by sliding the template over the image and measuring the similarity.
- **Signal Processing:** Detect patterns in time-series data.
- **Pattern Recognition:** Identifying and matching features in images.

Key Properties of Correlation:

- **Symmetry:** Correlation is symmetric, meaning the result is the same if the kernel and input are swapped.
- **Not Shift-Invariant:** Correlation depends on the relative positions of the signals.
- **No Kernel Flipping:** Unlike convolution, correlation doesn't flip the kernel.

Difference Between Convolution and Correlation:

Aspect	Convolution	Correlation
Operation	Flips the kernel before applying it.	Does not flip the kernel.
Mathematical Formula	$(f * g)(x) = \sum f(a) \cdot g(x - a)$	$(f * g)(x) = \sum f(a) \cdot g(x + a)$
Kernel Flipping	Yes, kernel is flipped both horizontally and vertically.	No, the kernel is applied directly as is.
Use Case	Used for tasks like blurring, sharpening, and edge detection in image processing, and feature extraction in CNNs.	Used for pattern recognition and template matching.
Properties	Shift invariant, associative.	Symmetric, but not shift invariant.

Visual Example of Convolution vs. Correlation:

Let's assume we have a simple kernel:

$$\text{Kernel} - \begin{bmatrix} 1 & 2 & 1 \\ 0 & 0 & 0 \\ -1 & -2 & -1 \end{bmatrix}$$

For convolution, this kernel is flipped horizontally and vertically before applying it to the image. In correlation, the kernel is applied directly without flipping.

- Convolution is commonly used in tasks like edge detection because the flipping of the kernel allows it to detect features like horizontal and vertical edges in an image.

- Correlation is useful for tasks like template matching, where you want to measure the similarity between parts of an image and a specific pattern.

Conclusion:

- **Convolution** and **correlation** are similar operations but differ in how the kernel is applied. Convolution flips the kernel and is widely used in image processing tasks like filtering, edge detection, and in Convolutional Neural Networks (CNNs).
- **Correlation** does not flip the kernel and is often used for template matching and finding patterns in signals and images. Both operations are essential in fields like image processing, machine learning, and signal processing.

Gaussian Smoothing

Gaussian smoothing, also known as **Gaussian blurring**, is a widely used technique in image processing and signal processing to reduce noise and detail in an image. It is a type of convolution operation where the image is convolved with a **Gaussian function** or **Gaussian kernel**. The result is a smoother version of the image, where sharp edges and noise are softened, making it useful for preprocessing tasks like noise reduction or preparing the image for further operations like edge detection.

Gaussian Function

The Gaussian function is a bell-shaped curve. defined as:

$$G(x, y) = \frac{1}{2\pi\sigma^2} e^{-\frac{x^2+y^2}{2\sigma^2}}$$

Where:

- x and y are the coordinates of the pixel relative to the center of the kernel.

- σ is the standard deviation of the Gaussian distribution. which controls the extent of the smoothing. A larger σ results in more blurring.

- The Gaussian function ensures that pixels closer to the center of the kernel have more weight than pixels further away. mimicking the way the human visual system perceives focus.

Gaussian Kernel

The Gaussian kernel is essentially a matrix derived from the Gaussian function. It is symmetric and normalized so that the sum of all elements equals 1. ensuring that the overall brightness of the image does not change after the convolution. A typical 3x3 Gaussian kernel might look like:

$$K = \frac{1}{16} \begin{bmatrix} 1 & 2 & 1 \\ 2 & 4 & 2 \\ 1 & 2 & 1 \end{bmatrix}$$

Larger kernels will provide more smoothing but can also reduce the level of detail in the image.

How Gaussian Smoothing Works:

1. **Kernel Creation:** A Gaussian kernel is generated based on the desired size and standard deviation σ\sigmaσ. Larger kernels and higher σ\sigmaσ values will result in more smoothing.
2. **Convolution:** The Gaussian kernel is applied over the image by performing a convolution operation. At each pixel, the weighted sum of the surrounding pixels is calculated, with the weights determined by the Gaussian function.
3. **Blurring:** As the kernel slides over the image, it produces a blurred version of the image, reducing sharp transitions in intensity, thus smoothing the image.

Python Implementation of Gaussian Smoothing

Below is an example of applying Gaussian smoothing to an image using Python with OpenCV and SciPy libraries:

```python
import cv2

import numpy as np

from scipy.ndimage import gaussian_filter


# Load the image in grayscale
image          =          cv2.imread('example_image.jpg',
cv2.IMREAD_GRAYSCALE)


# Apply Gaussian smoothing using OpenCV's built-in function
# Arguments: image, kernel size, standard deviation
smoothed_image = cv2.GaussianBlur(image, (5, 5), 1.0)


# Alternatively, using SciPy's gaussian_filter function
smoothed_image_scipy     =     gaussian_filter(image,
sigma=1.0)


# Show the original and smoothed image using OpenCV
cv2.imshow('Original Image', image)

cv2.imshow('Smoothed Image', smoothed_image)

cv2.waitKey(0)

cv2.destroyAllWindows()
```

Key Parameters:

- **Kernel Size (window size):** This determines the size of the area over which the smoothing is done. For example, a 3x3 or 5x5 kernel is commonly used. Larger kernels result in more blurring.
- **Standard Deviation σ\sigmaσ:** This determines the spread of the Gaussian function. A higher σ\sigmaσ leads to more blurring since the influence of farther pixels increases.

Effects of Gaussian Smoothing:

- **Noise Reduction:** Gaussian smoothing is very effective at reducing noise in an image. It achieves this by averaging out pixel values, reducing high-frequency components such as sharp noise.
- **Edge Preservation:** Although Gaussian smoothing blurs the image, it preserves edges better than uniform blurring techniques because of the weighted nature of the Gaussian kernel (where closer pixels contribute more to the average than farther ones).
- **Preprocessing for Edge Detection:** Smoothing is often applied before edge detection (like using the **Canny edge detector**) to reduce the effect of noise that can produce spurious edges.

Comparison with Other Smoothing Techniques:

Method	Description	Advantages	Disadvantages
Gaussian Blur	Uses a Gaussian kernel to blur the image. Weights pixels closer to the center.	Reduces noise while preserving edges to some extent.	Can still blur edges slightly.

Method	Description	Advantages	Disadvantages
Mean (Box) Blur	Averages pixel values equally over a neighborhood.	Simple and fast to compute.	Blurs edges more aggressively than Gaussian.
Median Blur	Replaces each pixel with the median of neighboring pixels.	Effective for removing salt-and-pepper noise.	Can distort small details.

Applications of Gaussian Smoothing:

- **Noise Reduction:** It is commonly used to remove noise from images, especially Gaussian noise.
- **Preprocessing in Computer Vision:** Often used before applying edge detection algorithms like the **Canny edge detector** or **Sobel operator** to make edge detection more robust to noise.
- **Blurring:** Gaussian smoothing is used to blur an image for artistic or functional purposes, such as creating background blurring in focus applications.

Conclusion:

Gaussian smoothing is a fundamental technique in image processing that uses the Gaussian function to blur an image, reducing noise and detail. It plays a crucial role in various preprocessing steps in tasks like edge detection and feature extraction. Its ability to smooth an image while maintaining some edge detail makes it more effective than simpler blurring methods like mean filtering.

Husn Ara

Edge Detection Techniques (Sobel, Canny)

Edge detection is a fundamental task in image processing and computer vision, used to identify points in an image where the brightness changes sharply, typically representing object boundaries. There are various edge detection techniques, but two widely used methods are the **Sobel operator** and the **Canny edge detector**.

Let's dive into these two techniques:

1. Sobel Edge Detection

The **Sobel operator** is a simple and efficient method for detecting edges based on computing the gradient of the image intensity at each pixel. It highlights regions where there is a sharp change in intensity, indicating the presence of an edge.

How Sobel Works:

- The Sobel operator uses two **convolution kernels**, one for detecting changes in the **horizontal direction** (Gx) and another for the **vertical direction** (Gy). The kernels are small 3x3 matrices that approximate the derivative in these directions.

Sobel Kernels:

- Horizontal Sobel kernel (Gx):

$$G_x = \begin{bmatrix} -1 & 0 & 1 \\ -2 & 0 & 2 \\ -1 & 0 & 1 \end{bmatrix}$$

- Vertical Sobel kernel (Gy):

$$G_y = \begin{bmatrix} -1 & -2 & -1 \\ 0 & 0 & 0 \\ 1 & 2 & 1 \end{bmatrix}$$

Steps in Sobel Edge Detection:

1. Grayscale Conversion: Convert the image to grayscale (since edge detection works on intensity values).

2. Apply Sobel Kernels: Convolve the image with the Gx and Gy kernels to compute the intensity gradients in the x and y directions.

3. Calculate Gradient Magnitude: The magnitude of the gradient at each pixel gives the strength of the edge:

$$G = \sqrt{G_x^2 + G_y^2}$$

4. Calculate Gradient Direction: The direction of the edge is given by:

$$\theta = \arctan\left(\frac{G_y}{G_x}\right)$$

5. Thresholding (optional): A threshold can be applied to the gradient magnitude to decide whether a pixel is an edge or not.

Python Implementation of Sobel:

import cv2

import numpy as np

Load the image

image   =   cv2.imread('example_image.jpg', cv2.IMREAD_GRAYSCALE)

Apply Sobel operator (Gx and Gy)

```
sobel_x = cv2.Sobel(image, cv2.CV_64F, 1, 0, ksize=3) #
Horizontal edges

sobel_y = cv2.Sobel(image, cv2.CV_64F, 0, 1, ksize=3) #
Vertical edges


# Compute the gradient magnitude
sobel_magnitude = np.sqrt(sobel_x**2 + sobel_y**2)


# Convert to 8-bit image (optional for display)
sobel_magnitude                                      =
cv2.convertScaleAbs(sobel_magnitude)


# Display the result
cv2.imshow('Sobel Magnitude', sobel_magnitude)

cv2.waitKey(0)

cv2.destroyAllWindows()
```

Advantages of Sobel:

- Simple and computationally efficient.
- Combines smoothing and differentiation, which helps reduce noise sensitivity.

Disadvantages of Sobel:

- Sensitive to noise in the image, even with some inherent smoothing.
- Only detects edges in horizontal and vertical directions (diagonal edges are less prominent).

2. Canny Edge Detection

The **Canny edge detector** is a more advanced edge detection algorithm designed to be less sensitive to noise and more accurate in detecting edges. It incorporates multiple steps, including noise reduction, gradient computation, and edge tracing.

Steps in Canny Edge Detection:

1. **Noise Reduction:** Before detecting edges, the image is smoothed using a **Gaussian filter** to reduce noise. This prevents false edge detection due to noise.
2. **Gradient Calculation:** The intensity gradient of the image is computed using operators like Sobel to get the edge strength (magnitude) and direction at each pixel.
3. **Non-Maximum Suppression:** The algorithm ensures that only the local maxima in the gradient direction are considered as edges, resulting in thin, sharp edges.
4. **Double Thresholding:** Two thresholds are applied (a **low threshold** and a **high threshold**):
    - Pixels with gradient magnitudes above the **high threshold** are marked as strong edges.
    - Pixels with magnitudes between the **low threshold** and the **high threshold** are marked as weak edges.
    - Pixels below the low threshold are discarded.
5. **Edge Tracking by Hysteresis:** Weak edges that are connected to strong edges are preserved, while other weak edges are discarded. This step refines the detected edges and reduces noise.

Python Implementation of Canny:

```
import cv2


# Load the image

image        =        cv2.imread('example_image.jpg',
cv2.IMREAD_GRAYSCALE)


# Apply Canny edge detection

edges    =    cv2.Canny(image,    threshold1=100,
threshold2=200)


# Display the result

cv2.imshow('Canny Edges', edges)

cv2.waitKey(0)

cv2.destroyAllWindows()
```

Key Parameters:

- **Threshold1:** The lower bound for edge detection.
- **Threshold2:** The upper bound for edge detection. Typically, Threshold2 is twice the value of Threshold1.

Advantages of Canny:

- **Multi-step process** reduces noise and produces thin edges.
- **Double thresholding** ensures robust edge detection and reduces false positives.
- **Edge tracking** enhances the continuity of edges, making it ideal for detecting clear and connected object boundaries.

Disadvantages of Canny:

- More computationally expensive than simpler edge detectors like Sobel.
- Sensitive to parameter tuning (low and high thresholds must be chosen carefully based on the image characteristics).

Comparison of Sobel and Canny Edge Detection

Aspect	Sobel Operator	Canny Edge Detector
Complexity	Simple, fast, and easy to implement.	More complex and computationally expensive.
Noise Sensitivity	Sensitive to noise, especially without preprocessing.	Less sensitive to noise due to Gaussian smoothing.
Edge Thickness	Produces thicker edges (gradient magnitude).	Produces thin, single-pixel-wide edges (non-maximum suppression).
Parameter Sensitivity	Not sensitive to parameter tuning.	Sensitive to threshold values.
Edge Continuity	Less effective at ensuring edge continuity.	Ensures continuous and connected edges.
Applications	Quick edge detection for basic tasks.	More robust edge detection, used in advanced applications (e.g., object recognition).

Applications of Edge Detection:

- **Object Detection and Recognition:** Edge detection is often the first step in identifying object boundaries in images.
- **Medical Imaging:** Used to detect contours and boundaries of tissues and organs.
- **Robotics:** Helps robots understand the environment by detecting shapes and obstacles.
- **Computer Vision Tasks:** Such as feature extraction, segmentation, and object tracking.

Conclusion:

- **Sobel edge detection** is a simple and fast method suitable for tasks requiring a quick approximation of edges.
- **Canny edge detection** is more sophisticated, offering better accuracy, noise resistance, and the ability to detect thin, connected edges, making it ideal for more advanced computer vision tasks.

The choice of method depends on the specific requirements of the task. If speed and simplicity are essential, Sobel is a good choice. If robustness and accuracy are priorities, especially in noisy images, Canny is preferable.

Image Transformation Techniques

Fourier Transform

The **Fourier Transform** (FT) is a mathematical tool used to transform signals between the time (or spatial) domain and the frequency domain. In image processing, it helps

Computer Vision:Tools & Algorithms for Analyzing Images analyse the frequency content of an image, allowing us to understand the distribution of spatial variations in intensity. This is especially useful for tasks like filtering, compression, and pattern recognition.

Fourier Transform Overview

The Fourier Transform decomposes a signal (such as an image) into its constituent frequencies. For a continuous signal $f(t)$, the continuous Fourier transform is defined as:

$$F(\omega) = \int_{-\infty}^{\infty} f(t)e^{-i\omega t}dt$$

Where:

- $f(t)$ is the original signal.

- $F(\omega)$ is the Fourier transform, which represents the signal in the frequency domain.

- ω is the angular frequency.

- $e^{-i\omega t}$ is the complex exponential term (Euler's formula).

In discrete contexts like digital image processing, we use the **Discrete Fourier Transform (DFT)**. The DFT transforms a discrete signal (or image) into its frequency components. The **2D Discrete Fourier Transform (2D DFT)** is particularly important in image processing.

2D Discrete Fourier Transform for Images

For a 2D image $f(x, y)$ of size $M \times N$, the 2D DFT is given by:

$$F(u, v) = \sum_{x=0}^{M-1} \sum_{y=0}^{N-1} f(x, y)e^{-2\pi i(\frac{ux}{M} + \frac{vy}{N})}$$

Where:

- $f(x, y)$ is the pixel value at coordinates (x, y).

- $F(u, v)$ is the frequency domain representation at frequency coordinates (u, v).

- u and v are the spatial frequencies in the horizontal and vertical directions, respectively.

The **Inverse Discrete Fourier Transform (IDFT)** is used to convert the frequency domain representation back to the spatial domain.

Key Properties of the Fourier Transform in Image Processing:

- **Frequency Domain Interpretation:** The result of the 2D Fourier Transform is a complex-valued function where each point represents a specific frequency component of the image.

- ○ **Low Frequencies:** These are located near the center of the transformed image and represent smooth variations (large-scale features).
- ○ **High Frequencies:** These are found near the edges and represent fine details, such as edges and noise.
- **Symmetry:** The DFT of a real-valued image produces a complex result, but the magnitude of the frequency components is symmetric about the origin.

Steps for Applying Fourier Transform to Images:

1. **Convert Image to Grayscale:** Since Fourier transforms work on intensity values, the image is often converted to grayscale first.
2. **Apply 2D DFT:** The image undergoes a 2D DFT to obtain the frequency domain representation.
3. **Shift the Zero Frequency to the Center:** By default, the zero frequency component (DC component) is at the top-left corner. It's common to shift it to the center for easier interpretation.
4. **Magnitude Spectrum:** The magnitude of the Fourier transform is computed to visualize the frequency content of the image.
5. **Inverse DFT (optional):** To reconstruct the image from its frequency domain representation, an inverse DFT is applied.

Python Implementation of 2D DFT (Fourier Transform)

Here's a Python example using the NumPy and OpenCV libraries to compute the Fourier Transform of an image:

```
import cv2
```

```python
import numpy as np

import matplotlib.pyplot as plt


# Load the image in grayscale

image          =          cv2.imread('example_image.jpg',
cv2.IMREAD_GRAYSCALE)


# Apply Fourier Transform using NumPy's FFT function

dft = np.fft.fft2(image)

dft_shifted = np.fft.fftshift(dft)  # Shift zero frequency to
center


# Compute the magnitude spectrum

magnitude_spectrum = 20 * np.log(np.abs(dft_shifted))


# Plot the original image and the magnitude spectrum

plt.subplot(121), plt.imshow(image, cmap='gray')

plt.title('Input Image'), plt.axis('off')


plt.subplot(122),          plt.imshow(magnitude_spectrum,
cmap='gray')

plt.title('Magnitude Spectrum'), plt.axis('off')


plt.show()
```

Explanation:

- np.fft.fft2(image) computes the 2D Fourier transform of the image.

- np.fft.fftshift(dft) shifts the zero frequency to the center for better visualization.
- The **magnitude spectrum** shows the frequency content, where bright spots represent higher magnitudes (stronger frequencies).

Inverse Fourier Transform:

To reconstruct the image from the frequency domain:

```
# Inverse Fourier Transform

idft_shifted = np.fft.ifftshift(dft_shifted)  # Shift back

reconstructed_image = np.fft.ifft2(idft_shifted)

reconstructed_image = np.abs(reconstructed_image)


# Display the reconstructed image

plt.imshow(reconstructed_image, cmap='gray')

plt.title('Reconstructed Image')

plt.axis('off')

plt.show()
```

Applications of Fourier Transform in Image Processing:

- **Image Filtering:** The Fourier transform is widely used in filtering operations, such as removing noise (low-pass filtering) or enhancing edges (high-pass filtering). By modifying certain frequency components and then applying the inverse Fourier transform, we can selectively remove or enhance image features.
- **Image Compression:** The transform helps reduce redundancy by representing the image in terms of its frequency components. Techniques like JPEG compression use a similar transform (Discrete Cosine Transform) for efficient image storage.

- **Pattern Recognition:** Fourier descriptors are often used to represent shapes in the frequency domain for recognition tasks.
- **Image Reconstruction:** The inverse Fourier transform allows us to reconstruct images from their frequency representations, which is useful in medical imaging (e.g., MRI and CT scans).

Low-Pass and High-Pass Filtering:

- **Low-Pass Filter (LPF):** A low-pass filter retains the low-frequency components (smooth regions) and suppresses high-frequency components (fine details or noise). In the frequency domain, this corresponds to retaining values near the center of the transformed image.
- **High-Pass Filter (HPF):** A high-pass filter retains the high-frequency components (sharp edges and details) and suppresses low-frequency components. In the frequency domain, this corresponds to retaining values far from the center of the transformed image.

Example of Low-Pass and High-Pass Filtering:

Low-pass filtering (keep low frequencies)

rows, cols = image.shape

crow, ccol = rows // 2, cols // 2 # Center of the frequency domain

Create a mask with a center square of 50x50, pass low frequencies

mask = np.zeros((rows, cols), np.uint8)

mask[crow-25:crow+25, ccol-25:ccol+25] = 1

```
# Apply mask and inverse DFT for LPF

dft_masked = dft_shifted * mask

idft_shifted = np.fft.ifftshift(dft_masked)

low_pass_image = np.fft.ifft2(idft_shifted)

low_pass_image = np.abs(low_pass_image)


plt.imshow(low_pass_image, cmap='gray')

plt.title('Low-Pass Filtered Image')

plt.axis('off')

plt.show()


# High-pass filtering (remove low frequencies)

mask_hp = 1 - mask

dft_masked_hp = dft_shifted * mask_hp

idft_shifted_hp = np.fft.ifftshift(dft_masked_hp)

high_pass_image = np.fft.ifft2(idft_shifted_hp)

high_pass_image = np.abs(high_pass_image)


plt.imshow(high_pass_image, cmap='gray')

plt.title('High-Pass Filtered Image')

plt.axis('off')

plt.show()
```

Conclusion:

The Fourier Transform is a powerful tool for analysing the frequency content of an image. It is widely used in image processing for tasks like filtering, noise reduction, and feature extraction. The ability to move between the spatial and frequency domains allows for flexibility in enhancing or suppressing different aspects of an image, making it a key technique in both theoretical and practical applications in image processing.

Wavelet Transform

The **Wavelet Transform** is another important mathematical tool used in image processing and signal analysis. Unlike the Fourier Transform, which decomposes a signal into sinusoids (sine and cosine functions) that extend over the entire domain, the Wavelet Transform decomposes a signal into localized, finite-duration "wavelets." This allows for both **frequency** and **spatial** (or time) information to be captured simultaneously, making it ideal for analyzing non-stationary signals where properties may vary over time or space.

In image processing, wavelet transforms are used for tasks like **image compression**, **denoising**, and **multiresolution analysis**.

Key Concepts of the Wavelet Transform

1. **Wavelets**: A wavelet is a small wave-like function that is localized in both time (or space) and frequency. Unlike sinusoids, wavelets start and stop in a finite time, making them useful for analyzing localized features of a signal, such as edges or transients.
2. **Multiresolution Analysis**: One of the key advantages of wavelets is their ability to represent data at multiple resolutions. This is especially useful in image processing, where wavelets can decompose an image into different frequency bands at different scales,

helping to capture both fine details and overall structures.

3. **Scaling and Translation**: The Wavelet Transform involves scaling (dilating or compressing) and translating (shifting) a wavelet function. By scaling, you can zoom in or out on different levels of detail, and by translating, you can move the wavelet across the signal or image to capture localized features.

Types of Wavelet Transforms

1. Continuous Wavelet Transform (CWT):

- The CWT provides a continuous decomposition of a signal into wavelets at different scales and positions.

- The CWT is useful for theoretical analysis but not practical for discrete signals (e.g., digital images).

- The transform is defined as:

$$W(s,\tau) = \int_{-\infty}^{\infty} f(t)\psi^*\left(\frac{t-\tau}{s}\right) dt$$

Where:

- $f(t)$ is the input signal.
- $\psi(t)$ is the mother wavelet (a base wavelet function).
- s is the scale factor (controls the width of the wavelet).
- τ is the translation factor (controls the location of the wavelet).
- $\psi^*(t)$ is the complex conjugate of the wavelet.

2. Discrete Wavelet Transform (DWT):

- The DWT is the discrete counterpart of the CWT and is widely used in practical applications like image compression (e.g., JPEG 2000).

- Instead of using every possible scale and translation, the DWT uses dyadic scales and translations (i.e. powers of two).

- The DWT is computed by passing the signal through a series of high-pass and low-pass filters to capture both the fine details and the overall structure of the signal.

Wavelet Transform in Image Processing

In image processing, the 2D Discrete Wavelet Transform (DWT) decomposes an image into different sub-bands, each representing specific

115

frequency components at different scales. After the first level of decomposition, an image is split into four sub-bands:

- **LL (Low-Low)**: Low-frequency components in both the horizontal and vertical directions (smooth, overall structure of the image).
- **LH (Low-High)**: Low-frequency components in the horizontal direction and high-frequency components in the vertical direction (horizontal edges).
- **HL (High-Low)**: High-frequency components in the horizontal direction and low-frequency components in the vertical direction (vertical edges).
- **HH (High-High)**: High-frequency components in both directions (diagonal edges).

Steps in the 2D DWT:

1. **Apply DWT to Rows**: Decompose each row of the image into low- and high-frequency components using a pair of filters.
2. **Apply DWT to Columns**: Decompose each column of the result from the first step.
3. **Obtain Four Sub-Bands**: The result is four sub-bands representing different combinations of low- and high-frequency components.

This process can be repeated for the **LL** sub-band (low frequencies) to obtain a **multilevel decomposition**. The more levels of decomposition, the better we can capture coarse details of the image.

Python Implementation of 2D DWT Using PyWavelets:

```
import cv2

import pywt

import matplotlib.pyplot as plt
```

```python
# Load the image in grayscale

image            =            cv2.imread('example_image.jpg',
cv2.IMREAD_GRAYSCALE)


# Perform 2D DWT on the image using Haar wavelet

coeffs2 = pywt.dwt2(image, 'haar')


# Extract the approximation and detail coefficients

LL, (LH, HL, HH) = coeffs2


# Plot the sub-bands

plt.figure(figsize=(8, 8))


plt.subplot(221), plt.imshow(LL, cmap='gray')

plt.title('Approximation (LL)'), plt.axis('off')


plt.subplot(222), plt.imshow(LH, cmap='gray')

plt.title('Horizontal (LH)'), plt.axis('off')


plt.subplot(223), plt.imshow(HL, cmap='gray')

plt.title('Vertical (HL)'), plt.axis('off')


plt.subplot(224), plt.imshow(HH, cmap='gray')

plt.title('Diagonal (HH)'), plt.axis('off')


plt.tight_layout()
```

plt.show()

Explanation:

- pywt.dwt2(image, 'haar') performs a 2D discrete wavelet transform using the **Haar wavelet** (a commonly used wavelet in image processing).
- The image is decomposed into four sub-bands: LL, LH, HL, and HH.
- The sub-bands are then plotted to visualize the different frequency components.

Wavelet-Based Image Compression

Wavelet-based image compression is a key application of wavelet transforms. One of the most well-known examples is **JPEG 2000**, which uses the DWT for compression, unlike the older JPEG format that relies on the Discrete Cosine Transform (DCT).

- **Steps in Wavelet-Based Compression:**
  1. **Wavelet Decomposition**: The image is decomposed into multiple sub-bands using the DWT.
  2. **Quantization**: The coefficients in the high-frequency sub-bands (HL, LH, HH) are quantized more aggressively than the low-frequency coefficients (LL), as humans are less sensitive to high-frequency details.
  3. **Encoding**: The quantized coefficients are encoded using an efficient algorithm (e.g., Huffman or arithmetic coding).
- **Advantages over JPEG**:
  - **Better Compression Ratios**: Wavelet-based compression achieves better compression ratios at the same quality levels compared to JPEG.
  - **Multiresolution Representation**: Wavelet compression can represent images at different resolutions, making it suitable for progressive image transmission.

Wavelet Transform vs Fourier Transform

Aspect	Wavelet Transform	Fourier Transform
Basis Functions	Wavelets (localized in both time/space and frequency).	Sinusoids (localized only in frequency, global in time/space).
Localization	Good localization in both time/space and frequency.	Good localization in frequency but poor in time/space.
Multiresolution Analysis	Yes, allows analyzing the signal at multiple resolutions.	No inherent multiresolution analysis.
Non-Stationary Signals	Handles non-stationary signals effectively.	Less effective for non-stationary signals.
Applications	Image compression, denoising, feature extraction.	Frequency analysis, filtering, global patterns in signals.

Applications of Wavelet Transform in Image Processing

1. **Image Compression**: JPEG 2000 uses the DWT for compression, offering better quality at lower file sizes compared to traditional JPEG.
2. **Image Denoising**: Wavelet transforms are effective in removing noise from images. High-frequency coefficients, which often correspond to

noise, can be suppressed while keeping important image details intact.

3. **Feature Extraction**: Wavelets are used for texture analysis and object recognition because of their ability to capture both local and global features.
4. **Edge Detection**: Wavelet transforms can be used to detect edges at multiple scales, capturing both fine and coarse edges.
5. **Medical Imaging**: Wavelets are used in medical imaging (e.g., MRI, CT scans) for noise reduction and feature enhancement.

Conclusion

The **Wavelet Transform** is a powerful tool for image processing due to its ability to represent both spatial and frequency information. It provides a multiresolution analysis that is highly useful for image compression, denoising, and texture analysis. Unlike the Fourier Transform, which only captures global frequency content, wavelets provide a localized analysis, making them particularly useful for images and signals with localized, transient features.

Chapter 4: Feature Detection and Description

Keypoint Detection

Keypoint Detection is a critical concept in computer vision and image processing. It refers to the process of identifying significant points, or "keypoints," in an image that are informative, robust, and repeatable under various conditions like scale, rotation, and lighting changes. These keypoints are typically located in regions of the image that have distinct textures, edges, or patterns, such as corners, blobs, or junctions.

Importance of Keypoint Detection

Keypoint detection is the foundation for many computer vision applications such as:

- **Feature Matching**: Matching corresponding keypoints between different images for tasks like image stitching.
- **Object Recognition**: Detecting and recognizing objects based on the keypoints in an image.

- **Structure from Motion**: Reconstructing 3D structures from 2D images by tracking keypoints across multiple images.
- **Augmented Reality**: Identifying anchor points in the real-world environment to overlay virtual content.

Types of Keypoint Detectors

1. **Corner Detectors**:
   - **Harris Corner Detector**: A classical method for detecting corners in images, using gradients to find areas where there is a large change in intensity in two orthogonal directions.
2. **Blob Detectors**:
   - **Laplacian of Gaussian (LoG)**: This method detects blobs by finding areas in the image that differ in intensity compared to surrounding pixels.
   - **Difference of Gaussian (DoG)**: An approximation of LoG used in the SIFT algorithm for detecting keypoints at multiple scales.
   - **Determinant of Hessian (DoH)**: This method uses the Hessian matrix to detect blob-like structures in images.
3. **Scale and Rotation-Invariant Detectors**:
   - **SIFT (Scale-Invariant Feature Transform)**: One of the most popular keypoint detectors, it finds keypoints that are invariant to scaling, rotation, and translation, making it very robust.
   - **SURF (Speeded-Up Robust Features)**: A faster alternative to SIFT that uses a Hessian matrix-based approach to detect keypoints.
4. **Other Modern Detectors**:
   - **ORB (Oriented FAST and Rotated BRIEF)**: A computationally efficient detector that combines the FAST keypoint detector with the BRIEF descriptor, useful for real-time applications.

- ○ **FAST (Features from Accelerated Segment Test)**: A fast and efficient corner detector often used in real-time vision systems.

Keypoint Detection Process

1. **Detect Keypoints**: Identify potential keypoints in the image. This involves detecting regions with significant changes in intensity values, such as corners or blobs.
2. **Compute Descriptors**: For each detected keypoint, compute a **descriptor**. A descriptor is a vector that encodes the local appearance around the keypoint. This allows keypoints to be compared and matched across images.
3. **Keypoint Matching**: Once keypoints are detected and described, they can be matched between images for tasks like image stitching, object recognition, or 3D reconstruction.

Popular Keypoint Detection Algorithms

1. Harris Corner Detector

The Harris Corner Detector is one of the earliest methods for keypoint detection, specifically for corner detection. It computes the gradient of the image and identifies regions with large variations in two orthogonal directions, typically indicating corners.

The Harris corner response function is given by:

$$R = \det(M) - k \cdot (\operatorname{trace}(M))^2$$

Where:

- M is the second-moment matrix (structure tensor) computed from image gradients.
- k is a sensitivity parameter.
- $\det(M)$ and $\operatorname{trace}(M)$ are the determinant and trace of M, respectively.

A high value of R indicates a corner.

Python Implementation of Harris Corner Detector:

import cv2

import numpy as np

123

```
# Load the image
image = cv2.imread('example_image.jpg')
gray = cv2.cvtColor(image, cv2.COLOR_BGR2GRAY)


# Harris corner detection
gray = np.float32(gray)
harris_corners = cv2.cornerHarris(gray, blockSize=2,
ksize=3, k=0.04)


# Dilate corner image to enhance the corners
harris_corners = cv2.dilate(harris_corners, None)


# Threshold to identify strong corners
image[harris_corners > 0.01 * harris_corners.max()] = [0,
0, 255]


# Show the result
cv2.imshow('Harris Corners', image)
cv2.waitKey(0)
cv2.destroyAllWindows()
```

2. SIFT (Scale-Invariant Feature Transform)

The **SIFT** algorithm is one of the most widely used keypoint detection methods. It detects keypoints that are invariant to scale and rotation, making it robust for many tasks. SIFT has two main stages:

1. **Keypoint Detection**: The image is convolved with **Difference of Gaussians (DoG)** at multiple scales to detect keypoints.
2. **Descriptor Computation**: A descriptor vector is computed based on the local image gradients around each keypoint, which captures the orientation and gradient structure of the region.

Python Implementation of SIFT using OpenCV:

```
import cv2

import matplotlib.pyplot as plt


# Load the image

image = cv2.imread('example_image.jpg')

gray = cv2.cvtColor(image, cv2.COLOR_BGR2GRAY)


# Create a SIFT detector

sift = cv2.SIFT_create()


# Detect keypoints and compute descriptors

keypoints, descriptors = sift.detectAndCompute(gray, None)


# Draw keypoints on the image

image_with_keypoints = cv2.drawKeypoints(image, keypoints, None, flags=cv2.DRAW_MATCHES_FLAGS_DRAW_RICH_KEYPOINTS)


# Display the image with keypoints
```

```
plt.imshow(cv2.cvtColor(image_with_keypoints,
cv2.COLOR_BGR2RGB))
```

```
plt.title('SIFT Keypoints')
```

```
plt.axis('off')
```

```
plt.show()
```

3. ORB (Oriented FAST and Rotated BRIEF)

ORB is a fast and efficient keypoint detector and descriptor that combines the **FAST** detector with the **BRIEF** descriptor. It's widely used in real-time applications due to its computational efficiency.

Python Implementation of ORB:

```
import cv2
```

```
import matplotlib.pyplot as plt
```

```
# Load the image
```

```
image = cv2.imread('example_image.jpg')
```

```
gray = cv2.cvtColor(image, cv2.COLOR_BGR2GRAY)
```

```
# Create an ORB detector
```

```
orb = cv2.ORB_create()
```

```
# Detect keypoints and compute descriptors
```

```
keypoints, descriptors = orb.detectAndCompute(gray,
None)
```

```
# Draw keypoints on the image
```

126

```
image_with_keypoints    =    cv2.drawKeypoints(image,
keypoints,                                    None,
flags=cv2.DRAW_MATCHES_FLAGS_DRAW_RICH_K
EYPOINTS)
```

```
# Display the image with keypoints
```

```
plt.imshow(cv2.cvtColor(image_with_keypoints,
cv2.COLOR_BGR2RGB))
```

```
plt.title('ORB Keypoints')
```

```
plt.axis('off')
```

```
plt.show()
```

Applications of Keypoint Detection

1. **Image Stitching**: Keypoints from multiple images are detected and matched to stitch together panoramic images.
2. **Object Recognition**: Keypoints and descriptors can be used to recognize objects in an image by matching them to a database of known objects.
3. **Tracking and Motion Estimation**: In video sequences, keypoints can be tracked over time to estimate motion or object trajectories.
4. **3D Reconstruction**: By matching keypoints across multiple images, 3D structures can be reconstructed using techniques like structure from motion.

Conclusion

Keypoint detection is a fundamental step in many computer vision tasks. Algorithms like SIFT, SURF, ORB, and Harris corner detectors offer various strengths, such as robustness to scale, rotation, and noise, making them suitable for diverse applications like object recognition, image stitching, and 3D reconstruction. The choice of keypoint detector depends on the application requirements, such as speed, accuracy, and computational resources.

Feature Descriptors

Feature Descriptors are mathematical representations of image features that describe the appearance or structure around keypoints or regions of interest. Once keypoints are detected in an image, feature descriptors provide a way to encode the local neighborhood around these keypoints into a vector or signature. This allows for comparing and matching keypoints between different images, which is essential for tasks like object recognition, image stitching, and motion tracking.

Feature descriptors are designed to be invariant to transformations such as scale, rotation, and lighting changes, making them robust for many computer vision applications.

Key Characteristics of Feature Descriptors

1. **Invariance**: Descriptors should be invariant to common transformations (e.g., scaling, rotation, affine transformations).
2. **Discriminative Power**: Descriptors should be distinct enough to differentiate between different keypoints or regions.
3. **Compactness**: Descriptors should be as compact as possible to enable efficient storage and matching.
4. **Robustness**: Descriptors should be robust to noise, occlusions, or minor distortions in the image.

Popular Feature Descriptors

1. SIFT (Scale-Invariant Feature Transform) Descriptor

The **SIFT** descriptor is one of the most widely used and influential descriptors in computer vision. It computes a descriptor based on the gradients of pixel intensities around each keypoint, making it invariant to scale and rotation.

- **How It Works**:
    - SIFT first detects keypoints using the Difference of Gaussians (DoG) approach.
    - For each keypoint, a local gradient histogram is computed from the surrounding pixels.
    - The descriptor is a 128-dimensional vector formed by 16 gradient histograms (each with 8 orientation bins) from a 4x4 grid around the keypoint.
- **Properties**:
    - Invariant to scale, rotation, and small distortions.
    - Robust to changes in illumination and noise.

Python Implementation of SIFT Descriptor Extraction:

```
import cv2


# Load the image

image = cv2.imread('example_image.jpg')

gray = cv2.cvtColor(image, cv2.COLOR_BGR2GRAY)


# Create a SIFT detector

sift = cv2.SIFT_create()
```

```
# Detect keypoints and compute descriptors
keypoints, descriptors = sift.detectAndCompute(gray, None)


print(f"Number of keypoints detected: {len(keypoints)}")

print(f"SIFT descriptors shape: {descriptors.shape}")  # Each descriptor is 128-dimensional
```

2. SURF (Speeded-Up Robust Features) Descriptor

SURF is an improvement over SIFT in terms of speed. It uses a Haar wavelet response and integral images to speed up the computation of both keypoints and descriptors.

- **How It Works**:
    - SURF uses a Hessian matrix-based blob detector to find keypoints.
    - It computes descriptors using Haar wavelets in a square region around each keypoint.
    - SURF uses a 64-dimensional descriptor (as opposed to SIFT's 128 dimensions) for efficiency.
- **Properties**:
    - Faster than SIFT but less accurate for fine details.
    - Scale and rotation-invariant.

Python Implementation of SURF Descriptor Extraction:

```
import cv2


# Load the image
image = cv2.imread('example_image.jpg')
```

130

gray = cv2.cvtColor(image, cv2.COLOR_BGR2GRAY)

Create a SURF detector (use SIFT in OpenCV since SURF is not included by default)

surf = cv2.xfeatures2d.SURF_create()

Detect keypoints and compute descriptors

keypoints, descriptors = surf.detectAndCompute(gray, None)

print(f"Number of keypoints detected: {len(keypoints)}")

print(f"SURF descriptors shape: {descriptors.shape}") # Each descriptor is 64-dimensional

3. BRIEF (Binary Robust Independent Elementary Features)

BRIEF is a compact and efficient binary descriptor. Unlike SIFT and SURF, which use floating-point vectors, BRIEF generates binary strings by comparing intensities of pixel pairs around the keypoints.

How It Works:

- BRIEF doesn't detect keypoints but relies on other detectors (e.g., FAST).
- For each keypoint, BRIEF creates a binary string by comparing the intensity of randomly selected pixel pairs in the keypoint's neighborhood.
- The descriptor is a compact binary string, making it very efficient to compute and compare.

Properties:

- Very fast and efficient.
- Not scale or rotation-invariant (can be combined with detectors that offer invariance).

Python Implementation of BRIEF Descriptor Extraction:

```
import cv2


# Load the image

image = cv2.imread('example_image.jpg')

gray = cv2.cvtColor(image, cv2.COLOR_BGR2GRAY)


# Create a FAST detector for keypoints

fast = cv2.FastFeatureDetector_create()


# Detect keypoints

keypoints = fast.detect(gray, None)


# Create a BRIEF extractor

brief = cv2.xfeatures2d.BriefDescriptorExtractor_create()


# Compute descriptors

keypoints, descriptors = brief.compute(gray, keypoints)


print(f"Number of keypoints detected: {len(keypoints)}")

print(f"BRIEF descriptors shape: {descriptors.shape}")  # Each descriptor is binary
```

4. ORB (Oriented FAST and Rotated BRIEF)

ORB is a combination of the FAST detector and the BRIEF descriptor, with added orientation information. It is designed to be efficient and effective for real-time applications, offering scale and rotation invariance.

How It Works:

- ORB uses the FAST detector to find keypoints and then assigns an orientation to each keypoint.
- The BRIEF descriptor is rotated according to the orientation of the keypoint, making it rotation-invariant.

Properties:

- Fast and suitable for real-time applications.
- Scale and rotation-invariant.
- Uses binary descriptors, making matching efficient.

Python Implementation of ORB Descriptor Extraction:

```
import cv2


# Load the image

image = cv2.imread('example_image.jpg')

gray = cv2.cvtColor(image, cv2.COLOR_BGR2GRAY)


# Create an ORB detector

orb = cv2.ORB_create()


# Detect keypoints and compute descriptors
```

```
keypoints, descriptors = orb.detectAndCompute(gray,
None)
```

```
print(f"Number of keypoints detected: {len(keypoints)}")
```

```
print(f"ORB descriptors shape: {descriptors.shape}")  #
Each descriptor is binary
```

5. HOG (Histogram of Oriented Gradients) Descriptor

HOG is a descriptor used primarily for object detection, especially for detecting humans in images. It works by computing histograms of gradients in localized regions of an image.

How It Works:

- The image is divided into small cells, and for each cell, a histogram of gradient orientations is computed.
- These histograms are then normalized over larger blocks to improve invariance to lighting and contrast changes.
- The final descriptor is a concatenation of these histograms.

Properties:

- Robust to lighting changes and small deformations.
- Commonly used for pedestrian detection.

Python Implementation of HOG Descriptor Extraction:

```
import cv2
```

```
from skimage.feature import hog
```

```
import matplotlib.pyplot as plt
```

```
# Load the image

image = cv2.imread('example_image.jpg')

gray = cv2.cvtColor(image, cv2.COLOR_BGR2GRAY)


# Compute HOG descriptor

hog_descriptor, hog_image = hog(gray, orientations=9,
pixels_per_cell=(8, 8),

                    cells_per_block=(2,             2),
block_norm='L2-Hys',

                    visualize=True, multichannel=False)


# Display HOG visualization

plt.imshow(hog_image, cmap='gray')

plt.title('HOG Descriptor Visualization')

plt.axis('off')

plt.show()
```

Feature Descriptor Matching

After computing descriptors for keypoints in an image, the next step is to match these descriptors across different images. This is commonly done using distance metrics such as:

- **Euclidean Distance**: For floating-point descriptors like SIFT and SURF.
- **Hamming Distance**: For binary descriptors like BRIEF and ORB.

Descriptor matching is used in various applications, such as **stereo vision**, **object recognition**, and **image stitching**.

Descriptor Matching Using BFMatcher in OpenCV:

```
# Create a BFMatcher object for matching descriptors

bf        =        cv2.BFMatcher(cv2.NORM_HAMMING,
crossCheck=True)


# Match descriptors between two images

matches = bf.match(descriptors1, descriptors2)


# Sort the matches based on distance

matches = sorted(matches, key=lambda x: x.distance)


# Draw matches

image_matches = cv2.drawMatches(image1, keypoints1,
image2,       keypoints2,       matches[:50],       None,
flags=cv2.DrawMatchesFlags_NOT_DRAW_SINGLE_P
OINTS)


# Display the matches

plt.imshow(image_matches)

plt.title('Descriptor Matches')

plt.axis('off')

plt.show()
```

Conclusion

Feature descriptors like **SIFT**, **SURF**, **ORB**, and **BRIEF** are powerful tools for encoding the local appearance around keypoints. They are essential for many computer vision tasks, including object recognition, tracking, and 3D reconstruction. The choice of descriptor depends on the application, with SIFT and SURF offering robust results

Husn Ara

but slower performance, while ORB and BRIEF offer faster, real-time capabilities with binary descriptors. Matching these descriptors between images allows for solving more complex problems such as image alignment, stereo vision, and recognition.

Feature Matching and Correspondence

Feature Matching and Correspondence are fundamental concepts in computer vision used to find similarities between images by identifying common points, or "features," across different images. The goal of feature matching is to determine which features in one image correspond to the same features in another image, enabling tasks such as object recognition, image stitching, and 3D reconstruction.

Overview

- **Feature Matching**: The process of finding similar features between two or more images.
- **Correspondence**: The concept of associating or matching points in one image with corresponding points in another image.

The process typically involves the following steps:

1. **Detect Keypoints**: Keypoints are detected in each image using techniques like SIFT, ORB, or FAST.
2. **Extract Descriptors**: Feature descriptors (e.g., SIFT, ORB, BRIEF) are calculated for each keypoint to describe its local neighborhood.
3. **Match Descriptors**: The descriptors between two images are compared to find the best matches

137

using distance metrics such as Euclidean or Hamming distance.

4. **Estimate Correspondence**: After matching, outliers are filtered out (using methods like RANSAC) to establish accurate correspondences.

Types of Matching

1. Brute Force Matching

The simplest approach to feature matching is brute force matching, where descriptors from one image are compared with descriptors from another image, and the best match is chosen based on a distance metric.

- **Euclidean Distance**: Used for floating-point descriptors like SIFT and SURF.
- **Hamming Distance**: Used for binary descriptors like ORB and BRIEF.

Python Implementation of Brute Force Matching with ORB:

```
import cv2

import matplotlib.pyplot as plt


# Load two images

image1           =           cv2.imread('image1.jpg',
cv2.IMREAD_GRAYSCALE)

image2           =           cv2.imread('image2.jpg',
cv2.IMREAD_GRAYSCALE)


# Detect ORB keypoints and descriptors

orb = cv2.ORB_create()
```

```
keypoints1, descriptors1 =
orb.detectAndCompute(image1, None)

keypoints2, descriptors2 =
orb.detectAndCompute(image2, None)


# Create BFMatcher object with Hamming distance (for
binary descriptors like ORB)

bf = cv2.BFMatcher(cv2.NORM_HAMMING,
crossCheck=True)


# Match descriptors

matches = bf.match(descriptors1, descriptors2)


# Sort them in the order of their distance (best matches
first)

matches = sorted(matches, key=lambda x: x.distance)


# Draw the first 50 matches

image_matches = cv2.drawMatches(image1, keypoints1,
image2, keypoints2, matches[:50], None,
flags=cv2.DrawMatchesFlags_NOT_DRAW_SINGLE_P
OINTS)


# Display the matches

plt.imshow(image_matches)

plt.title('ORB Feature Matching')

plt.axis('off')

plt.show()
```

2. K-Nearest Neighbors (KNN) Matching

Instead of finding only the single best match, **K-Nearest Neighbors (KNN)** matching finds the top **k** nearest matches for each descriptor. This can provide more robust matching, and combined with ratio tests (e.g., Lowe's ratio test), it can improve accuracy by eliminating ambiguous matches.

- **Lowe's Ratio Test**: Used to eliminate weak matches. It compares the distances of the two nearest neighbors for each feature. If the ratio of the closest to the second closest is below a certain threshold (usually 0.75), the match is considered good.

Python Implementation of KNN Matching with Lowe's Ratio Test (SIFT):

```
import cv2

import matplotlib.pyplot as plt


# Load two images

image1            =            cv2.imread('image1.jpg',
cv2.IMREAD_GRAYSCALE)

image2            =            cv2.imread('image2.jpg',
cv2.IMREAD_GRAYSCALE)


# Detect SIFT keypoints and descriptors

sift = cv2.SIFT_create()

keypoints1,            descriptors1            =
sift.detectAndCompute(image1, None)

keypoints2,            descriptors2            =
sift.detectAndCompute(image2, None)
```

```python
# Create BFMatcher object with L2 norm (for SIFT
descriptors)

bf = cv2.BFMatcher(cv2.NORM_L2, crossCheck=False)


# KNN matching

matches = bf.knnMatch(descriptors1, descriptors2, k=2)


# Apply Lowe's ratio test

good_matches = []

for m, n in matches:

    if m.distance < 0.75 * n.distance:

        good_matches.append(m)


# Draw matches

image_matches = cv2.drawMatches(image1, keypoints1,
image2,       keypoints2,       good_matches,       None,
flags=cv2.DrawMatchesFlags_NOT_DRAW_SINGLE_P
OINTS)


# Display the matches

plt.imshow(image_matches)

plt.title('SIFT Feature Matching with Lowe's Ratio Test')

plt.axis('off')

plt.show()
```

Outlier Removal and RANSAC

Even with good feature matching, some matches might still be incorrect due to noise, occlusion, or repeating patterns in the image. **Random Sample Consensus (RANSAC)** is a common technique used to filter out such outliers by estimating a transformation model (e.g., homography, fundamental matrix) and keeping only inliers that fit this model.

Steps in RANSAC:

1. Randomly select a subset of matches.
2. Compute a transformation (e.g., homography, fundamental matrix) based on this subset.
3. Measure how well the transformation fits all matches.
4. Repeat the process to find the transformation with the most inliers (good matches).
5. Use the best transformation to estimate accurate correspondences.

Python Implementation of RANSAC for Homography:

```
import cv2

import numpy as np

import matplotlib.pyplot as plt
```

```
# Load two images
image1           =           cv2.imread('image1.jpg',
cv2.IMREAD_GRAYSCALE)

image2           =           cv2.imread('image2.jpg',
cv2.IMREAD_GRAYSCALE)
```

```
# Detect ORB keypoints and descriptors
orb = cv2.ORB_create()
```

142

```python
keypoints1,                    descriptors1            =
orb.detectAndCompute(image1, None)

keypoints2,                    descriptors2            =
orb.detectAndCompute(image2, None)


# Create BFMatcher object with Hamming distance

bf         =          cv2.BFMatcher(cv2.NORM_HAMMING,
crossCheck=True)


# Match descriptors

matches = bf.match(descriptors1, descriptors2)


# Sort them in the order of their distance

matches = sorted(matches, key=lambda x: x.distance)


# Extract matched keypoints

points1 = np.zeros((len(matches), 2), dtype=np.float32)

points2 = np.zeros((len(matches), 2), dtype=np.float32)


for i, match in enumerate(matches):
    points1[i, :] = keypoints1[match.queryIdx].pt
    points2[i, :] = keypoints2[match.trainIdx].pt


# Compute the homography matrix using RANSAC

homography,  mask  =  cv2.findHomography(points1,
points2, cv2.RANSAC)
```

```
# Select only inliers (good matches)

inliers = [matches[i] for i in range(len(mask)) if mask[i]]


# Draw inlier matches

image_inliers = cv2.drawMatches(image1, keypoints1,
image2, keypoints2, inliers, None,
flags=cv2.DrawMatchesFlags_NOT_DRAW_SINGLE_P
OINTS)


# Display the result

plt.imshow(image_inliers)

plt.title('Inlier Matches with RANSAC')

plt.axis('off')

plt.show()
```

Applications of Feature Matching and Correspondence

1. **Image Stitching**: Multiple overlapping images can be stitched together into a panorama by matching features and finding correspondences between them.
2. **3D Reconstruction**: Feature correspondence between images taken from different viewpoints can be used to recover 3D structure.
3. **Object Recognition**: Correspondence between features in a query image and features in a database of known objects allows for object recognition.
4. **Motion Tracking**: Feature matching across frames in a video sequence enables motion tracking and trajectory estimation.

Conclusion

Husn Ara

Feature matching and correspondence play a crucial role in many computer vision tasks. By using feature detectors and descriptors like SIFT, ORB, and BRIEF, combined with robust matching techniques like KNN and RANSAC, we can identify corresponding points between images and achieve accurate results for applications such as image stitching, object recognition, and 3D reconstruction.

Chapter 5: Image Segmentation

Thresholding Techniques

Thresholding Techniques in image processing are methods used to convert grayscale images into binary images by segmenting the image based on pixel intensity values. The objective is to separate the foreground (object) from the background, which is particularly useful in object detection, image segmentation, and feature extraction.

Thresholding simplifies the image analysis process by converting a complex grayscale or color image into a binary image where each pixel is either "on" (white) or "off" (black), representing object and background, respectively.

Types of Thresholding Techniques

1. **Global Thresholding**
2. **Adaptive Thresholding**
3. **Otsu's Thresholding**

1. Global Thresholding

In global thresholding, a single threshold value is chosen for the entire image. All pixels with intensity values above this threshold are classified as one class (e.g., object), and those below are classified as another class (e.g., background).

Formula:

For a grayscale image I(x, y) and a threshold T:

- If I(x, y) > T, pixel becomes 1 (white).
- If I(x, y) <= T, pixel becomes 0 (black).

Python Implementation of Global Thresholding:

```python
import cv2

import matplotlib.pyplot as plt


# Load the grayscale image

image = cv2.imread('image.jpg', cv2.IMREAD_GRAYSCALE)


# Apply global thresholding

_, thresholded_image = cv2.threshold(image, 127, 255, cv2.THRESH_BINARY)


# Display the thresholded image

plt.imshow(thresholded_image, cmap='gray')

plt.title('Global Thresholding')

plt.axis('off')

plt.show()
```

2. Adaptive Thresholding

In adaptive thresholding, the threshold value is calculated for smaller regions of the image, allowing for different thresholds for different parts of the image. This method is useful when the lighting in the image is not uniform, and a single global threshold would not work effectively.

Types of Adaptive Thresholding:

- **Mean Adaptive Thresholding**: The threshold is the mean of the neighborhood area.
- **Gaussian Adaptive Thresholding**: The threshold is a weighted sum (Gaussian window) of the neighborhood values.

Python Implementation of Adaptive Thresholding:

```
import cv2

import matplotlib.pyplot as plt


# Load the grayscale image

image           =           cv2.imread('image.jpg',
cv2.IMREAD_GRAYSCALE)


# Apply adaptive mean thresholding

adaptive_mean = cv2.adaptiveThreshold(image, 255,
cv2.ADAPTIVE_THRESH_MEAN_C,

              cv2.THRESH_BINARY, 11, 2)


# Apply adaptive Gaussian thresholding

adaptive_gaussian = cv2.adaptiveThreshold(image, 255,
cv2.ADAPTIVE_THRESH_GAUSSIAN_C,

              cv2.THRESH_BINARY, 11, 2)
```

```
# Display the results
plt.figure(figsize=(10, 5))
plt.subplot(1, 2, 1)
plt.imshow(adaptive_mean, cmap='gray')
plt.title('Adaptive Mean Thresholding')
plt.axis('off')


plt.subplot(1, 2, 2)
plt.imshow(adaptive_gaussian, cmap='gray')
plt.title('Adaptive Gaussian Thresholding')
plt.axis('off')


plt.show()
```

3. Otsu's Thresholding

Otsu's method is an automatic global thresholding technique that calculates the optimal threshold value by minimizing the intra-class variance (the variance within the foreground and background pixel intensities). It is particularly useful when the image has a bimodal histogram, where pixel intensities are grouped into two peaks representing the background and foreground.

Otsu's thresholding can be combined with Gaussian filtering for better results on noisy images.

Python Implementation of Otsu's Thresholding:

```
import cv2
```

```python
import matplotlib.pyplot as plt

# Load the grayscale image
image = cv2.imread('image.jpg', cv2.IMREAD_GRAYSCALE)

# Apply Otsu's thresholding
_, otsu_thresholded_image = cv2.threshold(image, 0, 255, cv2.THRESH_BINARY + cv2.THRESH_OTSU)

# Display the result
plt.imshow(otsu_thresholded_image, cmap='gray')
plt.title("Otsu's Thresholding")
plt.axis('off')
plt.show()
```

Otsu's Thresholding with Gaussian Smoothing:

```python
# Apply Gaussian filtering
blurred_image = cv2.GaussianBlur(image, (5, 5), 0)

# Apply Otsu's thresholding
_, otsu_thresholded_blurred_image = cv2.threshold(blurred_image, 0, 255, cv2.THRESH_BINARY + cv2.THRESH_OTSU)

# Display the result
plt.imshow(otsu_thresholded_blurred_image, cmap='gray')
```

plt.title("Otsu's Thresholding with Gaussian Smoothing")

plt.axis('off')

plt.show()

Comparing Thresholding Techniques

- **Global Thresholding**: Works well for images with uniform lighting. It's fast and simple but ineffective when there are variations in illumination across the image.
- **Adaptive Thresholding**: Suitable for images with non-uniform lighting. It calculates different thresholds for different regions of the image, but it can be slower than global thresholding.
- **Otsu's Thresholding**: Automatically finds the optimal global threshold, but it assumes that the image has two distinct pixel intensity classes (bimodal histogram). Combining Otsu's thresholding with Gaussian filtering helps in removing noise before applying thresholding.

Applications of Thresholding

- **Document Binarization**: Separating text from the background in scanned documents.
- **Medical Imaging**: Segmenting regions of interest in X-rays or MRI scans.
- **Object Detection**: Isolating objects from the background in vision systems.
- **Face Detection**: Thresholding the skin color region in facial detection systems.

Conclusion

Thresholding is a crucial image segmentation technique that converts grayscale images into binary images. Depending on the image's characteristics and lighting conditions, global, adaptive, or Otsu's thresholding can be chosen to effectively segment foreground objects from the background.

Region-Based Segmentation

Region-based segmentation is a technique in image processing used to partition an image into different regions based on similarity in pixel properties, such as intensity or color. The goal is to group pixels that are similar to each other and separate them from dissimilar regions, effectively dividing the image into meaningful regions that correspond to different objects or parts of objects.

Region-based segmentation is often more effective than edge detection when the goal is to partition an image into large, contiguous regions. Unlike edge-based methods, which rely on detecting boundaries, region-based methods directly group pixels that belong to the same region.

Key Concepts of Region-Based Segmentation

1. **Region Growing**
2. **Region Splitting and Merging**
3. **Watershed Algorithm**

1. Region Growing

Region growing is a simple region-based segmentation method where the algorithm starts with a seed point and grows the region by adding neighboring pixels that are similar in terms of intensity, color, or texture.

Steps in Region Growing:

- Select one or more seed points in the image (either manually or automatically).
- Initialize a region with the seed points.
- For each pixel in the region, examine its neighboring pixels.
- Add neighboring pixels to the region if they meet the similarity criteria.
- Repeat the process until no more pixels can be added to the region.

Python Implementation of Region Growing:

```python
import numpy as np

import cv2

import matplotlib.pyplot as plt


# Load the grayscale image

image = cv2.imread('image.jpg', cv2.IMREAD_GRAYSCALE)


# Seed point and threshold

seed_point = (100, 100)  # Example seed point

threshold = 10


# Create a mask for the region growing process

mask = np.zeros_like(image)
```

```python
h, w = image.shape


# Region-growing function
def region_growing(image, mask, seed_point, threshold):
    x, y = seed_point
    region_mean = image[x, y]
    mask[x, y] = 255  # Mark the seed point in the mask
    stack = [(x, y)]

    while len(stack) > 0:
        x, y = stack.pop()

        # Check the 4-connected neighborhood
        for dx, dy in [(-1, 0), (1, 0), (0, -1), (0, 1)]:
            nx, ny = x + dx, y + dy

            if 0 <= nx < h and 0 <= ny < w and mask[nx, ny] == 0:
                if abs(int(image[nx, ny]) - int(region_mean)) < threshold:
                    mask[nx, ny] = 255
                    stack.append((nx, ny))

    return mask


# Perform region growing
```

```
segmented_image    =    region_growing(image,    mask,
seed_point, threshold)
```

Display the result

plt.imshow(segmented_image, cmap='gray')

plt.title('Region Growing Segmentation')

plt.axis('off')

plt.show()

2. Region Splitting and Merging

In this technique, the image is repeatedly subdivided into regions (splitting) and then adjacent regions are merged if they satisfy a predefined criterion (merging). The idea is to iteratively split the image into smaller regions that are homogeneous and then merge neighboring regions that are similar to each other.

Steps in Region Splitting and Merging:

- Start by considering the entire image as a single region.
- If a region is not homogeneous (based on a threshold), split it into smaller sub-regions (typically into quadrants).
- If adjacent regions are similar, merge them.
- Continue the process until no more splitting or merging is required.

This method is useful for images where regions may vary significantly in size but still have homogeneity within them.

3. Watershed Algorithm

The watershed algorithm is a powerful region-based segmentation technique that treats the image as a topographic surface, where the intensity of each pixel represents elevation. It segments the image by flooding the valleys of the topography. The algorithm identifies watershed lines (ridges) that separate different catchment basins (regions).

Steps in the Watershed Algorithm:

- The image is treated as a landscape or topography.
- Local minima in pixel intensity are considered as catchment basins.
- Water "floods" from these basins and merges neighboring basins based on their gradients, while watershed lines form the boundaries between different regions.

Watershed segmentation is especially useful when combined with other techniques such as **gradient-based segmentation** and **morphological operations** to remove noise before segmentation.

Python Implementation of the Watershed Algorithm:

```python
import cv2

import numpy as np

import matplotlib.pyplot as plt


# Load the image

image = cv2.imread('image.jpg')

gray = cv2.cvtColor(image, cv2.COLOR_BGR2GRAY)


# Apply a binary threshold to get a binary image
```

```
_,    binary_image    =    cv2.threshold(gray,    0,    255,
cv2.THRESH_BINARY_INV + cv2.THRESH_OTSU)
```

```
# Noise removal using morphological operations
```

```
kernel = np.ones((3, 3), np.uint8)
```

```
opening        =        cv2.morphologyEx(binary_image,
cv2.MORPH_OPEN, kernel, iterations=2)
```

```
# Sure background area (dilated image)
```

```
sure_bg = cv2.dilate(opening, kernel, iterations=3)
```

```
# Sure foreground area (using distance transform)
```

```
dist_transform    =    cv2.distanceTransform(opening,
cv2.DIST_L2, 5)
```

```
_,    sure_fg    =    cv2.threshold(dist_transform,    0.7    *
dist_transform.max(), 255, 0)
```

```
# Unknown region (subtracting sure foreground from sure
background)
```

```
sure_fg = np.uint8(sure_fg)
```

```
unknown = cv2.subtract(sure_bg, sure_fg)
```

```
# Marker labeling
```

```
_, markers = cv2.connectedComponents(sure_fg)
```

```
# Add 1 to all labels so that sure background is not 0 but
1
```

```
markers = markers + 1
```

```
# Mark the unknown region with zero
markers[unknown == 255] = 0


# Apply the watershed algorithm
markers = cv2.watershed(image, markers)


# Mark the boundaries of regions in red
image[markers == -1] = [255, 0, 0]


# Display the result
plt.imshow(cv2.cvtColor(image,
cv2.COLOR_BGR2RGB))
plt.title('Watershed Segmentation')
plt.axis('off')
plt.show()
```

Comparison of Region-Based Segmentation Methods

Technique	Advantages	Disadvantages
Region Growing	Simple, effective for homogeneous regions	Sensitive to noise, requires good seed point
Region Splitting & Merging	Adaptable to varying region sizes, no seed point needed	Can be slow, depends on homogeneity criterion

Technique	Advantages	Disadvantages
Watershed Algorithm	Useful for gradient-based segmentation, can separate touching objects	Sensitive to noise, can lead to over-segmentation

Applications of Region-Based Segmentation

- **Medical Imaging**: Segmenting regions of interest, such as tumors, organs, or other structures in CT or MRI scans.
- **Object Detection**: Identifying and isolating objects in a scene based on their homogeneity in color or texture.
- **Satellite Imagery**: Segmenting different land types (e.g., urban, forest, water) based on pixel intensity or texture.
- **Automated Quality Control**: Detecting defects in materials by segmenting the regions where the defect might occur.

Conclusion

Region-based segmentation techniques are essential tools in image processing for dividing an image into meaningful regions based on pixel similarity. While region growing and region splitting and merging are basic methods, more advanced techniques like the watershed algorithm provide powerful ways to segment images with varying intensities and gradients. Depending on the application, the appropriate region-based segmentation technique can lead to accurate image analysis and interpretation.

Edge-Based Segmentation

Edge-based segmentation is an image processing technique that focuses on detecting boundaries between regions in an image by identifying edges. An edge represents a sharp change in intensity or color, and edge-based segmentation methods aim to segment an image by detecting and tracing these edges. This method is widely used in applications like object detection, feature extraction, and image recognition.

Edge-based segmentation relies on edge detection algorithms, which highlight discontinuities in the image and use these edges to define region boundaries.

Key Concepts of Edge-Based Segmentation

1. **Edge Detection Operators**
   - Sobel operator
   - Prewitt operator
   - Roberts operator
   - Canny edge detector
2. **Edge Linking and Boundary Tracing**
3. **Gradient-based Techniques**
4. **Laplacian-based Techniques**

1. Edge Detection Operators

Edge detection operators are convolution kernels that are applied to the image to detect changes in intensity or gradient. These changes often represent object boundaries. Some common edge detection operators are:

Sobel Operator

The Sobel operator detects edges by computing the gradient of the image intensity in the horizontal and vertical directions. It uses two convolution masks, one for the horizontal gradient and one for the vertical gradient.

Python Implementation of Sobel Edge Detection:

import cv2

import numpy as np

import matplotlib.pyplot as plt

Load the image

image = cv2.imread('image.jpg', cv2.IMREAD_GRAYSCALE)

Apply Sobel edge detection

sobel_x = cv2.Sobel(image, cv2.CV_64F, 1, 0, ksize=3) # Horizontal edges

sobel_y = cv2.Sobel(image, cv2.CV_64F, 0, 1, ksize=3) # Vertical edges

Combine the results

sobel_combined = cv2.magnitude(sobel_x, sobel_y)

Display the result

```
plt.imshow(sobel_combined, cmap='gray')
```

```
plt.title('Sobel Edge Detection')
```

```
plt.axis('off')
```

```
plt.show()
```

Canny Edge Detector

The Canny edge detector is one of the most popular and effective edge detection algorithms. It uses a multi-stage process that includes noise reduction, gradient calculation, non-maximum suppression, and edge tracking through hysteresis. It's known for producing thin, precise edges.

Python Implementation of Canny Edge Detection:

```
# Load the image
```

```
image            =            cv2.imread('image.jpg',
cv2.IMREAD_GRAYSCALE)
```

```
# Apply Canny edge detection
```

```
edges = cv2.Canny(image, 100, 200)
```

```
# Display the result
```

```
plt.imshow(edges, cmap='gray')
```

```
plt.title('Canny Edge Detection')
```

```
plt.axis('off')
```

```
plt.show()
```

2. Edge Linking and Boundary Tracing

After detecting edges in the image, the next step in edge-based segmentation is to link these edges and trace the boundaries of objects. Edge linking is the process of connecting edge points to form continuous boundaries. This can be done using algorithms like **Hough transform** or using morphological operations to connect broken edges.

Hough Transform for Line Detection:

The Hough transform is a popular technique for detecting lines and shapes (like circles) in edge-detected images. It works by transforming points in the image into parameter space and identifying parameter values that form a straight line.

Python Implementation of Hough Line Transform:

```
# Apply Canny edge detection
edges = cv2.Canny(image, 100, 200)


# Apply Hough Line Transform
lines = cv2.HoughLines(edges, 1, np.pi / 180, 100)


# Draw the lines on the image
for line in lines:
    rho, theta = line[0]
    a = np.cos(theta)
    b = np.sin(theta)
    x0 = a * rho
    y0 = b * rho
    x1 = int(x0 + 1000 * (-b))
```

```
y1 = int(y0 + 1000 * (a))

x2 = int(x0 - 1000 * (-b))

y2 = int(y0 - 1000 * (a))

cv2.line(image, (x1, y1), (x2, y2), (0, 255, 0), 2)


# Display the result

plt.imshow(cv2.cvtColor(image,
cv2.COLOR_BGR2RGB))

plt.title('Hough Line Detection')

plt.axis('off')

plt.show()
```

3. Gradient-Based Techniques

Edge-based segmentation often involves calculating the gradient of the image intensity. The gradient is a vector that points in the direction of the greatest rate of change of intensity. High-gradient regions typically correspond to edges in the image.

- **Sobel operator** computes the gradient in both horizontal and vertical directions.
- **Prewitt operator** is similar to Sobel but uses a simpler kernel.
- **Roberts operator** is another gradient-based operator that detects diagonal edges.

Laplacian of Gaussian (LoG)

The Laplacian of Gaussian (LoG) combines the Laplacian operator with Gaussian smoothing to detect edges. It is useful for detecting edges in noisy images, as the Gaussian filter smooths the image before applying the Laplacian operator.

Python Implementation of LoG Edge Detection:

```
# Apply GaussianBlur to smooth the image
blurred_image = cv2.GaussianBlur(image, (3, 3), 0)


# Apply the Laplacian operator
laplacian = cv2.Laplacian(blurred_image, cv2.CV_64F)


# Display the result
plt.imshow(laplacian, cmap='gray')
plt.title('Laplacian of Gaussian Edge Detection')
plt.axis('off')
plt.show()
```

4. Laplacian-Based Techniques

The Laplacian operator calculates the second derivative of the image, highlighting regions where the intensity changes rapidly (edges). It is a non-directional operator, meaning it detects edges regardless of their orientation. However, because it is sensitive to noise, it is often used in combination with Gaussian smoothing (as seen in the Laplacian of Gaussian).

Zero-Crossings:

In Laplacian-based edge detection, edges are often identified as zero-crossings of the Laplacian, i.e., points where the intensity changes sign.

Comparison of Edge Detection Methods

Method	Advantages	Disadvantages
Sobel	Simple, fast, directional edge detection	Sensitive to noise, not very precise
Prewitt	Similar to Sobel, but computationally simpler	Less accurate for diagonal edges
Roberts	Effective for detecting diagonal edges	Sensitive to noise
Canny	Very precise, reduces noise, thin edges	More computationally expensive
LoG	Combines smoothing and edge detection	May detect false edges, sensitive to noise

Applications of Edge-Based Segmentation

1. **Object Detection**: Identifying the boundaries of objects in images for computer vision applications.
2. **Medical Imaging**: Detecting the boundaries of organs, tumors, or other structures in CT, MRI, or X-ray images.
3. **Document Image Analysis**: Detecting text, shapes, or figures in scanned documents.
4. **Robotics and Autonomous Systems**: Edge-based segmentation helps robots or autonomous vehicles recognize and navigate around objects in their environment.
5. **Face Detection**: Identifying edges of facial features like eyes, nose, and mouth.

Conclusion

Edge-based segmentation is a crucial technique in image processing that focuses on identifying regions based on

166

changes in intensity or color. Various edge detection algorithms, such as Sobel, Canny, and Laplacian of Gaussian, are used to detect edges, which are then linked to form boundaries between objects. The success of edge-based segmentation depends on factors like the image's noise level and the complexity of the objects within it.

Active Contour Models (Snakes)

Active Contour Models (Snakes) are energy-minimizing curves that evolve within an image to detect object boundaries. Introduced by Kass, Witkin, and Terzopoulos in 1987, they are used in image segmentation tasks, where the goal is to outline an object of interest based on image features such as edges. The curve (or snake) deforms under the influence of internal forces (which make the contour smooth) and external forces (derived from the image data) to align with object boundaries.

Key Concepts of Active Contour Models

1. **Energy Minimization Framework**
2. **Internal and External Forces**
3. **Active Contour Equation**
4. **Types of Snakes: Parametric and Geometric**
5. **Applications of Active Contour Models**

1. Energy Minimization Framework

The core idea behind active contour models is to minimize an energy function that governs the shape and position of the contour. The contour is represented as a parametric curve, denoted by $C(s) = (x(s), y(s))$, where s is the parametric variable. The energy function E_{snake} consists of internal energy, external energy, and image energy:

$$E_{snake} = \int [E_{internal}(C(s)) + E_{external}(C(s))]\, ds$$

- Internal Energy $E_{internal}$: Controls the smoothness of the contour, ensuring that the snake doesn't deform too irregularly.

- External Energy $E_{external}$: Derived from the image features (e.g., intensity gradients) to attract the contour to edges or features in the image.

2. Internal and External Forces

The snake is influenced by both internal and external forces:

Internal Forces

Internal forces maintain the smoothness and continuity of the snake. They are usually made up of two components:

- **Elasticity (first derivative)**: Ensures that the snake behaves like a string, resisting stretching.
- **Bending (second derivative)**: Ensures that the snake resists bending too sharply, promoting smooth curves.

Mathematically, the internal energy is given by:

$$E_{internal} = \alpha \left(\frac{dC(s)}{ds}\right)^2 + \beta \left(\frac{d^2 C(s)}{ds^2}\right)^2$$

where α controls the elasticity and β controls the bending stiffness.

External Forces

168

External forces pull the snake toward desired features such as object boundaries. These forces come from the image itself and guide the contour to high-intensity gradients (edges).

The external energy can be derived from:

- **Image gradient**: The contour is attracted to areas where the gradient magnitude is high, which usually corresponds to edges in the image.

A typical external energy term is:

$$E_{\text{external}} = -|\nabla I(x,y)|^2$$

where $I(x,y)$ is the image intensity at position (x,y), and ∇I is the gradient of the image.

3. Active Contour Equation

The active contour evolves iteratively by minimizing the total energy. This is achieved by solving the Euler-Lagrange equations, which govern the motion of the snake under the influence of internal and external forces. The resulting equation is:

$$\frac{\partial C(s,t)}{\partial t} = \alpha \frac{\partial^2 C(s,t)}{\partial s^2} - \beta \frac{\partial^4 C(s,t)}{\partial s^4} - \nabla E_{\text{external}}(C(s,t))$$

Here, $C(s,t)$ is the contour evolving over time t, and $\nabla E_{\text{external}}$ is the gradient of the external energy pulling the snake toward image features.

4. Types of Snakes: Parametric and Geometric

There are two main types of active contour models: **parametric snakes** and **geometric snakes**.

Parametric Snakes

These snakes are explicitly represented as parameterized curves, and their evolution depends on adjusting the curve's shape. They are sensitive to initialization, meaning they require an initial contour that is relatively close to the object's boundary.

- **Advantages**: Simple and intuitive, allows for explicit control over curve properties like elasticity and smoothness.
- **Disadvantages**: Sensitive to initialization, may struggle with topological changes (e.g., splitting or merging of contours).

Geometric Snakes (Level Set Method)

Geometric snakes represent the contour implicitly using a level set function. In this approach, the snake evolves by solving partial differential equations without explicitly tracking the curve. Geometric snakes can handle changes in topology, such as splitting or merging of the contour.

- **Advantages**: Can handle topological changes naturally, more robust to initialization.
- **Disadvantages**: Computationally expensive compared to parametric snakes.

5. Applications of Active Contour Models

- **Medical Imaging**: Used to segment structures like organs, tumors, or other anatomical features from medical scans (e.g., MRI, CT).
- **Object Detection**: Detecting objects in images by deforming the contour to fit the object boundaries.
- **Video Tracking**: Tracking objects in video sequences by evolving the contour over time.
- **Shape Modeling**: Modeling object shapes by fitting a deformable contour around them.

Python Implementation of Active Contour Model (Snakes)

Using the skimage library, we can implement active contour models easily with the following code:

```python
import numpy as np

import matplotlib.pyplot as plt

from skimage import data, color

from skimage.filters import gaussian

from skimage.segmentation import active_contour


# Load an example image

image = data.astronaut()

image_gray = color.rgb2gray(image)


# Smooth the image

image_smooth = gaussian(image_gray, 3)


# Initial contour (circle)

s = np.linspace(0, 2*np.pi, 400)

x = 220 + 100*np.cos(s)
```

```python
y = 100 + 100*np.sin(s)

init = np.array([x, y]).T


# Active contour model

snake    =    active_contour(image_smooth,    init,
alpha=0.015, beta=10, gamma=0.001)


# Plot the result

fig, ax = plt.subplots(figsize=(7, 7))

ax.imshow(image_gray, cmap='gray')

ax.plot(init[:, 0], init[:, 1], 'r--', lw=3, label='Initial
contour')

ax.plot(snake[:, 0], snake[:, 1], 'b-', lw=3, label='Final
contour')

ax.set_title('Active Contour Model (Snakes)')

ax.legend()

plt.show()
```

Explanation of Parameters:

- alpha: Controls the tension of the snake (elasticity).
- beta: Controls the smoothness (bending stiffness).
- gamma: A time step that affects the speed of snake evolution.

Advantages and Disadvantages of Active Contour Models

Advantages:

- **Flexibility**: Can detect complex object boundaries.
- **Smooth Contours**: Maintains smoothness of the contour, making it useful for natural shapes.
- **Versatility**: Can be applied to a wide range of segmentation tasks, from medical images to object detection in real-world scenes.

Disadvantages:

- **Sensitive to Initialization**: In the case of parametric snakes, the initial contour must be close to the object's boundary.
- **Parameter Sensitivity**: Requires tuning of parameters like α\alpha$\alpha$, β\beta$\beta$, and γ\gamma$\gamma$ for good results.
- **Computational Cost**: Can be computationally expensive, particularly with geometric snakes (level set methods).

Conclusion

Active contour models (snakes) are a powerful tool in image segmentation, especially for detecting and delineating object boundaries. By minimizing an energy function, snakes can adapt and evolve to fit complex shapes and structures. While parametric snakes are simple and intuitive, geometric snakes provide greater flexibility, particularly in handling topological changes. With proper initialization and parameter tuning, active contours can provide accurate and smooth object boundary detection in various applications.

Semantic and Instance Segmentation

Semantic segmentation and **instance segmentation** are two important tasks in computer vision, both aimed at segmenting objects in an image, but they differ in their goals and outputs. These techniques are widely used in applications such as autonomous driving, medical imaging, and scene understanding.

1. Semantic Segmentation

Semantic segmentation classifies each pixel in an image into a predefined class. The goal is to assign a class label (e.g., "car", "road", "tree") to every pixel. It does not differentiate between different instances of the same object; all objects of the same class are assigned the same label.

Characteristics of Semantic Segmentation:

- **Class-level Segmentation**: Pixels are labeled based on the class they belong to, without differentiating between instances of the same class.
- **Output**: A segmentation mask where each pixel is assigned a label corresponding to a class.

Example: In an image of a street, all cars will be classified as "car", all roads as "road", etc., but the system won't distinguish between individual cars.

Common Methods:

- **Fully Convolutional Networks (FCNs)**: Replace the fully connected layers in standard convolutional neural networks (CNNs) with convolutional layers to enable dense pixel-wise predictions.
- **U-Net**: A popular architecture in medical imaging that combines a contracting path (for feature extraction) with an expansive path (for localization).
- **DeepLab**: A series of models (DeepLabv1, v2, v3, and v3+) that use dilated convolutions and atrous spatial pyramid pooling (ASPP) to improve the receptive field and handle multi-scale objects.

Python Implementation of Semantic Segmentation (FCN):

```
import cv2

import numpy as np

import matplotlib.pyplot as plt

from tensorflow.keras.applications import vgg16

from tensorflow.keras.models import Model


# Load a pre-trained FCN model (VGG16 backbone)

base_model = vgg16.VGG16(weights="imagenet", include_top=False, input_shape=(224, 224, 3))


# Get the output of one of the deeper layers

layer = base_model.get_layer('block5_conv3').output


# Build the model that outputs the feature map for segmentation

model = Model(inputs=base_model.input, outputs=layer)
```

```
# Load an image and resize it to fit the model's input size

image = cv2.imread('street.jpg')

image_resized = cv2.resize(image, (224, 224))


# Preprocess the image

input_image                                        =
vgg16.preprocess_input(np.expand_dims(image_resized
, axis=0))


# Perform prediction

output = model.predict(input_image)


# Display the feature map as an example of semantic
segmentation

plt.imshow(np.mean(output[0], axis=-1), cmap='jet')

plt.title("Feature Map for Semantic Segmentation")

plt.show()
```

Use Cases:

- **Autonomous Driving**: Identifying drivable areas, pedestrians, and other vehicles on the road.
- **Medical Imaging**: Segmenting organs or tumors in medical scans.
- **Satellite Imaging**: Land use classification (e.g., roads, buildings, vegetation).

2. Instance Segmentation

Instance segmentation not only classifies each pixel but also distinguishes between different instances of the same object class. It provides both a class label

176

and an instance ID for each object. This makes it more challenging than semantic segmentation, as it requires detecting and separating individual instances of the same class.

Characteristics of Instance Segmentation:

- **Instance-level Segmentation**: Differentiates between different instances of the same class (e.g., multiple cars are detected separately).
- **Output**: A segmentation mask where each instance of an object class is uniquely labeled.

Example: In a street scene, each car is assigned a unique label (e.g., "car1", "car2"), so that multiple instances of "car" are separately segmented.

Common Methods:

- **Mask R-CNN**: A state-of-the-art instance segmentation method that extends Faster R-CNN (used for object detection) by adding a branch for predicting segmentation masks for each region of interest (RoI).
- **Panoptic FPN**: Combines semantic and instance segmentation to give a unified view of all pixels in an image.

Mask R-CNN Overview:

- **Backbone Network**: A CNN like ResNet or FPN for feature extraction.
- **Region Proposal Network (RPN)**: Generates object proposals.
- **RoIAlign**: Precisely aligns the feature maps of the proposed regions for mask prediction.
- **Segmentation Head**: Predicts a binary mask for each detected object instance.

Python Implementation of Instance Segmentation (Mask R-CNN):

```python
import cv2

import numpy as np

import matplotlib.pyplot as plt

from mrcnn.config import Config

from mrcnn import model as modellib

from mrcnn import visualize


# Load a pre-trained Mask R-CNN model
class InferenceConfig(Config):

    NAME = "coco_inference"

    NUM_CLASSES = 81  # 80 classes + 1 background

    GPU_COUNT = 1

    IMAGES_PER_GPU = 1


config = InferenceConfig()

model    =    modellib.MaskRCNN(mode="inference",
model_dir='./', config=config)

model.load_weights('mask_rcnn_coco.h5',
by_name=True)


# Load an image

image = cv2.imread('street.jpg')

image_rgb             =             cv2.cvtColor(image,
cv2.COLOR_BGR2RGB)


# Perform instance segmentation

results = model.detect([image_rgb], verbose=1)
```

Display the results

r = results[0]

visualize.display_instances(image_rgb, r['rois'], r['masks'], r['class_ids'], r['scores'])

Use Cases:

- **Autonomous Driving**: Detecting and segmenting individual vehicles and pedestrians.
- **Augmented Reality**: Segmenting and tracking objects in real-time for interaction.
- **Robotics**: Identifying and picking up individual objects in cluttered environments.

Key Differences between Semantic and Instance Segmentation:

Feature	Semantic Segmentation	Instance Segmentation
Pixel Classification	Classifies each pixel into a category	Classifies each pixel and distinguishes instances
Instance Differentiation	Does not differentiate between instances	Separates different instances of the same object
Example	All cars are labeled as "car"	Each car is labeled separately (e.g., "car1", "car2")
Complexity	Easier to implement, requires class-wise labeling	More complex, requires both class and instance labeling

Feature	Semantic Segmentation	Instance Segmentation
Common Techniques	FCN, U-Net, DeepLab	Mask R-CNN, Panoptic FPN

3. Panoptic Segmentation

Panoptic segmentation is a combination of both semantic and instance segmentation. It aims to label every pixel in an image with both the class (semantic segmentation) and unique instance (instance segmentation) where applicable. This method provides a comprehensive understanding of both things (instances) and stuff (regions like sky or road) in an image.

Conclusion

- **Semantic segmentation** classifies each pixel into a predefined class but doesn't distinguish between different instances of the same object.
- **Instance segmentation** not only classifies but also differentiates between different instances of the same class, making it more detailed and complex.
- Both tasks are essential for different computer vision applications and are often combined in advanced systems like panoptic segmentation for a more holistic scene understanding.

Chapter 6: Object Detection and Recognition

Traditional Object Detection Methods

Traditional object detection methods laid the groundwork for modern techniques and are still relevant in many applications. Two notable methods are **Histogram of Oriented Gradients (HOG)** and the **Viola-Jones detector**.

1. Histogram of Oriented Gradients (HOG)

HOG is a feature descriptor used for object detection that captures the distribution of gradients or edge directions in localized portions of an image. It is particularly effective for detecting objects such as pedestrians.

Key Steps in HOG:

1. **Gradient Computation**: Calculate the gradient of the image using filters (e.g., Sobel operators) to obtain edge information.
2. **Cell and Block Division**: Divide the image into small connected regions called cells. HOG features are calculated for each cell. For improved contrast and normalization, adjacent cells are grouped into larger blocks.
3. **Orientation Binning**: For each cell, the gradient directions are binned into a histogram, with the bin value weighted by the gradient magnitude.
4. **Normalization**: Normalize the histogram values over blocks to account for changes in lighting and contrast.
5. **Feature Vector**: The final HOG descriptor is formed by concatenating the histograms from all blocks.

Python Implementation of HOG:

Here's a simple implementation of HOG feature extraction using skimage:

```python
import cv2

import numpy as np

import matplotlib.pyplot as plt

from skimage.feature import hog

from skimage import exposure


# Load and preprocess the image

image = cv2.imread('pedestrian.jpg')

image_gray          =          cv2.cvtColor(image,
cv2.COLOR_BGR2GRAY)
```

Compute HOG features and visualize

```
hog_features, hog_image = hog(image_gray,
visualize=True, pixels_per_cell=(8, 8),
cells_per_block=(2, 2), block_norm='L2-Hys')
```

Improve contrast of HOG image for better visualization

```
hog_image = exposure.rescale_intensity(hog_image,
in_range=(0, 10))
```

Display the results

```
fig, ax = plt.subplots(1, 2, figsize=(12, 6))

ax[0].imshow(image_gray, cmap='gray')

ax[0].set_title('Original Image')

ax[0].axis('off')


ax[1].imshow(hog_image, cmap='gray')

ax[1].set_title('HOG Features')

ax[1].axis('off')


plt.show()
```

Advantages:

- Robust to lighting changes and noise.
- Effective for human detection and other objects with distinctive shapes.

Disadvantages:

- Sensitive to changes in pose and viewpoint.

- Requires careful tuning of parameters for optimal performance.

2. Viola-Jones Detector

The **Viola-Jones** detector is a pioneering framework for real-time face detection that combines several techniques to achieve high accuracy and speed. It was introduced by Paul Viola and Michael Jones in 2001.

Key Components:

1. **Haar Features**: The detector uses Haar-like features, which are simple rectangular features that capture the intensity differences between adjacent rectangular regions.
2. **Integral Image**: To compute Haar features efficiently, the Viola-Jones detector uses an integral image that allows for quick calculation of the sum of pixel values in a rectangular area.
3. **Adaboost**: The algorithm employs the Adaboost learning algorithm to select a small number of the most important features from a large set of Haar features. This reduces the complexity of the model.
4. **Cascade Classifier**: The Viola-Jones detector uses a cascade of classifiers that quickly eliminate non-object regions of the image. Each stage in the cascade focuses on classifying whether a sub-window contains a face. If a sub-window fails any stage, it is discarded, allowing the model to process images rapidly.

Python Implementation of Viola-Jones Detector:

Husn Ara

Using OpenCV, we can implement face detection using the Viola-Jones algorithm:

```
import cv2


# Load the pre-trained Haar cascade model for face detection

face_cascade                                =
cv2.CascadeClassifier(cv2.data.haarcascades      +
'haarcascade_frontalface_default.xml')


# Load the image

image = cv2.imread('group_photo.jpg')

gray_image                =                cv2.cvtColor(image,
cv2.COLOR_BGR2GRAY)


# Detect faces

faces   =   face_cascade.detectMultiScale(gray_image,
scaleFactor=1.1, minNeighbors=5)


# Draw rectangles around detected faces

for (x, y, w, h) in faces:

    cv2.rectangle(image, (x, y), (x + w, y + h), (255, 0, 0),
2)


# Display the result

cv2.imshow('Detected Faces', image)

cv2.waitKey(0)

cv2.destroyAllWindows()
```

Advantages:

- Fast and efficient, suitable for real-time applications.
- High detection rate for frontal faces.

Disadvantages:

- Limited to frontal face detection; struggles with occlusions, variations in pose, and non-frontal faces.
- Requires training for new objects or classes, which can be data-intensive.

Conclusion

- **HOG** is effective for shape-based object detection and is commonly used for pedestrian detection, while the **Viola-Jones detector** is specifically designed for fast and accurate face detection.
- Both methods have significantly influenced modern object detection techniques and remain relevant for specific applications due to their efficiency and simplicity.

Deep Learning for Object Detection

Deep learning has revolutionized object detection, leading to more accurate and efficient models. Some of the most popular architectures include **YOLO (You Only Look Once)**, **SSD (Single Shot MultiBox Detector)**, and the R-CNN family (R-CNN, Fast R-CNN, and Faster R-CNN). Each of these methods has its strengths and is suited to different use cases.

1. YOLO (You Only Look Once)

YOLO is a real-time object detection system that frames detection as a single regression problem. Instead of looking at the image in parts, YOLO processes the entire image in one go, which significantly speeds up the detection process.

Key Concepts:

- **Single Neural Network**: YOLO uses a single convolutional network to predict bounding boxes and class probabilities directly from the entire image.
- **Grid Division**: The image is divided into an S×SS \times SS×S grid. Each grid cell is responsible for predicting bounding boxes and the confidence score for objects whose center falls within the cell.
- **Bounding Box Prediction**: Each grid cell predicts a fixed number of bounding boxes along with their confidence scores and class probabilities.

Advantages:

- **Speed**: Very fast, making it suitable for real-time applications.
- **Global Context**: Considers the entire image context for predictions, reducing false positives.

Disadvantages:

- **Struggles with Small Objects**: Less effective for detecting small objects or when objects are close together.
- **Limited Generalization**: May perform poorly on objects that are not well-represented in the training dataset.

Python Implementation:

Using the darknet framework, YOLO can be implemented as follows:

```python
import cv2

import numpy as np


# Load YOLO

net = cv2.dnn.readNet("yolov3.weights", "yolov3.cfg")

layer_names = net.getLayerNames()

output_layers = [layer_names[i - 1] for i in net.getUnconnectedOutLayers()]


# Load an image

image = cv2.imread('image.jpg')

height, width = image.shape[:2]


# Prepare the image for YOLO

blob = cv2.dnn.blobFromImage(image, 0.00392, (416, 416), (0, 0, 0), True, crop=False)

net.setInput(blob)

outputs = net.forward(output_layers)


# Process the outputs

for output in outputs:

    for detection in output:

        scores = detection[5:]

        class_id = np.argmax(scores)

        confidence = scores[class_id]

        if confidence > 0.5:  # Confidence threshold
```

```
center_x = int(detection[0] * width)

center_y = int(detection[1] * height)

w = int(detection[2] * width)

h = int(detection[3] * height)

# Draw bounding box

cv2.rectangle(image, (center_x - w // 2, center_y - h // 2), (center_x + w // 2, center_y + h // 2), (255, 0, 0), 2)


# Display results

cv2.imshow("Image", image)

cv2.waitKey(0)

cv2.destroyAllWindows()
```

2. SSD (Single Shot MultiBox Detector)

SSD is another popular real-time object detection model that improves on the speed and accuracy of earlier models. It detects objects at different scales using feature maps from different layers of the convolutional network.

Key Concepts:

- **Multi-Scale Detection**: SSD uses feature maps at multiple scales to detect objects of various sizes. Each feature map corresponds to a different resolution, allowing the detection of both small and large objects.
- **Convolutional Filters**: For each location in the feature maps, SSD applies a set of convolutional filters to predict bounding boxes and class scores.

Advantages:

- **Speed**: Faster than many two-stage models like R-CNN, making it suitable for real-time applications.
- **Flexibility**: Can detect objects of various sizes more effectively due to multi-scale feature maps.

Disadvantages:

- **Accuracy**: Generally less accurate than more complex models like Faster R-CNN, especially for small objects.

Python Implementation:

Using TensorFlow's implementation of SSD:

```
import tensorflow as tf

import cv2

import numpy as np


# Load the pre-trained SSD model

model = tf.saved_model.load('ssd_model_directory')


# Load an image

image = cv2.imread('image.jpg')

input_tensor = tf.convert_to_tensor([image])


# Perform detection

detections = model(input_tensor)


# Process the results

for detection in detections['detection_boxes']:
```

```
box = detection.numpy()

cv2.rectangle(image,                    (int(box[1]*width),
int(box[0]*height)),  (int(box[3]*width),  int(box[2]*height)),
(255, 0, 0), 2)


# Display the result

cv2.imshow("SSD Detection", image)

cv2.waitKey(0)

cv2.destroyAllWindows()
```

3. R-CNN, Fast R-CNN, and Faster R-CNN

The R-CNN family of models represents a series of advancements in object detection, focusing on improving accuracy while reducing processing time.

R-CNN (Region-based Convolutional Neural Network)

- **Key Concepts**: R-CNN uses selective search to generate region proposals, which are then fed into a CNN for classification and bounding box regression.
- **Disadvantages**: Slow due to the separate steps of generating proposals and then processing them with a CNN.

Fast R-CNN

- **Key Improvements**: Instead of extracting features from each proposed region separately, Fast R-CNN processes the entire image through the CNN first. Region proposals are then used to extract features from the feature map.

- **Advantages**: Faster than R-CNN and improves accuracy due to the use of a single CNN for feature extraction.

Faster R-CNN

- **Key Enhancements**: Introduces a Region Proposal Network (RPN) that shares convolutional features with the detection network, eliminating the need for selective search.
- **Advantages**: Significantly faster and more accurate than both R-CNN and Fast R-CNN, making it a popular choice for object detection tasks.

Python Implementation of Faster R-CNN:

Using PyTorch for Faster R-CNN:

```
import torch

import torchvision

from torchvision.models.detection import fasterrcnn_resnet50_fpn

from torchvision.transforms import functional as F

import cv2


# Load the Faster R-CNN model

model = fasterrcnn_resnet50_fpn(pretrained=True)

model.eval()


# Load an image

image = cv2.imread('image.jpg')

image_tensor = F.to_tensor(image)
```

```
# Perform detection
with torch.no_grad():
    predictions = model([image_tensor])


# Process the results
boxes = predictions[0]['boxes'].numpy()
scores = predictions[0]['scores'].numpy()


# Filter out predictions with low confidence
for box, score in zip(boxes, scores):
    if score > 0.5:  # Confidence threshold
        x1, y1, x2, y2 = box.astype(int)
        cv2.rectangle(image, (x1, y1), (x2, y2), (255, 0, 0), 2)


# Display the result
cv2.imshow("Faster R-CNN Detection", image)
cv2.waitKey(0)
cv2.destroyAllWindows()
```

Comparison of Deep Learning Object Detection Methods

Feature	YOLO	SSD	R-CNN Family
Detection Type	Single-stage	Single-stage	Two-stage

Feature	YOLO	SSD	R-CNN Family
Speed	Very fast	Fast	Slower than YOLO and SSD
Accuracy	High	Moderate	High
Scale Handling	Limited for small objects	Better with multi-scale	Moderate, dependent on proposals
Use Case	Real-time applications	Real-time applications	High-accuracy applications

Conclusion

Deep learning has dramatically improved object detection capabilities, with models like **YOLO** and **SSD** offering real-time performance, while the **R-CNN family** provides high accuracy, especially in complex detection tasks. Each method has its strengths, making them suitable for different applications based on requirements for speed, accuracy, and computational resources.

Object Recognition Techniques

Object recognition involves identifying and classifying objects within an image. Several techniques have been developed, ranging from traditional methods such as **Bag** of Visual Words (BoVW) and **Fisher Vectors**, to modern deep learning-based methods like **ResNet** and **VGG**.

1. Bag of Visual Words (BoVW)

Bag of Visual Words (BoVW) is inspired by the bag-of-words model used in natural language processing. In this approach, visual features are extracted from images and treated as "visual words." The occurrence of these visual words in an image is used to build a histogram that serves as a feature vector for image classification.

Key Steps:

1. **Feature Extraction**: Keypoint detectors (like SIFT or SURF) are used to extract local features from the image.
2. **Clustering**: A clustering algorithm (e.g., K-means) is applied to group similar features into clusters, where each cluster represents a "visual word."
3. **Visual Word Vocabulary**: The centroids of these clusters form the vocabulary of visual words.
4. **Histogram Construction**: For a new image, features are extracted, and each feature is mapped to its closest visual word. A histogram is built to represent the frequency of each visual word in the image.
5. **Classification**: The histogram serves as a feature vector and is used as input to a machine learning classifier (e.g., SVM) to recognize objects.

Advantages:

- Simple and effective for certain tasks.
- Can be combined with various classifiers.

Disadvantages:

- Discards spatial information, making it less effective for more complex object recognition tasks.
- Requires manual feature extraction, which may not generalize well to different tasks.

Python Implementation of BoVW:

Using OpenCV to extract SIFT features and build a BoVW model:

```python
import cv2

import numpy as np

from sklearn.cluster import KMeans

from sklearn.preprocessing import StandardScaler

from sklearn.svm import SVC


# Load images and extract features using SIFT

sift = cv2.SIFT_create()

descriptors_list = []

for image_path in image_paths:

    image = cv2.imread(image_path, cv2.IMREAD_GRAYSCALE)

    keypoints, descriptors = sift.detectAndCompute(image, None)

    descriptors_list.append(descriptors)


# Stack all descriptors into a single numpy array

all_descriptors = np.vstack(descriptors_list)


# Perform K-means clustering to form visual vocabulary
```

```
k = 100  # Number of visual words

kmeans = KMeans(n_clusters=k)

kmeans.fit(all_descriptors)

visual_vocabulary = kmeans.cluster_centers_


# Build histograms for each image

histograms = []

for descriptors in descriptors_list:

    hist = np.zeros(k)

    for d in descriptors:

        idx = kmeans.predict([d])[0]

        hist[idx] += 1

    histograms.append(hist)


# Normalize histograms and train an SVM for classification

scaler = StandardScaler()

histograms = scaler.fit_transform(histograms)

svm = SVC(kernel='linear')

svm.fit(histograms, labels)
```

2. Fisher Vectors

Fisher Vectors (FV) extend BoVW by incorporating not just the occurrence of visual words, but also the distribution of features around each visual word. Fisher Vectors use a probabilistic model, typically a Gaussian Mixture Model (GMM), to describe the distribution of features and capture higher-order statistics (like mean and variance).

Key Steps:

1. **Feature Extraction**: Similar to BoVW, keypoints and local descriptors (SIFT, SURF, etc.) are extracted from the image.
2. **GMM Fitting**: A GMM is used to model the distribution of the extracted features.
3. **Encoding**: Fisher Vectors are computed by encoding how the local features deviate from the GMM's mean and variance.
4. **Classification**: Fisher Vectors serve as feature vectors and can be used for classification with an SVM or other classifiers.

Advantages:

- Captures higher-order statistics (mean, variance) about the distribution of features, making it more powerful than BoVW.
- More informative feature representation.

Disadvantages:

- More computationally expensive compared to BoVW.
- Still requires manual feature extraction, which may not generalize well to all object recognition tasks.

Python Implementation of Fisher Vectors:

Using scikit-learn and fvpy for Fisher Vectors:

```
import cv2

import numpy as np

from sklearn.mixture import GaussianMixture

from fvpy import fisher_vector
```

```
# Extract features (e.g., SIFT)

sift = cv2.SIFT_create()

descriptors_list = []

for image_path in image_paths:

    image               =               cv2.imread(image_path,
    cv2.IMREAD_GRAYSCALE)

    keypoints, descriptors = sift.detectAndCompute(image,
None)

    descriptors_list.append(descriptors)


# Fit a Gaussian Mixture Model (GMM) on all descriptors

gmm                                                         =
GaussianMixture(n_components=64).fit(np.vstack(descri
ptors_list))


# Compute Fisher Vectors for each image

fvs = [fisher_vector.compute_fisher_vector(gmm, desc)
for desc in descriptors_list]


# Train an SVM for classification

from sklearn.svm import SVC

svm = SVC(kernel='linear')

svm.fit(fvs, labels)
```

3. Deep Learning Approaches

Deep learning has dominated object recognition with models like **ResNet** and **VGG**. These models learn object representations directly from images without manual feature extraction, making them much more powerful and generalizable.

a. ResNet (Residual Networks)

ResNet introduced the concept of residual learning, which allows very deep networks to be trained by using skip connections (or residual connections) that bypass certain layers. This helps prevent the vanishing gradient problem.

Key Features:

- **Residual Blocks**: Introduces skip connections that allow gradients to flow through the network, improving the training of very deep networks.
- **Depth**: ResNet can be trained with hundreds of layers (e.g., ResNet-50, ResNet-101), achieving state-of-the-art results.

Advantages:

- Allows very deep networks to be trained efficiently.
- Excellent performance on large-scale object recognition tasks.

Python Implementation of ResNet:

Using PyTorch:

```
import torch

import torchvision

import torchvision.transforms as transforms


# Load ResNet pre-trained model

resnet = torchvision.models.resnet50(pretrained=True)

resnet.eval()
```

```
# Preprocess an input image
preprocess = transforms.Compose([
    transforms.Resize(256),
    transforms.CenterCrop(224),
    transforms.ToTensor(),
    transforms.Normalize(mean=[0.485,   0.456,   0.406],
std=[0.229, 0.224, 0.225])
])


image = Image.open('image.jpg')
image_tensor = preprocess(image).unsqueeze(0)


# Perform inference
with torch.no_grad():
    outputs = resnet(image_tensor)
    _, predicted = torch.max(outputs, 1)
    print('Predicted label:', predicted.item())
```

b. VGG (Visual Geometry Group Network)

VGG is a deep convolutional network known for its simplicity and depth. It uses small 3×33 \times 33×3 convolutional filters stacked on top of each other to increase the depth of the network.

Key Features:

- **Deep Architecture**: VGG-16 and VGG-19 have 16 and 19 weight layers, respectively.

- **Uniform Convolutional Filter Size**: Uses 3×33 \times 33×3 filters throughout, which makes the model easy to understand and implement.

Advantages:

- High accuracy for object recognition tasks.
- Simple design with uniform convolutional filters.

Disadvantages:

- High computational cost due to the large number of parameters.

Python Implementation of VGG:

Using PyTorch:

```
import torch

import torchvision

import torchvision.transforms as transforms


# Load VGG pre-trained model

vgg = torchvision.models.vgg16(pretrained=True)

vgg.eval()


# Preprocess an input image

preprocess = transforms.Compose([

    transforms.Resize(256),

    transforms.CenterCrop(224),

    transforms.ToTensor(),

    transforms.Normalize(mean=[0.485, 0.456, 0.406], std=[0.229, 0.224, 0.225])
```

```
])


image = Image.open('image.jpg')

image_tensor = preprocess(image).unsqueeze(0)


# Perform inference

with torch.no_grad():

    outputs = vgg(image_tensor)

    _, predicted = torch.max(outputs, 1)

    print('Predicted label:', predicted.item())
```

Comparison of Object Recognition Techniques

Technique	Feature Type	Complexity	Performance	Application
BoVW	Manually extracted (e.g., SIFT)	Low	Good for basic tasks	Simple object classification
Fisher Vectors	Manually extracted + higher-order statistics	Medium	More powerful than BoVW	Object detection and classification
ResNet	Automatically learned via CNN	High	State-of-the-art for many tasks	Large-scale image

Techniq ue	Feature Type	Complex ity	Performan ce	Applicatio n
				recognitio n
VGG	Automatic ally learned via CNN	High	High accuracy, large model	Image classificati on, pre-training

Conclusion

- **BoVW** and **Fisher Vectors** are traditional methods, useful when computational resources are limited or for simpler tasks.
- Deep learning approaches like **ResNet** and **VGG** offer state-of-the-art performance but require more computational power.

Husn Ara

Chapter 7: 3D Computer Vision

3D Reconstruction from Images

3D reconstruction from images is the process of recovering the three-dimensional structure of a scene or object from 2D images. It plays a critical role in fields such as computer vision, augmented reality, robotics, and medical imaging. Various techniques, including stereo vision, structure from motion (SfM), and multi-view stereo, are commonly used for 3D reconstruction.

Key Techniques for 3D Reconstruction

1. Stereo Vision

Stereo vision uses two or more images of the same scene taken from different angles (similar to how our eyes perceive depth) to infer depth information and reconstruct the 3D structure.

Steps:

- **Image Capture**: Capture two or more images of the scene from different perspectives.

- **Feature Matching**: Identify corresponding points (features) between the images.
- **Depth Calculation**: Using the disparity (difference in position of corresponding points), compute the depth based on the known distance between cameras (baseline).
- **3D Points**: Using the depth information and camera parameters, reconstruct the 3D points.

Advantages:

- Simple and effective when using calibrated cameras.
- Suitable for real-time systems like autonomous driving.

Disadvantages:

- Requires known camera parameters and calibration.
- Limited accuracy in regions with low texture or occlusion.

Python Implementation (Using OpenCV for Stereo Vision):

```python
import cv2

import numpy as np


# Load stereo images

img_left        =        cv2.imread('left_image.jpg',
cv2.IMREAD_GRAYSCALE)

img_right       =        cv2.imread('right_image.jpg',
cv2.IMREAD_GRAYSCALE)


# StereoBM (block matching) algorithm for depth map
```

```
stereo    =    cv2.StereoBM_create(numDisparities=16,
blockSize=15)

disparity_map = stereo.compute(img_left, img_right)


# Normalize the disparity map for display

disparity_map = cv2.normalize(disparity_map, None, 0,
255, cv2.NORM_MINMAX)


# Display the depth map

cv2.imshow('Disparity Map', np.uint8(disparity_map))

cv2.waitKey(0)

cv2.destroyAllWindows()
```

2. Structure from Motion (SfM)

Structure from Motion (SfM) is a technique that reconstructs 3D structure from a series of 2D images taken from different viewpoints, without requiring information about the camera's position or orientation. SfM simultaneously estimates the camera motion (pose) and the 3D scene structure.

Steps:

1. **Feature Extraction**: Extract features (e.g., SIFT, SURF) from the images.
2. **Feature Matching**: Match features between consecutive images.
3. **Camera Pose Estimation**: Estimate the relative motion of the camera between images.
4. **3D Point Cloud Reconstruction**: Triangulate matched feature points across multiple images to create a sparse 3D point cloud.

Advantages:

- Does not require calibrated cameras.
- Works well with unstructured image collections.

Disadvantages:

- Computationally expensive.
- Produces a sparse point cloud, requiring post-processing for dense reconstruction.

Python Implementation (Using OpenCV and COLMAP for SfM):

OpenCV provides basic functionality for SfM, but libraries like COLMAP or OpenMVG are more powerful for large-scale SfM tasks. The following example demonstrates SfM using OpenCV.

```python
import cv2

import numpy as np



# Load two consecutive images

img1              =              cv2.imread('img1.jpg',
cv2.IMREAD_GRAYSCALE)

img2              =              cv2.imread('img2.jpg',
cv2.IMREAD_GRAYSCALE)



# Extract features (e.g., SIFT)

sift = cv2.SIFT_create()

keypoints1,              descriptors1              =
sift.detectAndCompute(img1, None)
```

```
keypoints2,              descriptors2          =
sift.detectAndCompute(img2, None)


# Feature matching using FLANN-based matcher

index_params = dict(algorithm=1, trees=5)

search_params = dict(checks=50)

flann    =   cv2.FlannBasedMatcher(index_params,
search_params)

matches       =        flann.knnMatch(descriptors1,
descriptors2, k=2)


# Filter good matches using the ratio test

good_matches = []

for m, n in matches:

    if m.distance < 0.7 * n.distance:

        good_matches.append(m)


# Estimate Essential Matrix to find the camera pose

points1 = np.float32([keypoints1[m.queryIdx].pt for m
in good_matches])

points2 = np.float32([keypoints2[m.trainIdx].pt for m
in good_matches])
```

```
E, mask = cv2.findEssentialMat(points1, points2,
focal=1.0, pp=(0, 0), method=cv2.RANSAC,
prob=0.999, threshold=1.0)


# Recover the relative camera pose from the
Essential Matrix

_, R, t, mask = cv2.recoverPose(E, points1, points2)


# Use triangulation to find 3D points

points1 = points1[mask.ravel() == 1]

points2 = points2[mask.ravel() == 1]

points_4d                                        =
cv2.triangulatePoints(np.hstack([np.eye(3),
np.zeros((3, 1))]), np.hstack([R, t]), points1.T,
points2.T)

points_3d = points_4d[:3] / points_4d[3]


print("3D Points:\n", points_3d.T)
```

3. Multi-View Stereo (MVS)

Multi-View Stereo (MVS) extends stereo vision to
multiple images of the same scene from various
viewpoints. It refines the initial sparse point cloud
from SfM into a dense 3D reconstruction by matching
features across more images.

Steps:

1. **Initialize Point Cloud**: Use SfM to generate an initial sparse 3D point cloud.
2. **Depth Estimation**: For each image, estimate the depth of each pixel by matching it with corresponding pixels in other images.
3. **Dense Reconstruction**: Combine the depth maps from all images to produce a dense 3D model.

Advantages:

- Can produce dense 3D reconstructions with accurate depth information.
- Works well for detailed scene reconstruction.

Disadvantages:

- Computationally expensive.
- Sensitive to the number of images and their quality.

Tools: MVS libraries such as COLMAP, MVE (Multi-View Environment), and OpenMVS are widely used for dense reconstruction.

4. Volumetric Methods

Volumetric methods represent the scene using a 3D voxel grid. As the camera moves through the scene, each image is used to refine the voxel grid by updating the occupancy and color values of each voxel.

Popular volumetric methods include **Voxel Carving** and **TSDF (Truncated Signed Distance Function)** used in systems like **Kinect Fusion**.

Advantages:

- Good for reconstructing volumetric models of objects or indoor scenes.

- Can handle noisy depth data well.

Disadvantages:

- High memory requirements due to the voxel grid representation.
- Not well-suited for large outdoor scenes.

Applications of 3D Reconstruction

1. **Robotics**: 3D maps for navigation and obstacle avoidance.
2. **Medical Imaging**: Reconstructing 3D models from CT or MRI scans.
3. **Augmented Reality**: Scene understanding and interaction with virtual objects.
4. **Cultural Heritage**: 3D modeling of artifacts, monuments, and archaeological sites.
5. **Autonomous Vehicles**: Real-time 3D perception for obstacle detection and scene understanding.

Conclusion

3D reconstruction from images is a powerful and evolving field in computer vision. Techniques such as **Stereo Vision**, **Structure from Motion (SfM)**, and **Multi-View Stereo (MVS)** offer a range of solutions depending on the task, from real-time depth estimation to dense scene reconstruction. As the technology progresses, deep learning approaches and fusion with other sensing modalities like LiDAR are making 3D reconstruction more robust and applicable in real-world environments.

Husn Ara

Depth Estimation Techniques

Depth estimation is the process of determining the distance between objects in a scene and the camera. It's a critical task in computer vision and is widely used in robotics, autonomous vehicles, augmented reality, and 3D reconstruction. Several techniques have been developed for depth estimation, ranging from traditional methods such as stereo vision to more advanced deep learning techniques.

1. Stereo Vision

Stereo vision mimics human binocular vision by using two or more cameras placed at different viewpoints to estimate depth. By analyzing the disparity (shift) between corresponding pixels in the left and right images, the depth of points in the scene can be computed.

Steps:

1. **Capture Stereo Images**: Two images are captured from slightly different positions (e.g., left and right cameras).
2. **Feature Matching**: Corresponding points (features) in both images are matched.
3. **Disparity Calculation**: The disparity (pixel shift between corresponding points) is computed.
4. **Depth Calculation**: Depth is calculated using the formula:

$$Depth = \frac{f \cdot B}{Disparity}$$

where:

- f is the camera focal length.
- B is the baseline distance between the two cameras.
- $Disparity$ is the difference in pixel positions of corresponding points.

Advantages:

- Effective for real-time depth estimation.
- Well-suited for applications like autonomous driving and robotics.

Disadvantages:

- Requires good texture in the scene for feature matching.
- Struggles in occluded areas or low-texture regions.

Python Implementation of Stereo Vision:

Using OpenCV to calculate a depth map from stereo images:

```
import cv2

import numpy as np
```

```
# Load stereo images

img_left      =      cv2.imread('left_image.jpg',
cv2.IMREAD_GRAYSCALE)

img_right      =      cv2.imread('right_image.jpg',
cv2.IMREAD_GRAYSCALE)
```

```
# Create StereoBM object

stereo = cv2.StereoBM_create(numDisparities=16,
blockSize=15)


# Compute disparity map

disparity_map = stereo.compute(img_left, img_right)


# Normalize disparity map for visualization

disparity_map    =    cv2.normalize(disparity_map,
disparity_map, 0, 255, cv2.NORM_MINMAX)


# Display the result

cv2.imshow('Disparity                    Map',
np.uint8(disparity_map))

cv2.waitKey(0)

cv2.destroyAllWindows()
```

2. **Monocular Depth Estimation**

Monocular depth estimation refers to estimating depth from a single image. Since a single 2D image lacks explicit depth information, this is a more challenging problem. Modern techniques, especially deep learning-based approaches, have made significant progress in this area by learning depth cues from large datasets.

Deep Learning Approach:

Convolutional Neural Networks (CNNs) are commonly used for monocular depth estimation. These networks learn to infer depth from a single image by recognizing patterns like object size, shading, and perspective.

Popular Architectures:

- **MiDaS (Mixed Depth and Scale)**: A neural network model for monocular depth estimation, trained on multiple datasets with different depth ranges and scales.
- **UNet-like CNNs**: Often used for depth estimation tasks, with skip connections to recover fine details.

MiDaS (Mixed Depth and Scale) Overview

MiDaS (Mixed Depth and Scale) is a state-of-the-art deep learning model for monocular depth estimation. It was developed by the Intel Intelligent Systems Lab and can estimate depth from a single image. MiDaS is pre-trained on multiple datasets with different depth ranges and scales, allowing it to generalize well across various scenes and image types. It is particularly useful for applications such as 3D reconstruction, augmented reality, and robotics.

Key Features of MiDaS:

- **Monocular Depth Estimation**: Estimates depth from a single image without requiring stereo or RGB-D cameras.

- **Mixed Datasets**: Trained on a wide range of datasets, improving generalization.
- **Pre-trained Models**: Several pre-trained models are available for use with PyTorch.

Steps to Use MiDaS for Depth Estimation

- **Install Required Packages**:

    o PyTorch
    o OpenCV
    o NumPy

    You can install these dependencies via pip:

pip install torch torchvision opencv-python numpy

☐ **Load the MiDaS Model**: MiDaS models can be loaded directly using the PyTorch torch.hub interface.

☐ **Preprocess the Input Image**: MiDaS requires input images to be preprocessed into a specific format, which can be done using the transformation functions provided by MiDaS.

☐ **Run Depth Estimation**: Once the image is processed, pass it through the model to get the predicted depth map.

☐ **Post-process and Visualize the Depth Map**: The output from MiDaS can be normalized and displayed using OpenCV.

MiDaS Depth Estimation Code Example

Here is an implementation of MiDaS using PyTorch to estimate depth from a single image.

import torch

```python
import cv2

import numpy as np


# Load the MiDaS model

midas = torch.hub.load("intel-isl/MiDaS", "MiDaS")

midas.eval()


# Load the MiDaS transformation for preprocessing the input image

midas_transform = torch.hub.load("intel-isl/MiDaS", "transforms").default_transform


# Load the input image

img = cv2.imread('input_image.jpg')


# Convert the image to RGB

img = cv2.cvtColor(img, cv2.COLOR_BGR2RGB)


# Preprocess the image using the MiDaS transformation

input_batch = midas_transform(img).unsqueeze(0)
```

```
# Run the model to predict depth

with torch.no_grad():

    prediction = midas(input_batch)


# Remove the batch dimension and convert the
prediction to a NumPy array

depth_map = prediction.squeeze().cpu().numpy()


# Normalize the depth map for visualization

depth_map = cv2.normalize(depth_map, None, 0,
255,              norm_type=cv2.NORM_MINMAX,
dtype=cv2.CV_8U)


# Display the original image and the depth map

cv2.imshow('Original    Image',    cv2.cvtColor(img,
cv2.COLOR_RGB2BGR))

cv2.imshow('Depth Map', depth_map)


cv2.waitKey(0)

cv2.destroyAllWindows()
```

Explanation of the Code

- **Loading the MiDaS model**:

- o The model is loaded using torch.hub.load from the official MiDaS repository hosted on GitHub.
- **Image Preprocessing**:
  - o The input image is converted to RGB, as MiDaS works with RGB images.
  - o The image is transformed into a format that the model expects using the default_transform provided by MiDaS.
- **Running Inference**:
  - o The model is used in inference mode to predict the depth map.
- **Post-processing**:
  - o The output depth map is normalized to the range [0, 255] for easy visualization.
- **Displaying the Results**:

The original image and the estimated depth map are displayed using OpenCV.

Additional Notes

- **Model Options**: MiDaS offers different models optimized for various trade-offs between accuracy and speed. You can choose a different MiDaS model by specifying it when loading the model, such as MiDaS_small for faster inference.

midas = torch.hub.load("intel-isl/MiDaS", "MiDaS_small")

☐ **Resolution**: MiDaS operates on images at a fixed resolution. You can resize input images for faster processing or higher accuracy, depending on your application.

☐ **Real-time Applications**: By using MiDaS with a GPU, you can achieve real-time depth estimation for video streams, such as from a webcam or a video file.

Use Cases

- **3D Reconstruction**: Use MiDaS to estimate depth for 3D reconstruction pipelines.
- **Augmented Reality**: Apply depth estimation to improve object placement and interaction in AR applications.
- **Autonomous Driving**: Use depth information from MiDaS for navigation and obstacle avoidance.

Conclusion

MiDaS is a versatile and powerful tool for depth estimation from single images. Its deep learning-based architecture, trained on multiple datasets, allows it to generalize across a wide range of scenes. This makes it ideal for applications such as 3D reconstruction, robotics, and AR, where depth information is crucial.

UNet-like CNNs

UNet is a type of Convolutional Neural Network (CNN) architecture, originally developed for biomedical image segmentation but now widely used for various computer vision tasks such as depth estimation, semantic segmentation, and image generation. The key feature of UNet is its **U-shaped architecture**, which consists of an encoder (downsampling path) and a decoder (upsampling path), with skip connections between corresponding layers to capture fine details.

UNet Architecture:

1. **Encoder**: Extracts features using convolution and downsampling (max-pooling).

2. **Bottleneck**: The bridge between the encoder and decoder where the deepest, most abstract features are captured.
3. **Decoder**: Reconstructs the image or prediction map by upsampling and combining with features from the encoder.
4. **Skip Connections**: Connects the encoder layers to the decoder layers, helping to retain spatial information that is lost during downsampling.

PyTorch Implementation of UNet

```python
import torch

import torch.nn as nn

import torch.nn.functional as F


class UNet(nn.Module):

    def __init__(self):

        super(UNet, self).__init__()


        # Encoder

        self.enc1 = self.contracting_block(3, 64)

        self.enc2 = self.contracting_block(64, 128)

        self.enc3 = self.contracting_block(128, 256)

        self.enc4 = self.contracting_block(256, 512)


        # Bottleneck

        self.bottleneck = self.contracting_block(512, 1024)


        # Decoder

        self.dec4 = self.expansive_block(1024, 512)
```

```python
        self.dec3 = self.expansive_block(512, 256)

        self.dec2 = self.expansive_block(256, 128)

        self.dec1 = self.expansive_block(128, 64)


        # Final layer (1x1 convolution to get the desired
output channels)

        self.final_layer = nn.Conv2d(64, 1, kernel_size=1)


    def contracting_block(self, in_channels, out_channels):
        return nn.Sequential(

            nn.Conv2d(in_channels,                out_channels,
kernel_size=3, padding=1),

            nn.BatchNorm2d(out_channels),

            nn.ReLU(inplace=True),

            nn.Conv2d(out_channels,                out_channels,
kernel_size=3, padding=1),

            nn.BatchNorm2d(out_channels),

            nn.ReLU(inplace=True),

            nn.MaxPool2d(kernel_size=2)

        )


    def expansive_block(self, in_channels, out_channels):
        return nn.Sequential(

            nn.Conv2d(in_channels,                out_channels,
kernel_size=3, padding=1),

            nn.BatchNorm2d(out_channels),

            nn.ReLU(inplace=True),
```

```
        nn.Conv2d(out_channels,            out_channels,
kernel_size=3, padding=1),

        nn.BatchNorm2d(out_channels),

        nn.ReLU(inplace=True),

        nn.ConvTranspose2d(out_channels,
out_channels, kernel_size=2, stride=2)

    )


    def forward(self, x):
        # Encoder path
        enc1 = self.enc1(x)

        enc2 = self.enc2(enc1)

        enc3 = self.enc3(enc2)

        enc4 = self.enc4(enc3)


        # Bottleneck
        bottleneck = self.bottleneck(enc4)


        # Decoder path with skip connections
        dec4 = self.dec4(bottleneck) + enc4    # Skip
connection from encoder

        dec3 = self.dec3(dec4) + enc3

        dec2 = self.dec2(dec3) + enc2

        dec1 = self.dec1(dec2) + enc1


        # Final layer to reduce to the number of output
classes (e.g., 1 for binary segmentation)
```

```
out = self.final_layer(dec1)


    return torch.sigmoid(out)  # Use sigmoid for binary
segmentation, softmax for multi-class


# Example usage

if __name__ == "__main__":

  model = UNet()

  x = torch.randn((1, 3, 256, 256))  # Example input
tensor (batch_size, channels, height, width)

  output = model(x)

  print(output.shape)    # Expected output shape:
(batch_size, 1, 256, 256)
```

Explanation of the UNet Code

1. **Encoder (Downsampling Path)**:
   - The encoder uses contracting_block functions, which apply two convolutional layers followed by batch normalization and ReLU activations, and then perform downsampling using MaxPool2d.
2. **Bottleneck**:
   - The bottleneck is the deepest part of the network, containing the most abstract features. It has no max-pooling, just convolutions, batch normalization, and activations.
3. **Decoder (Upsampling Path)**:
   - The decoder uses expansive_block functions that mirror the encoder. These blocks perform convolution, batch normalization, ReLU activations, and then upsample the feature maps using ConvTranspose2d for upsampling.

- o Skip connections are added from the encoder to the corresponding layers in the decoder to retain spatial detail.

4. **Final Layer**:
   - o A Conv2d layer with a kernel size of 1 is applied at the end to reduce the feature map to a single channel for binary segmentation (or more channels for multi-class segmentation).

5. **Activation**:
   - o The output is passed through a sigmoid activation for binary segmentation (if you're working on multi-class segmentation, replace this with softmax).

Usage in Image Segmentation

You can apply this network to image segmentation tasks. Here's a small example of how to use it for segmentation:

```
# Assume we have an input image 'img' and its corresponding segmentation mask 'mask'

# Prepare the input image

img = cv2.imread('image.jpg')

img = cv2.resize(img, (256, 256))

img = img / 255.0  # Normalize the image

img = np.transpose(img, (2, 0, 1)) # Change the shape to (channels, height, width)

img = torch.Tensor(img).unsqueeze(0)  # Add batch dimension


# Prepare the ground truth segmentation mask

mask = cv2.imread('mask.jpg', cv2.IMREAD_GRAYSCALE)
```

Husn Ara

```
mask = cv2.resize(mask, (256, 256))

mask = mask / 255.0  # Normalize the mask

mask = torch.Tensor(mask).unsqueeze(0).unsqueeze(0)
# Add channel and batch dimensions


# Forward pass through the UNet model

model = UNet()

output = model(img)


# Calculate the loss (using BCE for binary segmentation)

criterion = nn.BCELoss()  # Binary Cross Entropy Loss

loss = criterion(output, mask)


# Print the loss

print(f"Loss: {loss.item()}")
```

Key Considerations

1. **Loss Functions**:
   - For **binary segmentation**, use BCELoss (Binary Cross Entropy Loss).
   - For **multi-class segmentation**, use CrossEntropyLoss.
2. **Data Preprocessing**:
   - Ensure the input images are normalized.
   - The input images should be resized to a resolution that is a power of 2, as the U-Net involves multiple downsampling and upsampling operations.
3. **Skip Connections**:
   - These help retain high-resolution information from earlier layers, which can be lost during downsampling, improving segmentation accuracy.

227

4. **Training and Fine-Tuning**:
   - o Train the model with a suitable dataset for segmentation, such as Cityscapes for semantic segmentation, or a custom dataset for your task.

Conclusion

UNet-like CNNs are versatile and powerful for image segmentation tasks, with applications in medical imaging, autonomous driving, and more. Their combination of encoding-decoding with skip connections makes them particularly well-suited for tasks requiring precise localization, such as semantic segmentation.

3. Depth from Motion (Structure from Motion - SfM)

Structure from Motion (SfM) is a technique that estimates depth and reconstructs a 3D scene from a series of 2D images taken from different viewpoints. It works by analyzing the relative motion of the camera between images to estimate both the camera pose and the 3D structure of the scene.

Steps:

1. **Feature Detection**: Detect keypoints and descriptors in the images.
2. **Feature Matching**: Match features between consecutive images.
3. **Camera Motion Estimation**: Estimate the relative motion of the camera between images.
4. **3D Point Cloud Reconstruction**: Use triangulation to compute the 3D location of matched points.

Advantages:

- Can reconstruct 3D scenes without knowing the exact camera position.
- Works with uncalibrated cameras and arbitrary camera motion.

Disadvantages:

- Requires multiple images with sufficient parallax.
- Computationally expensive.

4. **Time-of-Flight (ToF) Cameras**

Time-of-Flight (ToF) cameras estimate depth by measuring the time it takes for emitted light to return after reflecting off objects in the scene. The time delay is proportional to the distance of the object, allowing for direct depth estimation.

Advantages:

- Provides highly accurate and real-time depth information.
- Works well in low-light conditions.

Disadvantages:

- Limited range and can struggle with reflective surfaces.
- More expensive compared to traditional RGB cameras.

5. **Depth from Focus / Defocus**

Depth from focus/defocus techniques estimate depth by analyzing the sharpness of different regions in an image. Objects at different distances from the camera will appear more or less focused depending on the camera's focal plane.

Advantages:

- Useful in scenarios where the camera can adjust its focus.
- Does not require stereo cameras.

Disadvantages:

- Limited accuracy and range.
- Requires multiple images with varying focus settings.

6. **LIDAR (Light Detection and Ranging)**

LIDAR uses laser pulses to measure the distance to objects. It emits a laser beam and measures the time it takes for the beam to return after hitting an object, similar to ToF cameras but at longer ranges and with higher precision.

Advantages:

- Extremely accurate depth estimation over long distances.
- Works well for large-scale environments (e.g., autonomous driving).

Disadvantages:

- Expensive and requires specialized hardware.
- Performance can degrade in adverse weather conditions (e.g., rain, fog).

7. **RGB-D Cameras**

RGB-D Cameras capture both color (RGB) and depth (D) information simultaneously. Devices like Microsoft's Kinect sensor use an infrared projector and camera to calculate the depth of objects in the scene. Depth is calculated based on the deformation of the infrared pattern projected onto the scene.

Advantages:

- Provides dense and accurate depth information along with RGB data.
- Inexpensive and widely available for consumer applications (e.g., Kinect, Intel RealSense).

Disadvantages:

- Limited range and accuracy compared to LIDAR.
- Can struggle with reflective or transparent surfaces.

8. **Learning-Based Depth Estimation**

In recent years, **deep learning** models have been used to predict depth directly from images. Models like convolutional neural networks (CNNs) and transformers have shown great success in estimating depth from monocular, stereo, or RGB-D images.

Popular Models:

- **Monodepth**: A deep learning model for monocular depth estimation.
- **Deep3D**: A deep network that generates depth maps from 2D images.
- **PWC-Net**: A deep learning model used for optical flow, which can be adapted for depth estimation.

Advantages:

- Works well on large datasets with complex scenes.
- Can generalize across various environments when trained on diverse data.

Disadvantages:

- Requires large amounts of labeled data.
- May not perform well in unseen or highly varied environments.

Conclusion

There are many different techniques for depth estimation, each with its own strengths and limitations. The choice of technique depends on the application:

- **Stereo vision** and **SfM** are suitable for tasks like 3D reconstruction and autonomous driving.
- **Time-of-Flight** and **LIDAR** are useful for highly accurate real-time depth estimation in robotics and autonomous systems.
- **Monocular depth estimation** is particularly useful when working with single images or videos, especially in augmented reality applications.
- **RGB-D cameras** offer a cost-effective solution for consumer applications like gesture recognition and 3D scanning.

As deep learning continues to advance, learning-based methods are becoming increasingly accurate and efficient, further expanding the possibilities for depth estimation in computer vision.

3D Object Detection and Tracking

3D object detection and tracking play a crucial role in applications such as autonomous driving, augmented reality, robotics, and virtual environments. The key challenge is to detect and track objects in three-dimensional space accurately.

Key Components:

1. **Point Clouds and Voxel Grids**: Methods for representing 3D data.
2. **3D Bounding Boxes**: Used for detecting and locating objects in 3D space.
3. **SLAM (Simultaneous Localization and Mapping)**: A technique used to build maps and localize the system in unknown environments.

Point Clouds and Voxel Grids

Point Clouds:

- **Point clouds** are sets of points in 3D space, typically acquired from LiDAR or depth sensors. Each point in the cloud represents a point in space with x,y,zx, y, zx,y,z coordinates and optionally additional features such as intensity or color.
  - **Applications**: Autonomous driving, drone navigation, and 3D modeling.
  - **Challenges**: Large data size, sparse points, and lack of structure.

Voxel Grids:

- A **voxel grid** represents the 3D space by dividing it into a regular grid of volumetric elements (voxels), similar to 2D pixels but in 3D. Each voxel contains information about whether it is occupied by an object or free space.
  - **Advantages**: Voxel grids can be easier to process computationally, and convolutional operations can be applied,

making them suitable for CNN-based methods.

  o **Challenges**: Can be memory-intensive, especially for large 3D spaces.

3D Bounding Boxes

3D bounding boxes are a common method to localize and identify objects in 3D space. They are typically parameterized by:

- **Center position**: $(x,y,z)(x, y, z)(x,y,z)$ coordinates of the box's center.
- **Dimensions**: Width, height, and depth of the bounding box.
- **Orientation**: The rotation of the bounding box in 3D space.

In tasks like 3D object detection, algorithms aim to predict these bounding boxes around objects detected in point clouds or voxel grids.

Common 3D Bounding Box Methods:

- **Anchor-based methods**: Extend 2D bounding box anchor-based methods to 3D.
- **Anchor-free methods**: Directly predict the 3D bounding boxes without predefined anchors.

SLAM (Simultaneous Localization and Mapping)

SLAM is a computational problem where a system builds a map of an unknown environment while simultaneously keeping track of its position within that map. It is widely used in mobile robotics and autonomous navigation.

Key Concepts of SLAM:

- **Localization**: Estimating the system's position and orientation.
- **Mapping**: Building a map of the environment.
- **Sensors**: SLAM systems often rely on sensors like cameras, LiDAR, IMUs (Inertial Measurement Units), and depth sensors.

SLAM Techniques:

- **Visual SLAM**: Uses camera data to localize and map the environment.
- **LiDAR-based SLAM**: Uses point clouds generated by LiDAR to build maps.
- **RGB-D SLAM**: Uses RGB-D cameras (which provide both RGB and depth data) for 3D mapping.

Popular SLAM Algorithms:

- **ORB-SLAM**: A visual SLAM algorithm using feature points for localization.
- **LOAM (LiDAR Odometry and Mapping)**: A LiDAR-based method for real-time 3D SLAM.
- **Google Cartographer**: A SLAM framework that supports 2D and 3D mapping with LiDAR and IMU data.

3D Object Detection and Tracking Methods

Point-based Methods:

These methods operate directly on 3D point clouds.

- **PointNet/PointNet++**: Neural networks designed to directly process point clouds for classification and segmentation.

Voxel-based Methods:

Point clouds are converted into voxel grids for easier processing using convolutional networks.

- **VoxelNet**: A deep learning architecture that processes voxelized 3D point clouds for object detection.

Fusion-based Methods:

These methods combine multiple sensor inputs, such as LiDAR and camera data, for improved object detection and tracking.

- **MV3D (Multi-View 3D)**: Combines bird's-eye view of LiDAR with RGB images for object detection.

Example Code: 3D Bounding Box Estimation

Here's a simple example of how a 3D bounding box could be visualized in a point cloud using Python and Open3D (a library for 3D data processing).

Installation of Open3D:

pip install open3d

Visualizing Point Cloud and 3D Bounding Boxes:

import open3d as o3d

import numpy as np

Generate random point cloud data

pcd = o3d.geometry.PointCloud()

```
points = np.random.rand(1000, 3)  # 1000 random
points in 3D

pcd.points = o3d.utility.Vector3dVector(points)



# Create a 3D bounding box

bbox                                            =
o3d.geometry.OrientedBoundingBox(center=(0.5,
0.5, 0.5),

                            R=np.eye(3),

                            extent=(0.4, 0.3, 0.2))



# Visualize the point cloud and bounding box

o3d.visualization.draw_geometries([pcd, bbox])
```

SLAM Implementation: ORB-SLAM Example

ORB-SLAM2 is a popular visual SLAM system that can be used for both monocular, stereo, and RGB-D cameras.

- You can use the official ORB-SLAM2 implementation.
- This requires OpenCV and Pangolin for visualization, and can be used with ROS for real-time tracking and mapping in a robotic system.

Here's a high-level overview of how to run ORB-SLAM2 for monocular visual SLAM:

1. Clone the repository and install dependencies.
2. Prepare a dataset or video stream.
3. Run the SLAM system to track the camera and build a 3D map of the environment.

```
# Clone the repository

git clone https://github.com/raulmur/ORB_SLAM2.git



# Build the system and install dependencies

cd ORB_SLAM2

./build.sh



# Run SLAM on a dataset

./Examples/Monocular/mono_tum
Vocabulary/ORBvoc.txt
Examples/Monocular/TUM1.yaml
path_to_video_dataset
```

Conclusion

3D object detection and tracking are vital for applications like robotics, autonomous driving, and augmented reality. Techniques such as point clouds, voxel grids, 3D bounding boxes, and SLAM provide essential tools for solving these problems. Each approach has its strengths and challenges, and depending on the specific application (e.g., large outdoor scenes vs. indoor environments), the appropriate method (LiDAR-based SLAM, visual SLAM, or sensor fusion) should be selected.

Husn Ara

Chapter 8: Deep Learning in Computer Vision

Convolutional Neural Networks (CNNs)

Convolutional Neural Networks (CNNs) are a class of deep neural networks designed primarily for image-related tasks, such as image classification, object detection, segmentation, and more. CNNs leverage the spatial structure of images through specialized layers like convolutional layers, pooling layers, and fully connected layers.

1. Architecture and Layers of CNNs

Basic Layers in CNNs:

1. **Convolutional Layer**:
   o The core building block of a CNN.
   o This layer applies convolution operations between the input and a set of learnable filters (kernels), producing feature maps.
   o Helps capture local patterns, like edges or textures in images.

Formula: $Y_{ij} = \sum_{m,n} X_{i+m, j+n} \cdot K_{m,n}$, where X is the input, K is the kernel, and Y is the output.

PyTorch Convolutional Layer Example

```
conv_layer = nn.Conv2d(in_channels=3, out_channels=16, kernel_size=3, stride=1, padding=1)
```

2. **Activation Layer (ReLU)**:

- Introduces non-linearity to the network, allowing it to learn more complex patterns.
- **ReLU** (Rectified Linear Unit) is the most common activation function: $f(x)=max(0,x)$.

```
relu = nn.ReLU()
```

3. **Pooling Layer**:

- Reduces the spatial dimensions (width and height) of feature maps, preserving important features while reducing computation.
- **Max pooling** and **average pooling** are the most common pooling operations.
- Pooling layers help in reducing overfitting and make the model invariant to small translations in the input.

```
pooling_layer = nn.MaxPool2d(kernel_size=2, stride=2)
```

4. **Fully Connected Layer (Dense Layer)**:

- Found at the end of the network.
- Takes the flattened output from the convolutional and pooling layers and outputs predictions for the task (e.g., classification).

```
fc_layer          =          nn.Linear(in_features=256,
out_features=10)  # 10 classes output
```

CNN Architecture Example

A simple CNN for image classification:

```
import torch

import torch.nn as nn

import torch.nn.functional as F



class SimpleCNN(nn.Module):

    def __init__(self):

        super(SimpleCNN, self).__init__()

        self.conv1 = nn.Conv2d(3, 16, kernel_size=3,
padding=1)  # 3 input channels (RGB), 16 filters

        self.conv2 = nn.Conv2d(16, 32, kernel_size=3,
padding=1)

        self.pool = nn.MaxPool2d(2, 2)  # Max pooling
layer

        self.fc1 = nn.Linear(32 * 8 * 8, 128)  # Fully
connected layer

        self.fc2 = nn.Linear(128, 10)   # 10 output
classes (for classification)



    def forward(self, x):
```

```
    x   =   self.pool(F.relu(self.conv1(x)))      #
Convolution + ReLU + Pooling

    x   =   self.pool(F.relu(self.conv2(x)))      #
Convolution + ReLU + Pooling

    x = x.view(-1, 32 * 8 * 8)  # Flattening the tensor
for the FC layer

    x = F.relu(self.fc1(x))  # Fully connected layer +
ReLU

    x = self.fc2(x)  # Output layer

    return x
```

```
# Example usage

model = SimpleCNN()

input_tensor = torch.randn(1, 3, 32, 32)  # Batch size
of 1, 3 channels, 32x32 image

output = model(input_tensor)

print(output.shape)   # Output shape: [1, 10] (for
classification into 10 categories)
```

2. Training CNNs

The training process of CNNs follows the same principle as any deep learning model but leverages the special architecture of CNNs for image tasks.

Key Steps in Training CNNs:

    1. **Forward Propagation**:

- o The input passes through all layers, and the model generates a prediction.

2. **Loss Calculation**:
   - o Compute the loss using a suitable loss function (e.g., cross-entropy loss for classification).

```
criterion = nn.CrossEntropyLoss()

loss = criterion(output, labels)
```

3. **Backpropagation**:

- Compute gradients of the loss with respect to model parameters using backpropagation.

```
loss.backward()
```

4. **Optimization**:

- Update the model weights using an optimization algorithm like stochastic gradient descent (SGD) or Adam.

```
optimizer = torch.optim.SGD(model.parameters(), lr=0.01)

optimizer.step()
```

Example of a CNN Training Loop

```
# Example training loop

for epoch in range(num_epochs):

    optimizer.zero_grad()  # Clear previous gradients

    output = model(input_tensor)  # Forward pass

    loss = criterion(output, labels)  # Compute loss
```

```
loss.backward()  # Backward pass

optimizer.step()  # Update model weights



    print(f"Epoch    {epoch+1}/{num_epochs},    Loss:
{loss.item()}")
```

Loss Functions:

- **Cross-Entropy Loss**: Used for classification tasks.

  ```
  criterion = nn.CrossEntropyLoss()
  ```

Optimization Techniques:

- **SGD (Stochastic Gradient Descent)**: Basic and widely used optimizer.

  ```
  optimizer = torch.optim.SGD(model.parameters(),
  lr=0.01)
  ```

- **Adam Optimizer**: Adaptive learning rate algorithm, often used for faster convergence.

  ```
  optimizer                              =
  torch.optim.Adam(model.parameters(), lr=0.001)
  ```

3. Transfer Learning and Fine-Tuning

Transfer learning involves using pre-trained models that have been trained on large datasets (such as ImageNet) and adapting them to new tasks. This is particularly useful when you don't have a large dataset or when you want faster convergence.

Why Transfer Learning?

- **Pre-trained models** have already learned general features like edges, textures, and shapes.
- You can leverage this knowledge by **fine-tuning** the model for a new task, instead of training from scratch.

Two Approaches in Transfer Learning:

1. **Feature Extraction**:
   - Freeze the pre-trained model's weights and use the model as a feature extractor.
   - Replace the final classification layer to match the number of output classes for your task.

```
model = torchvision.models.resnet18(pretrained=True)

for param in model.parameters():

  param.requires_grad = False  # Freeze all layers




# Replace the final layer with a new one for your specific task

num_features = model.fc.in_features

model.fc = nn.Linear(num_features, num_classes)  # num_classes is the number of output classes
```

2. **Fine-Tuning**:

- Allow some of the pre-trained model layers (especially the later ones) to be trainable.
- Fine-tuning means adjusting these weights on your specific task dataset.

```
model = torchvision.models.resnet18(pretrained=True)
```

```
# Unfreeze some layers for fine-tuning

for param in model.layer4.parameters():

    param.requires_grad = True  # Fine-tune only the last
block


num_features = model.fc.in_features

model.fc = nn.Linear(num_features, num_classes)
```

Example: Fine-Tuning a Pre-trained CNN (ResNet18)

```
import torchvision.models as models

import torch.optim as optim


# Load a pre-trained ResNet model

model = models.resnet18(pretrained=True)


# Freeze early layers

for param in model.parameters():

    param.requires_grad = False


# Modify the fully connected layer for a new
classification task

num_classes = 5  # Number of classes for the new
task
```

num_features = model.fc.in_features

model.fc = nn.Linear(num_features, num_classes)

 # Define loss function and optimizer

criterion = nn.CrossEntropyLoss()

optimizer = optim.Adam(model.fc.parameters(), lr=0.001)

 # Example training loop (for fine-tuning)

for epoch in range(epochs):

    optimizer.zero_grad()

    outputs = model(inputs)

    loss = criterion(outputs, labels)

    loss.backward()

    optimizer.step()

    print(f'Epoch {epoch + 1}, Loss: {loss.item()}')

Conclusion

Convolutional Neural Networks (CNNs) are highly effective for image-based tasks due to their ability to capture spatial hierarchies in images. By stacking convolutional, pooling, and fully connected layers, CNNs learn complex patterns, making them suitable for tasks like image classification, object detection, and segmentation. Training CNNs involves proper data handling, loss calculation, and optimization techniques. Transfer learning and fine-tuning offer powerful strategies for leveraging pre-trained models, making CNNs adaptable to various tasks even with limited datasets.

Advanced Architectures

In modern deep learning, advanced architectures such as **ResNet**, **DenseNet**, and **EfficientNet** have been developed to improve training efficiency, accuracy, and generalization. These architectures introduced novel ideas like residual connections, dense connections, and compound scaling to address limitations like the vanishing gradient problem, inefficient use of parameters, and scalability across different tasks.

1. ResNet (Residual Networks)

ResNet was introduced by He et al. in the paper **"Deep Residual Learning for Image Recognition"** in 2015. It revolutionized deep learning by allowing networks to be much deeper (with hundreds of layers) without suffering from vanishing or exploding gradient problems, which are common in very deep networks.

Key Concept: Residual Block

- A **residual block** uses **skip connections**, also known as **shortcuts**, where the output of a layer is added directly to the input of that layer after passing through intermediate layers. This bypass connection helps gradients flow more easily during backpropagation, mitigating the vanishing gradient problem.

Residual Function:

$$y = F(x, \{W_i\}) + x$$

Where $F(x, \{W_i\})$ is the transformation learned by the intermediate layers, and x is the input that is directly added back to the output.

Architecture

A ResNet model consists of multiple residual blocks stacked together. For example, **ResNet-50** has 50 layers, while **ResNet-101** has 101 layers.

- **Key Layers in ResNet**:
    1. Convolution layers
    2. Batch Normalization
    3. ReLU activation
    4. Skip connections (residual connections)

ResNet Code Example (PyTorch):

```
import torch

import torch.nn as nn


class ResidualBlock(nn.Module):

    def __init__(self, in_channels, out_channels, stride=1):

        super(ResidualBlock, self).__init__()

        self.conv1 = nn.Conv2d(in_channels, out_channels, kernel_size=3, stride=stride, padding=1)

        self.bn1 = nn.BatchNorm2d(out_channels)

        self.relu = nn.ReLU(inplace=True)

        self.conv2 = nn.Conv2d(out_channels, out_channels, kernel_size=3, stride=1, padding=1)

        self.bn2 = nn.BatchNorm2d(out_channels)
```

```python
    # Skip connection if input and output channels are different
    self.skip_connection = nn.Sequential()
    if stride != 1 or in_channels != out_channels:
        self.skip_connection = nn.Sequential(
            nn.Conv2d(in_channels, out_channels, kernel_size=1, stride=stride),
            nn.BatchNorm2d(out_channels)
        )

    def forward(self, x):
        identity = self.skip_connection(x)
        out = self.conv1(x)
        out = self.bn1(out)
        out = self.relu(out)
        out = self.conv2(out)
        out = self.bn2(out)
        out += identity  # Add the skip connection
        out = self.relu(out)
        return out


# Example ResNet block with 64 input and output channels
res_block = ResidualBlock(64, 64)
```

2. DenseNet (Densely Connected Convolutional Networks)

DenseNet, introduced in the paper **"Densely Connected Convolutional Networks"** by Huang et al. in 2017, builds upon the idea of connecting each layer to every other layer in a **feed-forward fashion**. Instead of just using the output of the previous layer, each layer in a DenseNet receives the concatenated outputs of all preceding layers.

Key Concept: Dense Connectivity

- In DenseNet, each layer has access to the feature maps of all previous layers. This helps:
    1. Improve gradient flow during backpropagation.
    2. Promote feature reuse, making the model more efficient and reducing the number of parameters.

Dense Connectivity Formula:

$$x_l - H_l([x_0, x_1, \ldots, x_{l-1}])$$

Where x_l is the output of the l-th layer, and $[x_0, x_1, \ldots, x_{l-1}]$ represents the concatenation of feature maps from all previous layers.

Architecture

DenseNet is characterized by **dense blocks**, each containing several layers where the input to each layer is the concatenation of outputs from all preceding layers.

DenseNet Code Example (PyTorch):

```
class DenseBlock(nn.Module):
```

```python
    def     __init__(self,    num_layers,    in_channels,
growth_rate):

        super(DenseBlock, self).__init__()

        self.layers = nn.ModuleList()

        for i in range(num_layers):

            self.layers.append(self._make_layer(in_channels
+ i * growth_rate, growth_rate))


    def _make_layer(self, in_channels, growth_rate):

        layer = nn.Sequential(

            nn.BatchNorm2d(in_channels),

            nn.ReLU(inplace=True),

            nn.Conv2d(in_channels,                growth_rate,
kernel_size=3, padding=1)

        )

        return layer


    def forward(self, x):

        for layer in self.layers:

            out = layer(x)

            x = torch.cat([x, out], dim=1)  # Concatenate along
the channel dimension

        return x


# Example DenseBlock with 6 layers and a growth rate of
32

dense_block    =    DenseBlock(6,    in_channels=64,
growth_rate=32)
```

3. EfficientNet

EfficientNet, proposed by Tan and Le in **"EfficientNet: Rethinking Model Scaling for Convolutional Neural Networks"** in 2019, introduces a systematic way to scale neural networks using a technique called **compound scaling**. EfficientNet achieves state-of-the-art performance while using significantly fewer parameters than previous architectures.

Key Concept: Compound Scaling

EfficientNet uses a simple yet effective scaling strategy that uniformly scales the depth, width, and resolution of a network. The scaling factors are determined by a compound coefficient.

1. **Width scaling**: Increases the number of channels in each layer.
2. **Depth scaling**: Increases the number of layers.
3. **Resolution scaling**: Increases the input image resolution.

The compound scaling is done by a set of factors α, β, γ where:

- $d - \alpha^\phi$ (depth)

- $w - \beta^\phi$ (width)

- $r - \gamma^\phi$ (resolution)

Where ϕ is a user-defined scaling coefficient, and α, β, γ are constants that control how to scale the network.

Architecture

EfficientNet starts with a baseline network (EfficientNet-B0) and scales it to larger models (EfficientNet-B1 to EfficientNet-B7) using compound scaling.

254

EfficientNet also employs **MBConv blocks** (MobileNet Inverted Residuals) for efficient computation.

EfficientNet Code Example (PyTorch):

```python
import torch

import torch.nn as nn

import torch.nn.functional as F


class MBConvBlock(nn.Module):
    def __init__(self, in_channels, out_channels, expand_ratio, stride):
        super(MBConvBlock, self).__init__()
        hidden_dim = in_channels * expand_ratio
        self.use_res_connect = stride == 1 and in_channels == out_channels


        layers = []
        if expand_ratio != 1:
            layers.append(nn.Conv2d(in_channels, hidden_dim, kernel_size=1, bias=False))
            layers.append(nn.BatchNorm2d(hidden_dim))
            layers.append(nn.ReLU6(inplace=True))


        layers.extend([
            nn.Conv2d(hidden_dim, hidden_dim, kernel_size=3, stride=stride, padding=1, groups=hidden_dim, bias=False),
            nn.BatchNorm2d(hidden_dim),
```

```
        nn.ReLU6(inplace=True),

        nn.Conv2d(hidden_dim,              out_channels,
kernel_size=1, bias=False),

        nn.BatchNorm2d(out_channels)

    ])


    self.conv = nn.Sequential(*layers)


    def forward(self, x):
        if self.use_res_connect:
            return x + self.conv(x)
        else:
            return self.conv(x)


# Example MBConv block with 32 input channels, 64
output channels, expand ratio of 6, and stride 1

mbconv_block = MBConvBlock(32, 64, expand_ratio=6,
stride=1)
```

Conclusion

Each of these architectures — **ResNet**, **DenseNet**, and **EfficientNet** — offers unique innovations in deep learning:

- **ResNet** introduced residual connections, solving the vanishing gradient problem and enabling deeper networks.
- **DenseNet** enhanced feature reuse by connecting every layer to every other layer within dense blocks.

- **EfficientNet** achieved state-of-the-art performance by using a compound scaling method to balance depth, width, and resolution efficiently.

These architectures are fundamental to many state-of-the-art models used in image classification, object detection, and other computer vision tasks today.

Attention Mechanisms and Transformers

Attention mechanisms have become foundational in deep learning, originally introduced for natural language processing (NLP) tasks. In recent years, they've also shown tremendous potential in vision tasks, particularly through architectures like **Vision Transformers (ViT)** and **Hybrid CNN-Transformer models**. Self-attention allows models to weigh the importance of different parts of the input, making these mechanisms highly flexible for capturing global context in images.

1. Self-Attention in Vision

Self-attention mechanisms were first introduced in the paper **"Attention is All You Need"** (Vaswani et al., 2017) and later adapted for vision tasks. In the context of vision, self-attention helps a model understand global relationships between different parts of an image.

Key Idea:

- For each pixel (or patch) in an image, the self-attention mechanism computes a **weighted sum** of all other pixels/patches. This enables the model to capture long-range dependencies and global context, which is sometimes difficult with convolutional layers that only consider local neighborhoods.

How Self-Attention Works:

- **Query (Q), Key (K), and Value (V)** matrices are computed from the input image features.
- The attention weights are computed as the dot product between **Q** and **K**.
- These weights are then used to weigh the **Value** matrix, determining the contribution of each part of the image to the output.

Mathematically:

$$\text{Attention}(Q,K,V) = \text{softmax}\left(\frac{QK^T}{\sqrt{d_k}}\right)V$$

Where d_k is the dimensionality of the keys.

Self-Attention Code Example:

Here is a simplified version of the self-attention mechanism in PyTorch:

```
import torch

import torch.nn as nn

import torch.nn.functional as F


class SelfAttention(nn.Module):
    def __init__(self, embed_size, heads):
        super(SelfAttention, self).__init__()
        self.embed_size = embed_size
        self.heads = heads
```

```python
        self.head_dim = embed_size // heads

        assert self.head_dim * heads == embed_size,
"Embedding size must be divisible by heads"

        self.values = nn.Linear(self.head_dim,
self.head_dim, bias=False)
        self.keys = nn.Linear(self.head_dim, self.head_dim,
bias=False)
        self.queries = nn.Linear(self.head_dim,
self.head_dim, bias=False)
        self.fc_out = nn.Linear(embed_size, embed_size)


    def forward(self, values, keys, query, mask):
        N = query.shape[0]
        value_len, key_len, query_len = values.shape[1],
keys.shape[1], query.shape[1]


        # Split the embedding into multiple heads for multi-
head attention
        values = values.reshape(N, value_len, self.heads,
self.head_dim)
        keys = keys.reshape(N, key_len, self.heads,
self.head_dim)
        queries = query.reshape(N, query_len, self.heads,
self.head_dim)


        # Dot product attention: Q * K^T
```

```
energy = torch.einsum("nqhd,nkhd->nhqk", [queries,
keys])


        # Normalize energy values for numerical stability

        attention = torch.softmax(energy / (self.embed_size
** (1 / 2)), dim=3)


        # Get the weighted sum of values

        out  =  torch.einsum("nhql,nlhd->nqhd",  [attention,
values]).reshape(

            N, query_len, self.embed_size

        )


        # Pass through final fully connected layer

        out = self.fc_out(out)

        return out


# Example use case:

attention = SelfAttention(embed_size=256, heads=8)

x = torch.randn(64, 49, 256)  # Batch size 64, 49 patches,
256 feature size

out = attention(x, x, x, mask=None)

print(out.shape)  # Output shape: (64, 49, 256)
```

2. Vision Transformers (ViT)

The **Vision Transformer (ViT)**, introduced by Dosovitskiy et al. in the paper **"An Image is Worth 16x16 Words: Transformers for Image Recognition at Scale"** (2020), adapts the transformer architecture from NLP to computer vision. Instead of using convolutional layers, ViT directly applies transformers to image patches.

Key Concept: Patch Embeddings

- An image is split into fixed-size patches (e.g., 16×1616 \times 1616×16 pixels).
- These patches are then flattened and projected into a **linear embedding space**.
- Positional encodings are added to these embeddings to retain spatial information (since transformers are permutation-invariant).
- The resulting patch embeddings are then fed into the transformer layers.

Vision Transformer Architecture:

1. **Patch Extraction**: Split the input image into non-overlapping patches.
2. **Linear Projection**: Each patch is flattened and linearly projected into an embedding space.
3. **Transformer Encoder**: The transformer encoder consists of multi-head self-attention layers and feed-forward layers.
4. **Classification Head**: A special classification token is appended to the sequence of patch embeddings, and its final representation is used for classification.

ViT Code Example (Simplified):

```
import torch

import torch.nn as nn


class VisionTransformer(nn.Module):

    def __init__(self, img_size=224, patch_size=16, num_classes=1000, embed_size=768, depth=12, heads=12, mlp_dim=3072):
```

```python
        super(VisionTransformer, self).__init__()

        self.patch_size = patch_size

        num_patches = (img_size // patch_size) ** 2

        self.patch_embeddings = nn.Linear(patch_size *
patch_size * 3, embed_size)  # Project each patch into an
embedding

        self.position_embeddings                    =
nn.Parameter(torch.randn(1,    num_patches    +    1,
embed_size))  # Positional embeddings

        self.class_token = nn.Parameter(torch.randn(1, 1,
embed_size))  # Classification token

        self.transformer = nn.TransformerEncoder(

            nn.TransformerEncoderLayer(embed_size,
heads, mlp_dim), depth

        )

        self.fc = nn.Linear(embed_size, num_classes)


    def forward(self, x):

        B, _, _, _ = x.shape

        x         =         x.unfold(2,      self.patch_size,
self.patch_size).unfold(3,                self.patch_size,
self.patch_size)  # Extract patches

        x = x.flatten(2).transpose(1, 2)  # Flatten each patch
into a vector

        x = self.patch_embeddings(x)  # Linear projection

        class_tokens = self.class_token.expand(B, -1, -1)

        x = torch.cat((class_tokens, x), dim=1)  # Prepend
class token

        x += self.position_embeddings
```

```
    x = self.transformer(x)

    x = self.fc(x[:, 0])  # Use the output of the class token
for classification

    return x


# Example usage:

vit = VisionTransformer()

img = torch.randn(8, 3, 224, 224)  # Batch of 8 images,
each 224x224 with 3 color channels

out = vit(img)

print(out.shape)    # Output shape: (8, 1000) for
classification into 1000 categories
```

3. Hybrid CNN-Transformer Models

Hybrid models combine the strengths of **CNNs** for local feature extraction with the **transformer's global attention** mechanism. The idea is to use CNNs in the early stages of the network to extract rich spatial features and then apply transformers to model global relationships between the features.

Key Features of Hybrid Models:

- **CNN Backbone**: A CNN (like ResNet) is used to extract feature maps from the image. The feature maps are treated as a sequence of patches for the transformer.
- **Transformer for Global Attention**: The transformer processes the feature map patches, applying self-attention to capture long-range dependencies across the image.

Advantages:

- **Locality + Globality**: CNNs capture fine-grained local patterns, while transformers capture long-range dependencies and relationships.
- **Efficiency**: Hybrid models are more efficient than pure transformers for high-resolution images, as CNNs are computationally efficient in extracting features.

Example: Hybrid CNN-Transformer Model

```
class CNNTransformerHybrid(nn.Module):

    def __init__(self, num_classes=1000):

        super(CNNTransformerHybrid, self).__init__()

        # CNN backbone (e.g., ResNet)

        self.cnn_backbone                          =
torchvision.models.resnet50(pretrained=True)

        self.cnn_backbone.fc = nn.Identity()  # Remove the
final classification layer


        # Transformer encoder

        self.transformer_encoder = nn.TransformerEncoder(

            nn.TransformerEncoderLayer(d_model=2048,
nhead=8), num_layers=6

        )


        # Final classification layer

        self.fc = nn.Linear(2048, num_classes)


    def forward(self, x):

        # Extract features using CNN backbone
```

```
features = self.cnn_backbone(x)    # Shape:
[batch_size, 2048]

features = features.unsqueeze(1)  # Add sequence
dimension for transformer


# Apply transformer

x = self.transformer_encoder(features)


# Classification

out = self.fc(x[:, 0])    # Use the output of the
transformer for classification

return out


# Example: Hybrid CNN-Transformer model

hybrid_model                              =
CNNTransformerHybrid(num_classes=1000)

input_image = torch.randn(1, 3, 224, 224)

output = hybrid_model(input_image)

print(output.shape)  # Output shape: (1, 1000)
```

Conclusion

- **Self-attention** in vision allows models to capture global dependencies without relying solely on local convolutions.
- **Vision Transformers (ViT)** apply the transformer architecture directly to image patches, treating images as sequences, achieving state-of-the-art results in image classification.
- **Hybrid CNN-Transformer models** combine the strengths of CNNs for local feature extraction with transformers for modeling long-range

relationships, striking a balance between computational efficiency and performance.

Generative Models in Computer Vision

Generative models in computer vision are designed to model the underlying distribution of data, allowing them to generate new samples that resemble the training data. Two prominent generative models used in computer vision are **Generative Adversarial Networks (GANs)** and **Variational Autoencoders (VAEs)**. These models are widely applied in tasks like image synthesis, style transfer, and anomaly detection.

1. GANs (Generative Adversarial Networks)

Overview:

Generative Adversarial Networks (GANs), introduced by Ian Goodfellow in 2014, consist of two neural networks that compete with each other:

- **Generator (G)**: Attempts to generate realistic data (e.g., images).
- **Discriminator (D)**: Tries to distinguish between real data and data generated by the generator.

The generator's goal is to produce images that are indistinguishable from real images, while the discriminator learns to distinguish between real and generated images. The two networks are trained simultaneously in a min-max game where the generator improves its output, and the discriminator becomes more adept at identifying fake data.

Key Concepts:

- **Adversarial Training**: The two networks train in opposition, making GANs a form of unsupervised learning.
- **Loss Function**: GANs use a min-max loss function where the generator tries to minimize the probability of the discriminator being correct, while the discriminator tries to maximize this probability.

The loss function can be written as:

$$\min_{G} \max_{D} V(D, G) = \mathbb{E}_{x \sim p_{data}}[\log D(x)] + \mathbb{E}_{z \sim p_z}[\log(1 - D(G(z)))]$$

Where:

- $D(x)$ is the discriminator's estimate of the probability that x is a real sample.

- $G(z)$ is the generated sample from the generator, using random noise z.

Code   Example: GAN

```
import torch

import torch.nn as nn


class Generator(nn.Module):

    def __init__(self, input_dim=100, output_dim=3, img_size=64):

        super(Generator, self).__init__()

        self.init_size = img_size // 4

        self.fc = nn.Linear(input_dim, 128 * self.init_size ** 2)

        self.conv_blocks = nn.Sequential(

            nn.BatchNorm2d(128),
```

```python
            nn.Upsample(scale_factor=2),

            nn.Conv2d(128, 128, 3, stride=1, padding=1),

            nn.BatchNorm2d(128),

            nn.LeakyReLU(0.2, inplace=True),

            nn.Upsample(scale_factor=2),

            nn.Conv2d(128, output_dim, 3, stride=1,
padding=1),

            nn.Tanh()

        )


    def forward(self, z):

        out = self.fc(z)

        out = out.view(out.shape[0], 128, self.init_size,
self.init_size)

        img = self.conv_blocks(out)

        return img


class Discriminator(nn.Module):

    def __init__(self, input_dim=3, img_size=64):

        super(Discriminator, self).__init__()

        self.model = nn.Sequential(

            nn.Conv2d(input_dim, 64, 3, stride=2,
padding=1),

            nn.LeakyReLU(0.2, inplace=True),

            nn.Conv2d(64, 128, 3, stride=2, padding=1),

            nn.BatchNorm2d(128),

            nn.LeakyReLU(0.2, inplace=True),
```

```
    nn.Flatten(),

    nn.Linear(128 * (img_size // 4) ** 2, 1),

    nn.Sigmoid()

  )


 def forward(self, img):

   validity = self.model(img)

   return validity



# Example: Generator and Discriminator with image size 64x64

G = Generator()

D = Discriminator()


z = torch.randn(1, 100)  # Random noise for the generator

generated_img = G(z)

validity = D(generated_img)

print(validity)
```

Applications of GANs:

- **Image Generation**: GANs can generate high-quality images that resemble the training data.
- **Image Super-Resolution**: GANs are used to enhance image resolution (e.g., SRGAN).
- **Image-to-Image Translation**: Techniques like CycleGAN enable translation between domains (e.g., converting sketches to photos).
- **Style Transfer**: GANs can generate images in the style of another image while preserving the content of the original.

2. VAEs (Variational Autoencoders)

Overview:

Variational Autoencoders (VAEs) are probabilistic generative models that learn a latent representation of data by encoding input data into a continuous latent space. Unlike traditional autoencoders, which compress data into a deterministic latent vector, VAEs map data to a probability distribution in the latent space, allowing for random sampling.

Key Concepts:

- **Encoder**: Maps input data (images) to a latent space. The encoder outputs a mean and variance that parameterize the latent distribution.
- **Decoder**: Reconstructs data from the latent representation, allowing the model to generate new data by sampling from the latent space.
- **KL Divergence**: Ensures that the learned latent space is close to a standard Gaussian distribution, promoting smoothness and continuity in the latent space.

The loss function for VAEs consists of two terms:

1. **Reconstruction Loss**: Measures how well the reconstructed data matches the original input.
2. **KL Divergence**: Measures how closely the latent distribution matches a prior distribution (e.g., a Gaussian).

The total loss can be written as:

$$\mathcal{L} - \mathbb{E}_{q(z|x)}[\log p(x|z)] - D_{\mathrm{KL}}(q(z|x)\|p(z))$$

Where $q(z|x)$ is the encoder, $p(x|z)$ is the decoder, and $p(z)$ is the prior.

Code Example: VAE

```python
class VAE(nn.Module):

    def __init__(self, img_size=64, latent_dim=128):

        super(VAE, self).__init__()

        self.encoder = nn.Sequential(

            nn.Conv2d(3, 64, 4, stride=2, padding=1),

            nn.ReLU(),

            nn.Conv2d(64, 128, 4, stride=2, padding=1),

            nn.ReLU()

        )

        self.fc_mu = nn.Linear(128 * (img_size // 4) ** 2,
latent_dim)

        self.fc_logvar = nn.Linear(128 * (img_size // 4) ** 2,
latent_dim)

        self.decoder_fc  =  nn.Linear(latent_dim,  128  *
(img_size // 4) ** 2)

        self.decoder = nn.Sequential(

            nn.ConvTranspose2d(128,  64,  4,  stride=2,
padding=1),

            nn.ReLU(),

            nn.ConvTranspose2d(64,  3,  4,  stride=2,
padding=1),

            nn.Sigmoid()

        )


    def encode(self, x):

        h = self.encoder(x)

        h = h.view(h.size(0), -1)
```

```python
        mu, logvar = self.fc_mu(h), self.fc_logvar(h)

        return mu, logvar


    def reparameterize(self, mu, logvar):
        std = torch.exp(0.5 * logvar)

        eps = torch.randn_like(std)

        return mu + eps * std


    def decode(self, z):
        h = self.decoder_fc(z)

        h = h.view(h.size(0), 128, 16, 16)

        return self.decoder(h)


    def forward(self, x):
        mu, logvar = self.encode(x)

        z = self.reparameterize(mu, logvar)

        return self.decode(z), mu, logvar


# Example: VAE with image size 64x64

vae = VAE()

input_img = torch.randn(1, 3, 64, 64)

reconstructed_img, mu, logvar = vae(input_img)

print(reconstructed_img.shape)
```

Applications of VAEs:

- **Image Generation**: VAEs can generate novel images by sampling from the learned latent space.

- **Anomaly Detection**: VAEs can detect anomalies by measuring reconstruction error; if an image is difficult to reconstruct, it may be an outlier.
- **Latent Space Manipulation**: VAEs allow smooth interpolation between latent representations, useful for generating continuous variations of images.

3. Applications of Generative Models

Generative models like GANs and VAEs have wide-ranging applications in computer vision:

- **Image Synthesis**: GANs are particularly popular for synthesizing realistic images in fields such as art, gaming, and design.
- **Style Transfer**: Generative models can be used for style transfer, where the style of one image (e.g., Van Gogh painting) is applied to the content of another image.
- **Image Inpainting**: GANs and VAEs can be used to fill in missing parts of an image, enabling applications like photo restoration.
- **Super-Resolution**: GANs are applied to improve the resolution of images in fields like satellite imaging and medical imaging.

Generative models are fundamental to a variety of creative and practical tasks in modern computer vision.

Chapter 9: Video Analysis and Action Recognition

Motion Estimation

Motion estimation involves determining the movement of objects within a sequence of images or video. It is a critical task in various applications like video compression, object tracking, and autonomous driving. Two common approaches for motion estimation are **Optical Flow** and **Filtering techniques** (e.g., **Kalman Filter** and **Particle Filter**).

1. Optical Flow

Overview:

Optical flow refers to the apparent motion of objects between consecutive frames of a video, caused by the relative movement between the camera and the scene. Optical flow estimates the displacement vector for each pixel in the image, indicating how each pixel has moved between frames.

Key Concepts:

- **Flow Vector**: For each pixel, a vector is computed that indicates the direction and magnitude of motion between two frames.
- **Assumptions**:

- o **Brightness Constancy**: The intensity of a pixel remains constant over time.
- o **Small Motion**: The displacement between consecutive frames is small.
- o **Spatial Coherence**: Neighboring pixels have similar motion.

The optical flow equation is derived as:

$$I_x V_x + I_y V_y + I_t = 0$$

Where:

- I_x, I_y, and I_t are partial derivatives of the image intensity with respect to the x-axis, y-axis, and time, respectively.
- V_x and V_y are the components of the optical flow vector in the x and y directions.

Common Methods:

- **Lucas-Kanade Method**: A local method that assumes a constant motion over small patches of the image.
- **Horn-Schunck Method**: A global method that uses a smoothness constraint to enforce spatial coherence across the entire image.

Code Example: Optical Flow (Using OpenCV)

```
import cv2

import numpy as np



# Load two consecutive frames

prev_frame = cv2.imread('frame1.jpg', cv2.IMREAD_GRAYSCALE)

next_frame = cv2.imread('frame2.jpg', cv2.IMREAD_GRAYSCALE)
```

```
# Calculate optical flow using the Farneback method

flow = cv2.calcOpticalFlowFarneback(prev_frame,
next_frame, None, 0.5, 3, 15, 3, 5, 1.2, 0)


# Visualize the flow as HSV

hsv = np.zeros_like(cv2.cvtColor(prev_frame,
cv2.COLOR_GRAY2BGR))

mag, ang = cv2.cartToPolar(flow[..., 0], flow[..., 1])

hsv[..., 0] = ang * 180 / np.pi / 2

hsv[..., 1] = 255

hsv[..., 2] = cv2.normalize(mag, None, 0, 255,
cv2.NORM_MINMAX)


# Convert to RGB for display

rgb_flow = cv2.cvtColor(hsv,
cv2.COLOR_HSV2BGR)


cv2.imshow("Optical Flow", rgb_flow)

cv2.waitKey(0)

cv2.destroyAllWindows()
```

Applications of Optical Flow:

- **Object Tracking**: Optical flow can be used to track the movement of objects in a video sequence.

- **Video Compression**: By estimating motion between frames, optical flow is used to reduce redundancy in video data.
- **Autonomous Vehicles**: Optical flow is used for understanding the dynamic environment, including obstacle detection and navigation.

2. Kalman Filter

Overview:

The **Kalman Filter** is a recursive state estimation algorithm that uses a system's model and noisy measurements to estimate the state of a moving object. It is widely used in motion tracking and estimation due to its ability to handle noisy and uncertain sensor data.

Key Concepts:

- **State Prediction**: The Kalman Filter predicts the object's future state based on its previous state and the system model.
- **Measurement Update**: The filter updates the predicted state using new measurements, adjusting the prediction based on the error between predicted and actual measurements.
- **Gaussian Assumption**: The Kalman Filter assumes that both the system and measurement noise follow Gaussian distributions.

The Kalman Filter operates in two steps:

1. Prediction:

$$\hat{x}_k = F_k \hat{x}_{k-1} + B_k u_k$$

Where:

- $\hat{x}_k$ is the predicted state.
- F_k is the state transition model.
- B_k is the control input model.
- u_k is the control input.

2. **Update:**

$$\hat{x}_k = \hat{x}_k + K_k(z_k - H_k \hat{x}_k)$$

Where:

- K_k is the Kalman Gain.
- z_k is the measurement.
- H_k is the observation model.

Code Example: Kalman Filter

```python
import numpy as np



class KalmanFilter:

    def __init__(self):

        # Define initial state (position and velocity)

        self.x = np.array([[0], [0]])    # Initial state: [position, velocity]

        self.P = np.eye(2)  # Initial state covariance
```

Husn Ara

```python
    self.F = np.array([[1, 1], [0, 1]]) # State transition
matrix

    self.H = np.array([[1, 0]]) # Measurement matrix

    self.R = np.array([[1]])  # Measurement noise
covariance

    self.Q = np.eye(2)  # Process noise covariance

    self.I = np.eye(2)  # Identity matrix


  def predict(self):

    self.x = np.dot(self.F, self.x)  # Predict state

    self.P = np.dot(np.dot(self.F, self.P), self.F.T) +
self.Q  # Predict state covariance


  def update(self, z):

    y = z - np.dot(self.H, self.x)   # Measurement
residual

    S = np.dot(np.dot(self.H, self.P), self.H.T) +
self.R  # Residual covariance

    K    =    np.dot(np.dot(self.P,    self.H.T),
np.linalg.inv(S)) # Kalman gain

    self.x = self.x + np.dot(K, y)  # Update state

    self.P = (self.I - np.dot(K, self.H)) @ self.P  #
Update covariance
```

```
kf = KalmanFilter()

measurements = [1, 2, 3, 4, 5]    # Example
measurements


for z in measurements:

    kf.predict()

    kf.update(np.array([[z]]))

    print("Estimated state:", kf.x.ravel())
```

Applications of Kalman Filter:

- **Object Tracking**: Kalman Filters are widely used in tracking moving objects in video sequences (e.g., human tracking, vehicle tracking).
- **Sensor Fusion**: In robotics, the Kalman Filter is used to fuse data from multiple sensors (e.g., GPS, IMU) for accurate localization.
- **Prediction in Control Systems**: Kalman Filters are used to predict future states in dynamic control systems.

3. Particle Filter

Overview:

The **Particle Filter** is a non-parametric Bayesian filtering algorithm used for tracking and state estimation in non-linear, non-Gaussian systems. Unlike the Kalman Filter, which assumes Gaussian distributions, the Particle Filter represents the probability distribution of the state using a set of weighted particles (samples).

Key Concepts:

- **Particle Representation**: The state of the system is represented by a set of particles, where each particle represents a possible state of the system.
- **Resampling**: Particles with higher weights (those that better match the measurements) are more likely to survive, while low-weight particles are discarded.
- **Sequential Monte Carlo**: The Particle Filter uses a Monte Carlo approach to propagate and update particles over time.

Code Example: Particle Filter (Simplified)

```python
import numpy as np


class ParticleFilter:
    def __init__(self, num_particles=1000):
        self.num_particles = num_particles
        self.particles = np.random.uniform(0, 10, size=(num_particles, 2)) # Random initial particles
        self.weights = np.ones(num_particles) / num_particles # Initial weights


    def predict(self, move):
        self.particles[:, 0] += move + np.random.normal(0, 0.1, size=self.num_particles) # Update position


    def update(self, z):
        dist = np.abs(self.particles[:, 0] - z)   # Distance between particles and measurement
        self.weights = np.exp(-dist ** 2 / 2) # Update weights based on likelihood
```

```python
        self.weights += 1e-300  # Avoid division by zero

        self.weights /= np.sum(self.weights)   # Normalize
weights


    def resample(self):

        indices                                =
np.random.choice(range(self.num_particles),
size=self.num_particles, p=self.weights)

        self.particles = self.particles[indices]  # Resample
particles based on weights

        self.weights.fill(1.0 / self.num_particles)   # Reset
weights


pf = ParticleFilter()

measurements = [1, 2, 3, 4, 5]


for z in measurements:

    pf.predict(move=0.5) # Move particles

    pf.update(z)      #  Update  particles  based  on
measurement

    pf.resample() # Resample particles

    print("Estimated position:", np.mean(pf.particles[:, 0]))
```

Applications of Particle Filter:

- **Object Tracking**: Particle Filters are used to track non-linear and non-Gaussian systems, such as the trajectory of a moving object in cluttered environments.
- **Simultaneous Localization and Mapping (SLAM)**: Particle Filters are used in SLAM

algorithms to estimate the position of a robot while building a map of the environment.

- **Human Motion Tracking**: Particle Filters are employed for estimating human motion in complex scenes.

Summary

- **Optical Flow** is a fundamental technique used to estimate pixel-level motion between consecutive frames.
- **Kalman Filter** is an efficient state estimation method assuming linear, Gaussian models.
- **Particle Filter** is a more flexible approach that can handle non-linear and non-Gaussian processes but requires more computational resources.

These techniques are key components in dynamic vision tasks like tracking, motion estimation, and autonomous navigation.

Video Object Detection and Tracking

Video object detection and tracking is essential for understanding and analyzing moving objects in video sequences. It is used in applications such as surveillance, autonomous driving, and video editing. There are both traditional and deep learning-based methods for object detection and tracking. Here, we will explore some of these methods:

1. Mean-Shift and CAMShift (Traditional Methods)

1.1 Mean-Shift Algorithm

Mean-Shift is a non-parametric feature-space analysis technique used for locating the maxima of a density function. In the context of object tracking, Mean-Shift is used to find the region in an image where an object of interest is most likely to be located based on color or intensity histograms.

Key Steps:

- **Initial Region Selection**: The algorithm starts with a window or bounding box around the object to be tracked.
- **Mean Shift Iteration**: The algorithm iteratively shifts the window towards the region with the highest density of pixels similar to the object's features (e.g., color, texture).
- **Convergence**: The process continues until the window converges to the mode of the density, which is the new location of the object.

Code Example: Mean-Shift (Using OpenCV)

```
import cv2

import numpy as np


# Load video and initialize tracker window

cap = cv2.VideoCapture('video.mp4')

ret, frame = cap.read()

x, y, w, h = 300, 200, 100, 100  # Initial bounding box (x, y, width, height)

track_window = (x, y, w, h)


# Set up the ROI for tracking

roi = frame[y:y+h, x:x+w]

hsv_roi = cv2.cvtColor(roi, cv2.COLOR_BGR2HSV)
```

```python
roi_hist = cv2.calcHist([hsv_roi], [0], None, [180], [0, 180])

cv2.normalize(roi_hist,    roi_hist,    0,    255,
cv2.NORM_MINMAX)


# Set termination criteria: max iterations or move by at
least 1 point

term_crit    =    (cv2.TERM_CRITERIA_EPS    |
cv2.TERM_CRITERIA_COUNT, 10, 1)


while True:
    ret, frame = cap.read()
    if ret:
        hsv = cv2.cvtColor(frame, cv2.COLOR_BGR2HSV)
        dst = cv2.calcBackProject([hsv], [0], roi_hist, [0, 180],
1)


        # Apply mean shift to get the new location
        ret,    track_window    =    cv2.meanShift(dst,
track_window, term_crit)


        # Draw the tracking window on the frame
        x, y, w, h = track_window
        img2 = cv2.rectangle(frame, (x, y), (x+w, y+h), 255,
2)
        cv2.imshow('Tracking', img2)


        if cv2.waitKey(30) & 0xFF == 27:
            break
```

else:

```
break
```

```
cap.release()
```

```
cv2.destroyAllWindows()
```

1.2 CAMShift (Continuously Adaptive Mean-Shift)

CAMShift is an extension of the Mean-Shift algorithm that adapts the size and shape of the tracking window during the tracking process. It was designed for better handling of scale and rotation changes in object tracking. CAMShift recalculates the size of the window dynamically based on the color distribution around the object.

Key Differences from Mean-Shift:

- CAMShift adapts to changes in the size of the object as well as rotations.
- More robust in handling non-uniform object shapes and scale changes.

Code Example: CAMShift (Using OpenCV)

```python
import cv2
import numpy as np


cap = cv2.VideoCapture('video.mp4')
ret, frame = cap.read()
x, y, w, h = 300, 200, 100, 100  # Initial bounding box
track_window = (x, y, w, h)
```

```python
# Set up the ROI for tracking

roi = frame[y:y+h, x:x+w]

hsv_roi = cv2.cvtColor(roi, cv2.COLOR_BGR2HSV)

roi_hist = cv2.calcHist([hsv_roi], [0], None, [180], [0, 180])

cv2.normalize(roi_hist,      roi_hist,      0,      255,
cv2.NORM_MINMAX)


# Set termination criteria

term_crit    =    (cv2.TERM_CRITERIA_EPS    |
cv2.TERM_CRITERIA_COUNT, 10, 1)


while True:
    ret, frame = cap.read()
    if ret:
        hsv = cv2.cvtColor(frame, cv2.COLOR_BGR2HSV)
        dst = cv2.calcBackProject([hsv], [0], roi_hist, [0, 180],
1)


        # Apply CAMShift to get the new location
        ret,     track_window    =    cv2.CamShift(dst,
track_window, term_crit)


        # Draw the rotated rectangle
        pts = cv2.boxPoints(ret)
        pts = np.int0(pts)
        img2 = cv2.polylines(frame, [pts], True, 255, 2)
        cv2.imshow('Tracking', img2)
```

```
    if cv2.waitKey(30) & 0xFF == 27:

        break

else:

    break


cap.release()

cv2.destroyAllWindows()
```

2. Deep Learning-Based Trackers

2.1 Siamese Networks for Object Tracking

Siamese networks are widely used for object tracking tasks. The idea is to train a network to compare an exemplar (the object to be tracked) with candidates from the search area (current frame) and determine the best match.

Key Features:

- **Template Matching**: Siamese networks learn a feature space where the object's representation in one frame is compared to potential objects in subsequent frames.
- **End-to-End Learning**: These networks are trained end-to-end to directly optimize the similarity between the exemplar and candidate regions.
- **Lightweight Architecture**: Siamese networks can be lightweight, making them fast enough for real-time object tracking.

Common Networks:

- **SiamFC (Fully-Convolutional Siamese Networks)**: A simple and efficient architecture for real-time tracking. It compares the template and search region using convolutional layers.
- **SiamRPN (Region Proposal Network)**: An extension of SiamFC with a region proposal mechanism, improving accuracy by proposing more precise bounding boxes.

Code Example: Siamese Network for Object Tracking (Pseudocode)

```
class SiameseNetwork(nn.Module):

    def __init__(self):

        super(SiameseNetwork, self).__init__()

        # Define CNN layers for extracting features from the exemplar and search region

        self.conv_layers = nn.Sequential(

            nn.Conv2d(3, 96, kernel_size=11, stride=2),

            nn.ReLU(),

            nn.MaxPool2d(kernel_size=3, stride=2),

            nn.Conv2d(96, 256, kernel_size=5, stride=1),

            nn.ReLU(),

            nn.MaxPool2d(kernel_size=3, stride=2)

        )


    def forward(self, exemplar, candidate):

        # Extract features from both exemplar and candidate

        feat_exemplar = self.conv_layers(exemplar)

        feat_candidate = self.conv_layers(candidate)
```

```
    # Compute similarity between features (e.g., using cross-correlation)

    similarity_map = cross_correlation(feat_exemplar, feat_candidate)

    return similarity_map


# Pseudocode for tracking

# Load pre-trained Siamese model

model = SiameseNetwork()


# Load video and get initial bounding box for object

for frame in video_frames:

    if first_frame:

        exemplar = extract_patch(frame, initial_bbox)

    else:

        candidate = extract_patch(frame, search_region)

        similarity_map = model(exemplar, candidate)

        new_bbox = update_bbox(similarity_map)
```

Applications of Siamese Networks:

- **Real-Time Tracking**: Siamese trackers like **SiamFC** are designed for real-time applications such as autonomous driving and drone navigation.
- **Visual Object Tracking**: Used in surveillance to track moving objects across frames.

Summary

- **Mean-Shift** is a traditional algorithm for object tracking, relying on histogram back-projection and iterative shifting of a window.

- **CAMShift** extends Mean-Shift by dynamically adapting the size and shape of the window, making it better suited for tracking objects with varying scale and orientation.
- **Siamese Networks** represent modern deep learning-based trackers that use similarity learning to track objects in a video efficiently. They are fast, lightweight, and capable of handling challenging scenarios like occlusion and fast motion.

Each of these methods has its own strengths and weaknesses, and the choice of technique depends on the specific application and computational constraints.

Action and Activity Recognition

Action and activity recognition involves identifying and classifying actions or activities in video data. This is crucial for applications like video surveillance, human-computer interaction, sports analytics, and more. Different neural network architectures are employed to effectively analyze spatial and temporal information in videos. Here, we'll explore three key approaches: **3D Convolutional Networks**, **Recurrent Neural Networks (RNNs)**, and **Temporal Action Detection and Segmentation**.

1. 3D Convolutional Networks (3D CNNs)

Overview:

3D Convolutional Networks extend the traditional 2D convolutional networks by adding a third dimension, which allows them to capture both spatial and temporal features in video data. The third dimension corresponds to time, making it suitable for action recognition.

Key Features:

- **3D Convolutions**: Instead of convolving over height and width (2D), 3D convolutions convolve over height, width, and time. This enables the network to learn features that represent motion across frames.
- **Temporal Context**: 3D CNNs can learn both short-term and long-term temporal relationships by processing a sequence of frames simultaneously.

Architecture:

A typical architecture might include:

- **3D Convolutional Layers**: To learn spatiotemporal features.
- **Pooling Layers**: To reduce dimensionality while retaining important features.
- **Fully Connected Layers**: For classification of actions based on the learned features.

Code Example: 3D CNN (Using PyTorch)

```
import torch

import torch.nn as nn


class Simple3DCNN(nn.Module):
    def __init__(self):
        super(Simple3DCNN, self).__init__()

        self.conv3d_1 = nn.Conv3d(3, 16, kernel_size=(3, 3, 3), stride=(1, 1, 1))

        self.pool = nn.MaxPool3d(kernel_size=(1, 2, 2), stride=(1, 2, 2))
```

```
    self.conv3d_2 = nn.Conv3d(16, 32, kernel_size=(3,
3, 3), stride=(1, 1, 1))

    self.fc = nn.Linear(32 * 3 * 5 * 5, 10)   # Adjust
according to input size


  def forward(self, x):

    x = self.pool(F.relu(self.conv3d_1(x)))

    x = self.pool(F.relu(self.conv3d_2(x)))

    x = x.view(x.size(0), -1)  # Flatten

    x = self.fc(x)

    return x


# Example usage

model = Simple3DCNN()

input_data = torch.randn(1, 3, 16, 112, 112)  # Batch size
of 1, 16 frames, 112x112 RGB

output = model(input_data)
```

2. Recurrent Neural Networks (RNNs) in Video Analysis

Overview:

Recurrent Neural Networks (RNNs) are well-suited for sequential data analysis due to their ability to maintain hidden states and capture temporal dependencies. In video analysis, RNNs can be used to process sequences of features extracted from individual frames.

Key Features:

- **Temporal Dependencies**: RNNs maintain an internal state that helps to remember previous inputs, making them effective for capturing temporal relationships in action sequences.
- **Long Short-Term Memory (LSTM)**: LSTM networks, a type of RNN, address the vanishing gradient problem and can learn long-term dependencies better than standard RNNs.

Architecture:

- **Feature Extraction**: Typically, features are extracted from each video frame using a CNN (2D).
- **RNN Layers**: The extracted features are then fed into RNN or LSTM layers to learn temporal dynamics.
- **Classification Layer**: Finally, a dense layer is used for action classification.

Code Example: RNN with LSTM (Using PyTorch)

```python
import torch

import torch.nn as nn


class RNNVideoClassifier(nn.Module):
    def __init__(self, input_size, hidden_size, num_classes):
        super(RNNVideoClassifier, self).__init__()
        self.lstm = nn.LSTM(input_size, hidden_size, batch_first=True)
        self.fc = nn.Linear(hidden_size, num_classes)

    def forward(self, x):
        # x shape: (batch_size, seq_length, input_size)
```

```
out, _ = self.lstm(x)

out = out[:, -1, :]  # Get the last time step output

out = self.fc(out)

return out


# Example usage

model        =        RNNVideoClassifier(input_size=512,
hidden_size=256, num_classes=10)

input_data = torch.randn(1, 30, 512)  # Batch size of 1, 30
frames, 512 features

output = model(input_data)
```

3. Temporal Action Detection and Segmentation

Overview:

Temporal action detection involves not only classifying the action being performed but also identifying when it occurs in a video. This is particularly useful for videos with multiple actions or varying action durations.

Key Techniques:

- **Action Proposals**: Generate potential segments of the video that may contain actions using techniques like sliding windows or dense sampling.
- **Temporal Segment Networks (TSN)**: A popular architecture that segments the video into multiple clips, processes each clip independently, and aggregates results for action classification.

Segmentation Methods:

- **Two-Stream Networks**: Combines spatial and temporal streams (e.g., RGB frames and optical flow) to better capture action dynamics.
- **Temporal Convolutional Networks (TCN)**: Uses 1D convolutions along the time dimension to model long-range dependencies effectively.

Code Example: Temporal Segment Network (Pseudocode)

```
class TemporalSegmentNetwork(nn.Module):

    def __init__(self):

        super(TemporalSegmentNetwork, self).__init__()

        # Define spatial and temporal branches

        self.spatial_branch = Simple3DCNN()

        self.temporal_branch = RNNVideoClassifier(input_size=512, hidden_size=256, num_classes=10)


    def forward(self, rgb_clips, flow_clips):

        spatial_features = self.spatial_branch(rgb_clips)

        temporal_features = self.temporal_branch(flow_clips)

        # Combine features

        combined_features = (spatial_features + temporal_features) / 2

        return combined_features


# Example usage

model = TemporalSegmentNetwork()

rgb_clips = torch.randn(1, 3, 16, 112, 112) # RGB clips
```

```
flow_clips = torch.randn(1, 30, 512)   # Optical flow
features

output = model(rgb_clips, flow_clips)
```

Summary

- **3D Convolutional Networks (3D CNNs)** are effective for capturing spatiotemporal features in videos, allowing for direct action recognition.
- **Recurrent Neural Networks (RNNs)**, particularly LSTMs, excel at modeling temporal relationships in sequential data, making them suitable for analyzing video sequences after feature extraction.
- **Temporal Action Detection and Segmentation** techniques aim to identify not only the actions in a video but also when they occur, using advanced architectures like Temporal Segment Networks and two-stream networks.

These approaches collectively enhance the capability of systems to understand and interpret complex activities in video data.

Chapter 10: Advanced Topics in Computer Vision

Multi-Task Learning in Vision

Multi-task learning (MTL) is a machine learning approach where a model is trained on multiple tasks simultaneously. In computer vision, this allows models to leverage shared representations to improve performance on all tasks. MTL is particularly useful in situations where tasks have shared underlying structures, such as **object detection**, **segmentation**, and **pose estimation**. By training on related tasks, MTL can lead to improved generalization, reduced computational cost, and increased robustness.

1. Joint Object Detection and Segmentation

Overview:

Joint object detection and segmentation is a prime example of multi-task learning in vision. Here, the goal is to detect objects in an image and simultaneously segment them at the pixel level, producing both bounding boxes and segmentation masks. Combining these tasks allows the model to share features between object detection and segmentation, leading to more accurate results.

Common Architectures:

- **Mask R-CNN**: One of the most widely used architectures for joint object detection and instance segmentation.
    - ○ **Object Detection**: Based on Faster R-CNN, the network detects objects using a region proposal network (RPN) that generates bounding boxes.
    - ○ **Segmentation Mask**: A small fully convolutional network (FCN) is added to predict a segmentation mask for each detected object.

Key Components of Mask R-CNN:

- **Backbone**: Typically a CNN like ResNet or ResNeXt is used to extract features from the input image.
- **Region Proposal Network (RPN)**: Proposes candidate object regions, which are then refined.
- **Bounding Box Regression**: Predicts the coordinates of the bounding boxes for detected objects.
- **Segmentation Head**: A parallel branch that outputs binary masks for each object, providing pixel-level segmentation.

Code Example: Mask R-CNN (Using PyTorch)

```
import torch

import torchvision

from        torchvision.models.detection        import
maskrcnn_resnet50_fpn
```

```
# Load a pre-trained Mask R-CNN model

model = maskrcnn_resnet50_fpn(pretrained=True)


# Set model to evaluation mode

model.eval()


# Example usage on a sample image

image = torch.randn(1, 3, 300, 300)  # Replace with
real image tensor

output = model(image)


# Output includes bounding boxes, labels, scores,
and segmentation masks

boxes = output[0]['boxes']

masks = output[0]['masks']
```

Applications:

- **Autonomous Driving**: Detect and segment vehicles, pedestrians, and road signs.
- **Medical Imaging**: Detect and segment tumors or lesions in medical scans.
- **Robotics**: Detect and segment objects for grasping and manipulation.

2. Pose Estimation

Overview:

Pose estimation is the task of detecting the key points or landmarks of a human body, which are then used to infer the pose (position and orientation) of the person. It is another area where multi-task learning is highly beneficial, especially when combined with other vision tasks like object detection or segmentation.

Common Architectures:

- **OpenPose**: A multi-task CNN that detects body, hand, and facial keypoints in real-time.
  - o **Multi-Scale Predictions**: OpenPose processes images at multiple scales to accurately detect small and large key points.
  - o **Part Affinity Fields**: In addition to keypoint detection, OpenPose predicts part affinity fields that describe the spatial relationships between body parts.
- **Hourglass Networks**: These networks are commonly used for pose estimation and have a U-shaped architecture that captures both local and global features by repeatedly downsampling and upsampling the input.
- **HRNet (High-Resolution Network)**: Instead of repeatedly downsampling the image, HRNet maintains high-resolution representations throughout the network. This leads to more accurate localization of keypoints, especially for small details.

Pose Estimation as a Multi-Task Problem:

- **Pose Estimation + Action Recognition**: Estimating human pose while simultaneously recognizing the action being performed.
- **Pose Estimation + Object Detection**: Estimating human keypoints while detecting objects in the

301

scene, useful in sports analytics or human-robot interaction.

Key Components:

- **Backbone**: Similar to detection tasks, networks like ResNet are used to extract features.
- **Keypoint Prediction**: Heatmaps are generated for each keypoint, indicating the probability of the keypoint being at a particular location in the image.
- **Post-Processing**: Techniques like Non-Maximum Suppression (NMS) are used to select the most likely keypoints.

Code Example: Pose Estimation with HRNet (Pseudocode)

```
import torch

import torchvision



# Load a pre-trained HRNet model for pose estimation

hrnet_model                                    =
torchvision.models.detection.keypointrcnn_resnet50
_fpn(pretrained=True)



# Set model to evaluation mode

hrnet_model.eval()



# Example usage on an image
```

```
image = torch.randn(1, 3, 300, 300)  # Replace with
a real image tensor

output = hrnet_model(image)



# Output includes keypoint predictions

keypoints = output[0]['keypoints']
```

Applications:

- **Sports Analytics**: Pose estimation is used to analyze athlete performance, recognize actions like running or jumping, and measure biomechanical efficiency.
- **Virtual Reality (VR)**: Pose estimation is used in VR applications to track user movements and adjust the virtual environment accordingly.
- **Surveillance**: Pose estimation is used in crowd analysis or abnormal behavior detection in public spaces.

3. Benefits of Multi-Task Learning in Vision

- **Shared Representations**: Learning multiple tasks together allows the model to learn shared features, leading to better generalization across tasks.
- **Efficiency**: A single model can be trained to perform multiple tasks simultaneously, reducing computational cost and memory usage.
- **Robustness**: Multi-task learning can make models more robust to overfitting, as they are required to generalize across different but related tasks.

Example: Combining Object Detection, Segmentation, and Pose Estimation

Imagine a system that needs to detect people in a video, segment them at the pixel level, and estimate their body poses. In a multi-task framework, the shared features extracted by the backbone CNN can be reused by the detection, segmentation, and pose estimation heads, as shown below:

```
class MultiTaskModel(nn.Module):

    def __init__(self):

        super(MultiTaskModel, self).__init__()

        # Shared backbone for feature extraction

        self.backbone                                =
torchvision.models.resnet50(pretrained=True)



        # Detection head (bounding boxes)

        self.detection_head      =      nn.Linear(2048,
num_classes * 4)  # For bounding box regression



        # Segmentation head (pixel-level masks)

        self.segmentation_head = nn.Conv2d(2048, 1,
kernel_size=1)



        # Pose estimation head (keypoint prediction)

        self.pose_head          =          nn.Conv2d(2048,
num_keypoints, kernel_size=1)
```

```python
def forward(self, x):

    features = self.backbone(x)


    # Multi-task outputs

    detection_output                        =
self.detection_head(features)

    segmentation_output                     =
self.segmentation_head(features)

    pose_output = self.pose_head(features)


    return detection_output, segmentation_output,
pose_output


# Example usage

model = MultiTaskModel()

input_data = torch.randn(1, 3, 256, 256)  # Example
input

detection, segmentation, pose = model(input_data)
```

Summary

- **Joint Object Detection and Segmentation**:
  Techniques like **Mask R-CNN** allow
  simultaneous object detection and pixel-level
  segmentation by leveraging shared
  convolutional features. This is crucial for

applications requiring fine-grained understanding of images, such as in medical imaging and autonomous driving.

- **Pose Estimation**: Pose estimation benefits from multi-task learning when combined with other vision tasks like object detection or action recognition. Architectures like **OpenPose**, **Hourglass Networks**, and **HRNet** are widely used for accurate keypoint localization in complex environments.

Multi-task learning in vision enables more efficient and robust models that can perform several related tasks at once, improving overall performance and reducing computational overhead.

Domain Adaptation and Transfer Learning

Domain adaptation and transfer learning aim to generalize a model trained on one domain to perform well in another domain, especially when the two domains have different data distributions. These methods are particularly useful in computer vision tasks, where collecting and labeling large datasets for every possible domain is impractical.

- **Transfer Learning**: Reusing a model trained on a large dataset for a new task with little data.
- **Domain Adaptation**: Adapting a model to a target domain with little or no labeled data, using knowledge from a source domain.

1. Adversarial Domain Adaptation

Overview:

Adversarial Domain Adaptation uses concepts from **Generative Adversarial Networks (GANs)** to align the feature distributions of the source and target domains. The goal is to train a model that can generalize across both domains despite differences in data distribution.

Key Components:

- **Feature Extractor**: A shared feature extractor is used to extract features from both source and target domain data.
- **Domain Discriminator**: A domain discriminator is trained to distinguish between the source and target domain features.
- **Adversarial Training**: The feature extractor is trained adversarially to "fool" the domain discriminator, making the feature distributions from both domains indistinguishable. This forces the model to learn domain-invariant features.

Architecture:

- **Feature Extractor**: Extracts features from both domains.
- **Task Classifier**: Classifies the source domain data (e.g., object classification).
- **Domain Discriminator**: Tries to distinguish between source and target domain features.

The loss function typically consists of:

- **Task Loss**: Measures the classification performance on the source domain.
- **Adversarial Loss**: Encourages the feature extractor to produce domain-invariant features by minimizing the discriminator's ability to distinguish between source and target domains.

Code Example: Adversarial Domain Adaptation (Pseudocode using PyTorch)

```
import torch

import torch.nn as nn


class FeatureExtractor(nn.Module):
    def __init__(self):
        super(FeatureExtractor, self).__init__()
        self.conv1 = nn.Conv2d(3, 64, kernel_size=3, stride=1, padding=1)
        self.conv2 = nn.Conv2d(64, 128, kernel_size=3, stride=1, padding=1)


    def forward(self, x):
        x = F.relu(self.conv1(x))
        x = F.relu(self.conv2(x))
        return x


class DomainDiscriminator(nn.Module):
    def __init__(self):
        super(DomainDiscriminator, self).__init__()
        self.fc1 = nn.Linear(128 * 32 * 32, 100)
        self.fc2 = nn.Linear(100, 2)  # Binary classification: source vs target


    def forward(self, x):
        x = x.view(x.size(0), -1)  # Flatten
```

```
        x = F.relu(self.fc1(x))

        x = self.fc2(x)

        return x


class TaskClassifier(nn.Module):

    def __init__(self):

        super(TaskClassifier, self).__init__()

        self.fc1 = nn.Linear(128 * 32 * 32, 10)  # Example for
10 classes


    def forward(self, x):

        x = x.view(x.size(0), -1)

        return self.fc1(x)



# Adversarial training loop would alternate between
optimizing the discriminator and feature extractor.
```

Applications:

- **Cross-Domain Image Classification**: When a model trained on clear, well-lit images needs to be adapted to work with low-light or blurred images.
- **Medical Imaging**: Adapting a model trained on data from one type of scanner to another type, or from one hospital to another.

2. Few-Shot and Zero-Shot Learning

Overview:

Few-shot and zero-shot learning aim to recognize new categories with very few or no labeled examples, respectively. These methods leverage prior knowledge, often in the form of pre-trained models or auxiliary information like semantic attributes, to generalize to new tasks.

1. **Few-Shot Learning**:

Few-shot learning deals with training a model to recognize new classes using only a few labeled examples (e.g., 1-5 samples per class). It is especially important in scenarios where gathering large datasets is difficult, such as rare medical conditions or specific types of wildlife.

- **Meta-Learning**: One approach to few-shot learning is meta-learning, where the model learns to learn. It is trained on many small tasks (meta-tasks) and learns to generalize quickly to new tasks with few samples.
  - ○ **Prototypical Networks**: This method calculates a prototype (mean) for each class in the feature space and classifies new examples based on their distance to these prototypes.
  - ○ **Matching Networks**: Matches new examples with a small support set by comparing them in an embedding space.

Code Example: Prototypical Networks (Pseudocode)

```
import torch

import torch.nn as nn


class PrototypicalNetwork(nn.Module):
    def __init__(self, embedding_dim):
        super(PrototypicalNetwork, self).__init__()
        self.encoder = nn.Sequential(
            nn.Conv2d(3, 64, kernel_size=3),
```

```python
        nn.ReLU(),

        nn.MaxPool2d(2),

        nn.Conv2d(64, embedding_dim, kernel_size=3)

    )


    def forward(self, x):

        return self.encoder(x)


def calculate_prototypes(support_set, labels, model):

    # Calculate the prototype (mean) for each class

    prototypes = []

    for class_id in torch.unique(labels):

        class_examples = support_set[labels == class_id]

        prototype = class_examples.mean(0)

        prototypes.append(prototype)

    return torch.stack(prototypes)


# Example usage with support set and query set

support_set = torch.randn(5, 3, 28, 28)  # 5 samples, 3 channels, 28x28 images

labels = torch.tensor([0, 1, 0, 1, 0])    # Labels for the support set

query_set = torch.randn(1, 3, 28, 28)   # Query sample


model = PrototypicalNetwork(embedding_dim=64)

prototypes = calculate_prototypes(support_set, labels, model)
```

2. **Zero-Shot Learning (ZSL):**

Zero-shot learning refers to recognizing classes that the model has never seen during training. This is achieved by leveraging auxiliary information like semantic attributes, class descriptions, or relationships between classes.

- **Attribute-Based Models**: These models use attributes shared between classes to generalize to unseen categories. For example, if the model knows attributes like "has wings" or "is a mammal," it can recognize unseen animals by these characteristics.
- **Embedding-Based Models**: In embedding-based ZSL, both seen and unseen classes are embedded into a common space (e.g., using word embeddings like Word2Vec). A new image is classified by finding its closest class in the embedding space.

Code Example: Zero-Shot Learning with Attribute Embedding (Pseudocode)

import torch

Example: Embedding space for seen and unseen classes

seen_class_embeddings = torch.randn(5, 300) # 5 seen classes, 300-dim embeddings

unseen_class_embedding = torch.randn(1, 300) # 1 unseen class embedding

Feature of a new (unseen) image in the same embedding space

image_feature = torch.randn(1, 300)

```
# Classify the image by finding the closest class in the
embedding space

distances = torch.norm(seen_class_embeddings -
image_feature, dim=1)

closest_class = torch.argmin(distances)



# The model can generalize to the unseen class based on
the shared embedding space
```

Applications:

- **Image Retrieval**: Matching unseen categories of images using semantic descriptions (e.g., "red car" or "striped cat").
- **Fine-Grained Classification**: Recognizing unseen species or breeds of animals by leveraging shared attributes.
- **Natural Language Processing**: ZSL is also used in NLP for tasks like zero-shot text classification based on semantic information.

Summary

- **Adversarial Domain Adaptation** uses adversarial training to learn domain-invariant features, enabling models to generalize across different data distributions.
- **Few-Shot Learning** focuses on learning new tasks with only a few labeled examples, often leveraging meta-learning approaches like Prototypical Networks and Matching Networks.
- **Zero-Shot Learning** allows models to recognize new classes without any labeled examples, using auxiliary information like semantic attributes or embedding spaces.

These techniques enable robust generalization to new domains and tasks, which is critical for real-world applications where large, labeled datasets are scarce.

Explainable AI in Computer Vision

Explainable AI (XAI) in computer vision focuses on making deep learning models, especially Convolutional Neural Networks (CNNs), more interpretable and transparent. Since CNNs are often considered "black-box" models, understanding how they make decisions is crucial for applications in sensitive domains like healthcare, autonomous vehicles, and legal systems.

1. Interpretability of CNNs

Overview:

CNNs are highly effective for image-related tasks such as classification, detection, and segmentation. However, their decision-making process can be difficult to interpret due to the complex and hierarchical nature of learned features. **Interpretability** refers to understanding the inner workings of CNNs and how the model arrives at specific decisions for a given input.

Key Concepts:

- **Feature Visualization**: One approach to interpretability is visualizing the features learned by the network at different layers. Early layers typically learn simple features like edges, while

314

deeper layers learn more abstract patterns (e.g., textures, objects).

- **Class Activation Mapping (CAM)**: CAM techniques are used to highlight the regions in an image that contributed most to the CNN's prediction. These maps help identify which parts of an image the model focused on for classification.
- **Filter Visualization**: Filters (or kernels) in CNN layers can be visualized to understand what types of features the network is detecting. For example, early filters might detect edges or colors, while deeper filters capture more complex patterns.

Feature Visualization Example:

1. **Layer-Wise Activations**: By inputting an image into the network and visualizing the activation maps at different layers, we can see what the network "focuses on" at various stages of its decision-making process.
2. **DeconvNets and Gradient-Ascent**: These techniques reconstruct input images that strongly activate a specific neuron, allowing us to interpret what the neuron is sensitive to.

Example Code: Visualizing Activations in a CNN (PyTorch)

```
import torch

import torchvision.models as models

import matplotlib.pyplot as plt


# Load a pre-trained ResNet model

model = models.resnet18(pretrained=True)

model.eval()


# Sample input image (1 batch, 3 channels, 224x224)
```

```
input_image = torch.randn(1, 3, 224, 224)


# Hook to capture activations of intermediate layers

activations = {}


def hook_fn(module, input, output):

    activations[module] = output


# Attach hooks to desired layers

layer_to_hook = model.layer1[0].conv1

hook = layer_to_hook.register_forward_hook(hook_fn)


# Forward pass

output = model(input_image)


# Visualize the activations of the hooked layer

activation                                        =
activations[layer_to_hook].detach().squeeze(0)

fig, axes = plt.subplots(1, 4, figsize=(12, 3))

for i in range(4):

    axes[i].imshow(activation[i].cpu(), cmap='viridis')

    axes[i].axis('off')

plt.show()


# Don't forget to remove the hook after usage

hook.remove()
```

2. Visual Saliency Maps

Overview:

Saliency maps provide a visual representation of the important regions in an image that contribute most to a model's prediction. They are widely used to explain decisions made by CNNs in image classification and other vision tasks. Saliency maps typically highlight pixels or regions that strongly influence the model's output, helping humans understand which parts of the image are driving the decision.

Types of Saliency Map Techniques:

1. **Gradient-Based Methods**:
   - These methods compute the gradient of the output with respect to the input image. The magnitude of the gradient at each pixel indicates how sensitive the model's prediction is to changes in that pixel.
   - **Vanilla Saliency**: The most basic approach computes the gradient of the class score with respect to the input image. High-gradient pixels are considered salient.
   - **SmoothGrad**: A variant that reduces noise by averaging the gradients over multiple noisy copies of the input.

2. **Class Activation Mapping (CAM)**:
   - CAM methods provide heatmaps indicating the importance of different regions of an image for a specific class prediction.
   - **Grad-CAM**: Extends CAM by applying it to any CNN architecture. It computes gradients of the class score concerning feature maps and uses these gradients to weight the feature maps, producing class-specific heatmaps.

3. **Integrated Gradients**:
   - This method attributes the prediction to pixels by integrating gradients along a path

from a baseline image (e.g., a black image) to the original input. It provides more stable and interpretable explanations compared to vanilla gradients.

Grad-CAM: How It Works

Grad-CAM generates visual explanations for CNN decisions by using the gradients of the output (for a specific class) flowing into the final convolutional layer to produce a heatmap highlighting important regions of the input image.

- **Input**: An image.
- **Target Class**: The class for which you want the saliency map (e.g., "cat").
- **Final Convolutional Layer**: The layer before the fully connected layers.
- **Gradients**: Gradients of the target class with respect to the feature maps of the final convolutional layer.

Code Example: Generating a Grad-CAM Heatmap (PyTorch)

```
import torch

import torch.nn.functional as F

import cv2

import numpy as np

import torchvision.models as models


# Load a pre-trained CNN model

model = models.resnet18(pretrained=True)

model.eval()


# Function to compute Grad-CAM
```

Husn Ara

```python
def generate_gradcam(input_image, model, target_layer,
target_class):
    gradients = []

    def save_gradients(grad):
        gradients.append(grad)

    # Hook to get gradients from the target layer
    hook = target_layer.register_hook(save_gradients)

    # Forward pass to get feature maps
    features = input_image
    for name, layer in model.named_children():
        features = layer(features)
        if name == 'layer4':  # Change to target layer
            break

    # Backpropagation for the target class
    target_class_score = F.softmax(features, dim=1)[0,
target_class]
    model.zero_grad()
    target_class_score.backward()

    # Gradients and feature maps
    grad = gradients[0].squeeze(0)  # Gradients from the
target class
    feature_maps = features.squeeze(0)
```

```python
    # Global average pooling of gradients over feature
maps
    weights = torch.mean(grad, dim=[1, 2])
    gradcam = torch.zeros_like(feature_maps[0])
    for i, w in enumerate(weights):
        gradcam += w * feature_maps[i]


    # Apply ReLU
    gradcam = F.relu(gradcam)


    # Convert to numpy for visualization
    gradcam = gradcam.cpu().detach().numpy()
    gradcam = cv2.resize(gradcam, (input_image.size(2),
input_image.size(3)))
    gradcam = gradcam - np.min(gradcam)
    gradcam = gradcam / np.max(gradcam)


    return gradcam


# Input image
input_image = torch.randn(1, 3, 224, 224)  # Replace with
real image


# Generate Grad-CAM heatmap
target_layer = model.layer4
```

```
gradcam = generate_gradcam(input_image, model,
target_layer, target_class=243)  # 243 = "bull mastiff"
```

Visualize the heatmap

```
plt.imshow(gradcam, cmap='jet')

plt.colorbar()

plt.show()
```

Applications of Explainability in Computer Vision:

1. **Healthcare**: In medical imaging, doctors rely on explanations from AI models for diagnoses. For example, in X-ray or MRI scans, saliency maps can highlight regions of interest (e.g., tumors), ensuring that the AI model is focusing on relevant areas.
2. **Autonomous Vehicles**: Understanding how AI models detect obstacles or interpret road signs is crucial for safety. Saliency maps can help explain which parts of the scene the model focused on when making driving decisions.
3. **Security**: In surveillance systems, saliency maps can show which areas of an image or video a model is focusing on for detecting suspicious activities, enhancing transparency and accountability.
4. **Legal and Compliance**: In regulatory environments, explainability is essential for proving that AI models are not biased or making unfair decisions based on irrelevant features.

Summary:

- **Interpretability of CNNs** involves understanding the inner workings of models and how features are learned. Techniques like **feature visualization**, **filter visualization**, and **class activation maps** help interpret the decision-making process.
- **Visual Saliency Maps** (such as Grad-CAM) provide a heatmap indicating important regions in the input image that contributed most to a model's prediction, improving transparency and trust in AI decisions.

Explainability is crucial for increasing user trust, identifying biases, and ensuring that models are making decisions based on relevant information in safety-critical or regulated industries.

Robustness and Adversarial Attacks

Adversarial attacks in computer vision involve creating small, often imperceptible, changes to input images that can cause deep learning models (especially CNNs) to make incorrect predictions. These **adversarial examples** pose significant challenges to the robustness and reliability of vision models in real-world applications like facial recognition, autonomous driving, and medical diagnostics.

1. Adversarial Examples in Vision Models

Overview:

Adversarial examples are specially crafted inputs designed to "fool" a model into making wrong predictions by introducing minimal perturbations to the original input. These perturbations are often so small that they are invisible to the human eye but are enough to mislead deep learning models.

Key Concepts:

- **Perturbation**: A small, human-imperceptible noise added to the original image, often computed based on the gradient of the model's loss function with respect to the input.
- **Adversarial Attack**: The process of generating adversarial examples by finding perturbations that maximize the model's prediction error.
- **Targeted vs. Untargeted Attacks**:
  - **Targeted Attack**: The attacker manipulates the input to cause the model to predict a specific (incorrect) class.
  - **Untargeted Attack**: The attacker aims to make the model misclassify the input, but the incorrect class is not predetermined.

Adversarial Attack Techniques:

1. **Fast Gradient Sign Method (FGSM)**:
   - One of the simplest adversarial attack methods. It adds a small perturbation to the input image in the direction of the gradient of the loss function.

- Formula:

$$\text{Adversarial Image} = \text{Original Image} + \epsilon \cdot \text{sign}(\nabla_x J(\theta, x, y))$$

Where:

- ϵ is a small scalar controlling the size of the perturbation.
- $\nabla_x J(\theta, x, y)$ is the gradient of the loss function J with respect to the input image x, parameters θ, and target label y.

1. **Projected Gradient Descent (PGD)**:
   - An iterative version of FGSM, which applies multiple small perturbations to the

image. After each step, the perturbation is "projected" back to ensure that the perturbation size does not exceed a predefined limit.

2. **Carlini-Wagner (C&W) Attack**:
   - A more sophisticated attack that minimizes a loss function to find the smallest possible perturbation that causes a misclassification. It is effective against many defense strategies.

Code Example: FGSM Attack (PyTorch)

```
import torch

import torch.nn as nn

import torch.optim as optim


# Load a pre-trained CNN model (e.g., ResNet)

model = models.resnet18(pretrained=True)

model.eval()


# Loss function

criterion = nn.CrossEntropyLoss()


# Function to generate an adversarial example using FGSM

def fgsm_attack(image, epsilon, data_grad):

    # Get the sign of the gradients

    sign_data_grad = data_grad.sign()

    # Create the perturbed image

    perturbed_image = image + epsilon * sign_data_grad
```

```python
# Clip the image to stay within the valid range [0, 1]

perturbed_image = torch.clamp(perturbed_image, 0, 1)

return perturbed_image


# Example forward pass and adversarial attack generation
def generate_adversarial_example(model, image, label, epsilon):

    image.requires_grad = True

    output = model(image)

    loss = criterion(output, label)

    model.zero_grad()

    loss.backward()

    data_grad = image.grad.data

    # Generate the adversarial example

    adv_image = fgsm_attack(image, epsilon, data_grad)

    return adv_image


# Example usage
image = torch.randn(1, 3, 224, 224)  # Input image

label = torch.tensor([243]) # True label (e.g., "bull mastiff")

epsilon = 0.01  # Perturbation magnitude


adversarial_image = generate_adversarial_example(model, image, label, epsilon)
```

Applications of Adversarial Attacks:

- **Security**: Adversarial examples can deceive facial recognition systems or bypass security checks by tricking models into misclassifying malicious images as benign.
- **Autonomous Vehicles**: Small changes to traffic signs (e.g., placing stickers) can lead to incorrect detections, posing safety risks.
- **Healthcare**: Adversarial attacks can cause medical image classifiers to misinterpret scans, potentially leading to incorrect diagnoses.

2. Defense Mechanisms

Overview:

To counter adversarial attacks, several **defense mechanisms** have been developed. These defenses aim to either make models more robust to adversarial examples or detect such attacks before they affect model performance.

Defense Techniques:

1. **Adversarial Training**:
   - In adversarial training, the model is trained with a mixture of clean and adversarial examples. By augmenting the training dataset with adversarial examples, the model learns to recognize and resist adversarial perturbations.
   - **Key Idea**: The model becomes robust by seeing adversarial examples during training, which makes it harder to fool the model with new attacks.
2. **Gradient Masking**:
   - **Gradient masking** hides or reduces the gradient information to prevent attackers from easily computing perturbations. However, this defense can sometimes be circumvented by more advanced attacks.
   - **Example**: Non-differentiable layers or noisy gradients can hinder the attacker's

ability to compute meaningful perturbations.

3. **Defensive Distillation**:
   - A technique where a model is first trained on clean data and then distilled into a smaller model with softened output probabilities. The distillation process smoothens the decision boundary, making it harder for adversarial examples to exploit.
   - **Distillation** reduces the sensitivity of the model to small input changes by "teaching" the final model to focus on general patterns rather than sharp decision boundaries.

4. **Input Preprocessing**:
   - Simple preprocessing techniques, such as image smoothing, adding random noise, or JPEG compression, can sometimes disrupt adversarial perturbations and prevent them from fooling the model.
   - **Example**: Gaussian blurring or median filtering may remove the small pixel-level perturbations that adversarial attacks introduce, leading to more robust predictions.

5. **Certified Defenses**:
   - These methods provide mathematical guarantees about a model's robustness within a certain range of perturbations. **Randomized smoothing** is one such technique, where the model's prediction is smoothed over multiple noisy versions of the input to ensure stability against small adversarial changes.
   - **Key Advantage**: These defenses offer theoretical guarantees of robustness, unlike empirical methods like adversarial training, which may not work against all attack types.

Code Example: Adversarial Training (PyTorch)

```
import torch.optim as optim
```

```python
# Adversarial training loop
def adversarial_training(model, dataloader, epsilon, num_epochs):
    optimizer = optim.Adam(model.parameters(), lr=0.001)
    criterion = nn.CrossEntropyLoss()

    for epoch in range(num_epochs):
        for images, labels in dataloader:
            # Create adversarial examples
            images.requires_grad = True
            outputs = model(images)
            loss = criterion(outputs, labels)
            model.zero_grad()
            loss.backward()
            data_grad = images.grad.data
            adv_images = fgsm_attack(images, epsilon, data_grad)

            # Forward pass with adversarial examples
            outputs_adv = model(adv_images)
            loss_adv = criterion(outputs_adv, labels)

            # Backpropagation and optimization
            optimizer.zero_grad()
            loss_adv.backward()
```

```
        optimizer.step()


        print(f"Epoch    [{epoch+1}/{num_epochs}],    Loss:
{loss_adv.item()}")


# Usage: Train the model with adversarial examples

#    dataloader    =    DataLoader(training_dataset,
batch_size=32, shuffle=True)

adversarial_training(model,   dataloader,   epsilon=0.03,
num_epochs=10)
```

Applications of Defense Mechanisms:

- **Robust AI Systems**: In mission-critical systems like healthcare or autonomous driving, adversarial robustness is essential for ensuring that models make reliable decisions under real-world conditions.
- **Cybersecurity**: Defenses against adversarial attacks can enhance the security of face authentication systems, biometric identification, and other AI-driven security measures.
- **Model Certification**: Certified defenses provide guarantees of robustness, which are important in regulated industries that require compliance with safety and performance standards.

Summary

- **Adversarial Attacks**: Small perturbations can deceive deep learning models into making incorrect predictions. Techniques like FGSM and PGD exploit the model's gradients to craft these adversarial examples.
- **Defense Mechanisms**: Various methods such as adversarial training, gradient masking, defensive distillation, input

preprocessing, and certified defenses aim to improve model robustness against adversarial examples.

Robustness and defense against adversarial attacks are essential for building trustworthy and secure AI systems in real-world applications. As adversarial attack techniques evolve, defenses must continue to improve to protect AI models from these vulnerabilities.

Chapter 11: Computer Vision in Industry

Real-Time Computer Vision Systems

Real-time computer vision systems are designed to process and analyze visual data (images or video) instantly or with minimal delay. These systems are widely used in applications like autonomous vehicles, surveillance, robotics, augmented reality, and smart devices. Achieving real-time performance involves optimizing algorithms to run efficiently on various hardware, including embedded systems and edge computing platforms.

1. Optimization for Embedded Systems

Overview:

Embedded systems in computer vision are low-power, resource-constrained devices that often operate in real-time, such as smartphones, drones, and IoT devices. The challenge is to implement computationally intensive tasks like image classification, object detection, or tracking on hardware with limited memory, processing power, and battery life.

Techniques for Optimization:

1. **Quantization**:
   - Reducing the precision of model parameters and activations from 32-bit floating-point to 8-bit integers or even lower, which reduces memory usage and increases speed.
   - **Benefit**: Lower precision means less data to process, leading to faster computations and reduced energy consumption.
   - Example: TensorFlow Lite and PyTorch Mobile support quantization for neural networks running on mobile or edge devices.

2. **Pruning**:
   - Pruning involves removing unnecessary or less critical weights from a trained neural network to reduce its size. This reduces the number of computations required without significantly affecting accuracy.
   - **Structured pruning** removes entire filters or channels, while **unstructured pruning** removes individual weights.

3. **Model Compression**:
   - Compressing models involves reducing the number of parameters, making the model lightweight. Techniques like **knowledge distillation** transfer knowledge from a large, complex model (teacher) to a smaller, simpler model (student), retaining much of the performance while reducing the model's size.

4. **Hardware-Specific Optimization**:
   - Utilizing hardware accelerators like GPUs, TPUs, or custom-designed chips (e.g., NVIDIA Jetson, Google Edge TPU) to speed up vision tasks.
   - Using libraries such as OpenCV, Intel OpenVINO, and NVIDIA TensorRT, which

offer optimized functions tailored to the hardware capabilities.

5. **Efficient CNN Architectures**:
   - Efficient architectures like **MobileNet**, **ShuffleNet**, and **EfficientNet** are designed specifically for embedded devices. These models use depthwise separable convolutions, group convolutions, and squeeze-and-excitation layers to reduce computational complexity.
   - **MobileNetV2**: Uses inverted residuals and linear bottlenecks to improve efficiency while maintaining accuracy.

Code Example: Quantization (PyTorch)

```python
import torch

import torchvision.models as models


# Load a pre-trained model

model = models.resnet18(pretrained=True)

model.eval()


# Convert the model to a quantized version

model_fp32 = model  # Full-precision model

model_int8 = torch.quantization.quantize_dynamic(

    model_fp32, {torch.nn.Linear}, dtype=torch.qint8

)


# Example forward pass with quantized model

input_data = torch.randn(1, 3, 224, 224)

output = model_int8(input_data)
```

Applications:

- **Smart Cameras**: Real-time vision processing on low-power embedded devices for surveillance and monitoring applications.
- **Autonomous Drones**: Embedded vision systems help in obstacle detection, object recognition, and navigation.
- **Mobile Augmented Reality (AR)**: Optimized vision algorithms are used to provide real-time AR experiences on smartphones.

2. Edge Computing in Vision

Overview:

Edge computing refers to performing computation near the source of data generation (on edge devices such as cameras, sensors, or mobile devices) rather than relying on cloud-based servers. For real-time computer vision, edge computing minimizes latency, reduces bandwidth usage, and enhances privacy by processing data locally.

Key Concepts:

- **Low Latency**: Edge computing reduces the delay caused by data transmission to and from the cloud, making it ideal for applications requiring instantaneous feedback, like autonomous driving or real-time surveillance.
- **Data Privacy**: Processing sensitive data on the edge rather than in the cloud protects user privacy since less data is sent over the network.
- **Reduced Bandwidth**: Edge computing minimizes the amount of data transmitted to centralized cloud servers, reducing network congestion and associated costs.

Techniques for Efficient Vision on the Edge:

1. **Model Partitioning**:
   - o Splitting a vision model into parts, where the first layers run on the edge device, and the rest run in the cloud. This reduces the amount of data that needs to be transmitted and enables larger models to be used.

2. **On-Device Inference**:
   - o Running lightweight models entirely on the edge device. Frameworks like TensorFlow Lite, ONNX, and PyTorch Mobile enable on-device inference of deep learning models, optimized for mobile and embedded platforms.

3. **Edge AI Hardware**:
   - o Devices like **NVIDIA Jetson**, **Google Coral**, **Intel Movidius**, and **Qualcomm Snapdragon** are designed for efficient AI computation on the edge, providing hardware accelerators like GPUs, NPUs (Neural Processing Units), or VPUs (Vision Processing Units) for vision tasks.

4. **Distributed Processing**:
   - o Distributing processing tasks between the edge and the cloud based on the complexity of the task. For example, simple tasks like object detection can run on the edge, while more computationally expensive tasks like 3D reconstruction can be offloaded to the cloud.

5. **Federated Learning**:
   - o Instead of sending data to the cloud for model training, federated learning enables multiple edge devices to collaboratively learn a shared model while keeping the data localized on each device. This preserves privacy while reducing cloud dependency.

Code Example: TensorFlow Lite Model Inference on Edge

```
import tensorflow as tf
```

```python
# Load TensorFlow Lite model
interpreter = tf.lite.Interpreter(model_path="mobilenet_v2.tflite")

interpreter.allocate_tensors()


# Get input and output tensors
input_details = interpreter.get_input_details()

output_details = interpreter.get_output_details()


# Prepare input data
input_data = np.array(np.random.random_sample(input_details[0]['shape']), dtype=np.float32)


# Perform inference
interpreter.set_tensor(input_details[0]['index'], input_data)

interpreter.invoke()


# Get output result
output_data = interpreter.get_tensor(output_details[0]['index'])

print(output_data)
```

Applications:

- **Autonomous Vehicles**: Edge computing allows for real-time object detection, lane recognition, and pedestrian tracking without needing to rely on cloud communication.

- **Smart Cities**: Real-time surveillance systems in smart cities can detect and respond to traffic violations, accidents, or suspicious activities using edge devices.
- **Industrial IoT**: Edge devices in manufacturing can monitor quality control, detect defects in products, and ensure real-time feedback for operational efficiency.

Summary

- **Optimization for Embedded Systems**: Techniques like quantization, pruning, model compression, and efficient CNN architectures (e.g., MobileNet, EfficientNet) enable computer vision models to run efficiently on resource-constrained hardware.
- **Edge Computing in Vision**: Performing real-time inference on edge devices reduces latency, enhances privacy, and reduces bandwidth usage. Edge AI hardware (e.g., Jetson, Coral) and frameworks like TensorFlow Lite or ONNX support efficient deployment of vision models on the edge.

Real-time computer vision systems are becoming increasingly vital across industries, from autonomous vehicles to smart devices, where quick and accurate processing is essential. Optimization and edge computing are central to achieving these objectives efficiently.

Autonomous Systems and Robotics

Autonomous systems, particularly in the context of robotics, rely on advanced computer vision techniques to perceive, navigate, and interact with their environment. In this section, we focus on two critical aspects of autonomous robotics: **perception in autonomous vehicles** and **vision-based navigation**. These are key to enabling robots and autonomous systems to operate safely and effectively in dynamic, unstructured environments.

1. Perception in Autonomous Vehicles

Overview:

In autonomous vehicles (AVs), perception refers to the ability of the vehicle to "see" and understand its surroundings using various sensors and algorithms. This includes recognizing objects (e.g., pedestrians, cars), identifying lanes, detecting road signs, and understanding the overall scene to make safe driving decisions.

Key Sensors Used in Perception:

- **Cameras**: Used for capturing visual data, object recognition, and lane detection.
- **LiDAR (Light Detection and Ranging)**: Measures distances to objects by illuminating them with laser light and analyzing the reflected light.
- **Radar**: Detects objects and their speed, especially in poor weather conditions or low visibility.

- **Ultrasonic Sensors**: Used for short-range object detection (e.g., parking assistance).

Perception Tasks in Autonomous Vehicles:

1. **Object Detection and Classification**:
   - **Real-time object detection** algorithms identify vehicles, pedestrians, cyclists, and other objects in the environment. This is often done using deep learning models like YOLO, SSD, and Faster R-CNN.
   - **Object classification** ensures that the vehicle can distinguish between different types of objects and react accordingly.

Example: YOLOv4 for real-time object detection in AV systems.

```
import cv2
import numpy as np


# Load YOLO model
net = cv2.dnn.readNet("yolov4.weights", "yolov4.cfg")
layer_names = net.getLayerNames()
output_layers = [layer_names[i[0] - 1] for i in net.getUnconnectedOutLayers()]


# Load an image
img = cv2.imread("road_image.jpg")
height, width, channels = img.shape


# Prepare the image for YOLO
blob = cv2.dnn.blobFromImage(img, 0.00392, (416, 416), (0, 0, 0), True, crop=False)
```

```python
net.setInput(blob)


# Perform forward pass

outputs = net.forward(output_layers)


# Process the detections (example)

for output in outputs:

    for detection in output:

        scores = detection[5:]

        class_id = np.argmax(scores)

        confidence = scores[class_id]

        if confidence > 0.5:

            center_x = int(detection[0] * width)

            center_y = int(detection[1] * height)

            w = int(detection[2] * width)

            h = int(detection[3] * height)


            # Bounding box coordinates

            x = int(center_x - w / 2)

            y = int(center_y - h / 2)

            cv2.rectangle(img, (x, y), (x + w, y + h), (0, 255, 0), 2)

            cv2.putText(img, "Object", (x, y - 10), cv2.FONT_HERSHEY_SIMPLEX, 0.5, (0, 255, 0), 2)


# Display the image with detections
```

```
cv2.imshow("Detected Objects", img)

cv2.waitKey(0)
```

2. Semantic and Instance Segmentation:

- **Semantic segmentation** labels each pixel of an image with a corresponding class (e.g., road, vehicle, pedestrian), while **instance segmentation** differentiates between multiple objects of the same class (e.g., two pedestrians).
- Autonomous vehicles use segmentation to understand the drivable space, obstacles, and the environment structure.

Example: **DeepLab** or **Mask R-CNN** can be used for this task.

3. Lane Detection:

- Lane detection is crucial for vehicle localization and maintaining proper lane positioning. Traditional methods rely on edge detection and Hough transforms, but deep learning-based approaches like **CNNs** are becoming more popular due to their robustness against noise and challenging conditions.

Example: **Hough Line Transform** for traditional lane detection.

```
# Hough Line Transform for lane detection (OpenCV)

gray = cv2.cvtColor(img, cv2.COLOR_BGR2GRAY)

edges = cv2.Canny(gray, 50, 150)

lines = cv2.HoughLinesP(edges, 1, np.pi / 180, threshold=100, minLineLength=50, maxLineGap=10)
```

```
for line in lines:

    x1, y1, x2, y2 = line[0]

    cv2.line(img, (x1, y1), (x2, y2), (0, 255, 0), 3)


cv2.imshow("Lane Detection", img)

cv2.waitKey(0)
```

4. **Sensor Fusion**:

- To improve perception accuracy and robustness, AVs use **sensor fusion**, combining data from cameras, LiDAR, radar, and other sensors to create a complete, reliable understanding of the environment.
- **Kalman filters** and **Bayesian filters** are used to fuse sensor data and track objects over time.

2. Vision-Based Navigation

Overview:

Vision-based navigation uses visual data (images or video) from cameras to guide the movement of robots or vehicles. It involves recognizing the environment, avoiding obstacles, and localizing the robot in space.

Vision-Based Navigation Techniques:

1. **Visual SLAM (Simultaneous Localization and Mapping)**:
   - SLAM is the process of building a map of an environment while simultaneously keeping track of the robot's position within that environment. **Visual SLAM** uses

camera data instead of (or in addition to) other sensors like LiDAR.

- ○ Key components of SLAM include **feature extraction**, **feature matching**, and **pose estimation**.

Common algorithms: **ORB-SLAM, LSD-SLAM**.

2. **Optical Flow for Navigation**:
   - ○ **Optical flow** measures the motion of objects, surfaces, and edges between frames in a video sequence. It can be used for estimating the robot's speed and direction or for avoiding dynamic obstacles.

Example: Optical flow using the **Lucas-Kanade method**.

```
import cv2

import numpy as np


# Capture video from camera

cap = cv2.VideoCapture(0)


# Take the first frame and convert it to grayscale

ret, old_frame = cap.read()

old_gray        =        cv2.cvtColor(old_frame,
cv2.COLOR_BGR2GRAY)


# Parameters for Lucas-Kanade Optical Flow
```

```
lk_params = dict(winSize=(15, 15), maxLevel=2,
criteria=(cv2.TERM_CRITERIA_EPS                        |
cv2.TERM_CRITERIA_COUNT, 10, 0.03))


# Detect good features to track

p0 = cv2.goodFeaturesToTrack(old_gray, mask=None,
maxCorners=100, qualityLevel=0.3, minDistance=7,
blockSize=7)


while True:
    ret, frame = cap.read()

    frame_gray             =             cv2.cvtColor(frame,
cv2.COLOR_BGR2GRAY)


    # Calculate optical flow
    p1, st, err = cv2.calcOpticalFlowPyrLK(old_gray,
frame_gray, p0, None, **lk_params)


    # Select good points
    good_new = p1[st == 1]
    good_old = p0[st == 1]


    # Draw the tracks
    for i, (new, old) in enumerate(zip(good_new,
good_old)):
        a, b = new.ravel()
        c, d = old.ravel()
        cv2.line(frame, (a, b), (c, d), (0, 255, 0), 2)
```

```
cv2.circle(frame, (a, b), 5, (0, 255, 0), -1)


cv2.imshow('Optical Flow', frame)


# Break on key press

if cv2.waitKey(30) & 0xFF == ord('q'):

    break


# Update the previous frame and previous points

old_gray = frame_gray.copy()

p0 = good_new.reshape(-1, 1, 2)


cap.release()

cv2.destroyAllWindows()
```

3. **Path Planning**:

- In vision-based navigation, **path planning** involves determining the optimal route from the robot's current location to its destination while avoiding obstacles. Algorithms such as **A***, **RRT (Rapidly-exploring Random Trees)**, and **Dijkstra** are commonly used for this purpose.
- Deep reinforcement learning is also increasingly applied to train robots to navigate complex environments autonomously.

4. **Visual Odometry**:

- Visual odometry estimates the motion of the robot by analyzing the change in visual

345

information between consecutive frames. It provides an estimate of the robot's position and orientation over time.

- This can be achieved through feature-based methods or dense image alignment.

Summary

- **Perception in Autonomous Vehicles**: Involves using various sensors (cameras, LiDAR, radar) to detect objects, segment the environment, and perform lane detection. Techniques like object detection (YOLO, Faster R-CNN) and semantic segmentation help AVs understand their surroundings.
- **Vision-Based Navigation**: Techniques like Visual SLAM, optical flow, and visual odometry enable robots and autonomous vehicles to navigate dynamically and build a map of the environment while localizing themselves.

Both perception and navigation are critical for enabling the autonomy of robotic systems and vehicles, making them safer, more reliable, and efficient.

Medical Image Analysis

Medical image analysis leverages advanced image processing and machine learning techniques, particularly deep learning, to assist in diagnosis, treatment planning, and research. Two key areas where this is applied include **deep learning in radiology and pathology** and **image segmentation in medical imaging**.

1. Deep Learning in Radiology and Pathology

Overview:

Radiology and pathology are central to the diagnosis of many diseases, including cancer, cardiovascular conditions, and neurological disorders. Deep learning models, particularly Convolutional Neural Networks (CNNs), have been applied extensively to analyze radiological images (X-rays, CT, MRI, PET) and pathology slides for detecting abnormalities, automating tasks, and improving diagnostic accuracy.

Applications of Deep Learning in Radiology and Pathology:

1. **Disease Detection and Diagnosis**:
   - Deep learning models are used to automatically detect diseases like cancer, pneumonia, and brain tumors from radiological images.
   - **CNN-based models** like ResNet, VGG, and DenseNet are commonly used to classify images based on pathology, often outperforming traditional machine learning models.

Example: Pneumonia Detection from Chest X-rays:

```
import torch

import torchvision.models as models

from torchvision import transforms

from PIL import Image


# Load a pre-trained model (e.g., ResNet)
```

```python
model = models.resnet50(pretrained=True)

model.eval()


# Preprocess image (resize, normalize, etc.)

preprocess = transforms.Compose([

    transforms.Resize(256),

    transforms.CenterCrop(224),

    transforms.ToTensor(),

    transforms.Normalize(mean=[0.485,        0.456,
0.406], std=[0.229, 0.224, 0.225]),

])


img = Image.open("chest_xray.png")

img_tensor = preprocess(img)

img_tensor = img_tensor.unsqueeze(0)


# Perform prediction

with torch.no_grad():

    output = model(img_tensor)

    _, predicted = output.max(1)

print(f"Predicted class: {predicted.item()}")
```

2. **Tumor Detection in Pathology**:
   - ○ **Whole Slide Images (WSIs)** are high-resolution images of tissue slides used in pathology. Deep learning models are used to identify tumor regions, measure tumor size, and classify tissue abnormalities from WSIs.
   - ○ **Patch-based CNNs** break WSIs into smaller patches and perform classification on each patch, then aggregate results to generate a global prediction for the slide.
3. **Medical Image Enhancement**:
   - ○ Enhancing image quality and resolution through super-resolution techniques is another area where deep learning plays a role. GANs (Generative Adversarial Networks) are often used to improve low-quality images for better diagnostic performance.
   - ○ For instance, improving MRI resolution to make subtle abnormalities visible.
4. **Predictive Modeling**:
   - ○ Deep learning models can analyze imaging data over time (e.g., brain scans) to predict disease progression or treatment response. This is particularly valuable in chronic conditions like Alzheimer's or cancer.

2. Image Segmentation in Medical Imaging

Overview:

Image segmentation is a crucial task in medical imaging that involves partitioning an image into meaningful regions (e.g., organs, tumors, lesions) for diagnosis, surgery planning, and treatment. Medical image segmentation can be challenging due to noise, low contrast, and variability in anatomy and pathology, making deep learning-based approaches highly useful.

Techniques for Medical Image Segmentation:

1. UNet for Medical Image Segmentation:

- **UNet** is a widely used CNN architecture designed for biomedical image segmentation. Its symmetric encoder-decoder structure captures both low-level details and high-level context, making it ideal for tasks like organ or tumor segmentation.
- The encoder extracts features from the input image, and the decoder reconstructs the image while predicting pixel-wise segmentation labels.

UNet Architecture:

- **Encoder**: Series of convolutional layers followed by downsampling (max-pooling).
- **Decoder**: Up-sampling layers with concatenation from corresponding encoder layers for feature fusion.
- **Skip Connections**: Between the encoder and decoder layers to preserve spatial information.

Example: UNet for Brain Tumor Segmentation in MRI:

import torch

import torch.nn as nn

import torch.nn.functional as F

Define UNet model architecture

350

```python
class UNet(nn.Module):

    def __init__(self, in_channels, out_channels):

        super(UNet, self).__init__()

        self.encoder1 = self.conv_block(in_channels, 64)

        self.encoder2 = self.conv_block(64, 128)

        self.encoder3 = self.conv_block(128, 256)

        self.decoder1 = self.conv_block(256, 128)

        self.decoder2 = self.conv_block(128, 64)

        self.final_conv = nn.Conv2d(64, out_channels, kernel_size=1)


    def conv_block(self, in_channels, out_channels):

        return nn.Sequential(

            nn.Conv2d(in_channels, out_channels, kernel_size=3, padding=1),

            nn.ReLU(inplace=True),

            nn.Conv2d(out_channels, out_channels, kernel_size=3, padding=1),

            nn.ReLU(inplace=True)

        )
```

```python
def forward(self, x):

    enc1 = self.encoder1(x)

    enc2 = self.encoder2(F.max_pool2d(enc1, 2))

    enc3 = self.encoder3(F.max_pool2d(enc2, 2))

    dec1    =    self.decoder1(F.interpolate(enc3,
scale_factor=2))

    dec2    =    self.decoder2(F.interpolate(dec1,
scale_factor=2))

    return self.final_conv(dec2)



# Instantiate and test the model

model = UNet(in_channels=1, out_channels=2)   #
MRI images often have 1 channel (grayscale)

sample_input = torch.randn(1, 1, 256, 256) # Batch
of 1, 256x256 image

output = model(sample_input)

print(output.shape)  # Output segmentation mask
```

2. **3D Segmentation**:
   - Medical images like CT and MRI scans are often 3D, requiring models that can handle 3D data for segmentation. **3D UNet** and **VNet** architectures extend 2D segmentation techniques to 3D.
   - These networks take volumetric data as input and generate 3D segmentations for tasks like organ delineation or tumor tracking across multiple slices.

3. **Multi-Class Segmentation**:
   - o Multi-class segmentation involves labeling each pixel with one of several classes (e.g., different organs or regions of interest). For example, in a CT scan, each pixel might represent the liver, kidneys, or lungs.
4. **Attention Mechanisms in Segmentation**:
   - o **Attention mechanisms** are integrated into segmentation networks to focus on relevant regions of the image, especially useful when the object of interest (e.g., a small lesion) is hard to detect.

Summary

- **Deep Learning in Radiology and Pathology**: CNNs are used for disease detection, tumor classification, and predictive modeling from medical images. These models provide automated, accurate analysis in tasks like pneumonia detection or tumor segmentation from WSIs.
- **Image Segmentation in Medical Imaging**: UNet and its variants (3D UNet, VNet) are commonly used for medical image segmentation tasks, helping in detecting and delineating organs, tumors, and other anatomical structures in 2D and 3D scans.

Medical image analysis continues to evolve with deep learning, helping to improve diagnostic accuracy, automate time-consuming tasks, and personalize treatment strategies.

Ethical Considerations and Bias in Computer Vision

As computer vision systems become more integrated into everyday life—from facial recognition to medical imaging—there are growing concerns about the ethical implications of these technologies. Two critical areas of focus are **fairness in AI models** and **privacy concerns in surveillance systems**.

1. Fairness in AI Models

Overview:

Bias in AI models, including those used in computer vision, can arise due to imbalanced datasets, flawed labeling processes, or societal biases reflected in the data. When left unaddressed, these biases can lead to unequal outcomes across different demographic groups, especially in sensitive applications like facial recognition, medical diagnostics, or autonomous driving.

Key Issues and Challenges:

1. **Bias in Training Data**:
   o AI models trained on biased datasets may perform well on the majority class but poorly on underrepresented groups. For instance, facial recognition systems have historically struggled to accurately identify people with darker skin tones, leading to racial disparities in performance.

Example: The Gender Shades study found that commercial facial recognition systems from major tech companies performed much worse on darker-skinned women than on lighter-skinned men. This is attributed to the underrepresentation of diverse skin tones in the training data.

2. **Algorithmic Fairness**:
   - Fairness involves creating models that make equitable predictions across different population groups. Researchers propose several fairness metrics, such as **demographic parity** and **equalized odds**, to evaluate whether models treat different groups fairly.

   Demographic Parity: Ensuring that predictions (e.g., facial recognition or classification) are equally distributed across demographic groups.

   Equalized Odds: Ensuring that the true positive and false positive rates are equal across different groups.

3. **Model Interpretability**:
   - Understanding why a model makes certain predictions is critical for identifying bias. Techniques like **saliency maps** and **attention mechanisms** allow us to visualize which parts of an image a model focuses on when making predictions, potentially revealing hidden biases in decision-making.
4. **Bias in Medical Image Analysis**:
   - In medical imaging, AI models can exhibit biases due to unequal representation of diseases in different demographics. For example, an AI trained predominantly on images of lighter-skinned patients might

perform worse on detecting skin conditions in darker-skinned individuals.

Addressing Fairness:

- **Diverse and Representative Datasets**: Ensuring that training data is representative of all demographics is the first step in reducing bias. Researchers are working on building more diverse datasets, such as **Diverse Faces in the Wild (DiF)**, to improve fairness in facial recognition.
- **Fairness-Aware Algorithms**: Techniques such as adversarial debiasing and reweighting algorithms have been developed to reduce bias in model training.

2. Privacy Concerns in Surveillance Systems

Overview:

Computer vision is increasingly used in surveillance systems for monitoring public spaces, law enforcement, and even in commercial applications (e.g., retail stores). While these systems offer efficiency and security, they also raise significant privacy concerns, particularly regarding the collection, storage, and misuse of personal data.

Key Issues:

1. **Mass Surveillance**:
   - **Facial Recognition Technology (FRT)** is widely deployed in surveillance systems, raising concerns about its potential for mass surveillance. Governments and private companies can track individuals in real time, leading to a loss of privacy and civil liberties.
   - The use of FRT in public spaces without consent creates a scenario where

individuals may be continuously monitored without their knowledge, infringing on the right to privacy.

2. **Data Collection and Storage**:
   - Surveillance systems collect large amounts of sensitive data, including images, videos, and biometric information. The storage and handling of this data pose significant risks, particularly if the data is hacked, leaked, or misused.
   - **GDPR (General Data Protection Regulation)** and other privacy regulations attempt to govern the use of personal data, but their enforcement in the context of AI-driven surveillance is still a challenge.

3. **Re-identification**:
   - Even when personal data is anonymized, re-identification techniques using computer vision can piece together seemingly anonymous data to re-identify individuals. For instance, gait recognition can identify people based on the way they walk, even when their faces are obscured.

   Example: In some studies, anonymized footage from surveillance cameras could be linked back to individuals by cross-referencing the data with other public datasets.

4. **Surveillance Creep**:
   - The concept of **"surveillance creep"** refers to the gradual expansion of surveillance technologies beyond their intended use. For instance, a system designed for security purposes may eventually be used for purposes like targeted advertising or behavioral profiling, raising ethical concerns.

Mitigating Privacy Concerns:

1. **Regulations and Legislation**:

- o Governments and organizations are increasingly looking to regulate the use of surveillance technologies. For example, several U.S. cities have banned the use of facial recognition in public spaces due to privacy concerns.
- o **Data Anonymization**: Ensuring that collected data is properly anonymized to prevent misuse or unauthorized identification of individuals.

2. **Privacy-Preserving Techniques**:
   - o **Federated Learning**: Instead of collecting and storing data centrally, federated learning enables AI models to be trained locally on devices, reducing the risk of data breaches.
   - o **Homomorphic Encryption**: Protecting data while still allowing computations on encrypted data can be useful in privacy-sensitive applications, such as medical image analysis or surveillance.

3. **Transparency and Consent**:
   - o Ensuring that individuals are informed about the use of surveillance technologies and giving them control over how their data is used is crucial for maintaining trust. This includes obtaining explicit consent for data collection and providing mechanisms for opting out.

Summary

- **Fairness in AI Models**: Bias in computer vision models, often stemming from imbalanced datasets, can lead to unfair outcomes, especially in applications like facial recognition and medical imaging. Addressing fairness requires diverse datasets, fairness-aware algorithms, and interpretability tools.
- **Privacy Concerns in Surveillance Systems**: The widespread use of computer vision in surveillance systems raises ethical concerns

about mass surveillance, data privacy, and misuse. Privacy-preserving techniques and stronger regulations are needed to mitigate these concerns.

Ethics in computer vision is a growing field, as society navigates the balance between technological innovation and human rights.

Chapter 12: Tools and Frameworks

Computer vision tasks, ranging from image processing to deep learning-based recognition, are often implemented using powerful libraries such as **OpenCV**, **TensorFlow**, **Keras**, and **PyTorch**. Each library serves different purposes, from traditional image processing to deep learning for object detection and classification.

OpenCV (Open Source Computer Vision Library)

Overview:

OpenCV is a widely used open-source library designed for real-time computer vision applications. It provides tools for basic image processing tasks like filtering, edge detection, and feature extraction, and more advanced applications like face detection and object tracking.

Key Features:

- **Image Processing**: OpenCV offers a wide range of image processing techniques, including smoothing, thresholding, morphological transformations, and edge detection.

- **Feature Detection**: Algorithms like SIFT, SURF, and ORB can be used for keypoint detection and feature matching.
- **Object Detection**: OpenCV supports traditional object detection techniques such as the Haar Cascade for face detection.
- **Video Processing**: OpenCV can process video frames in real time, making it useful for applications like motion detection and tracking.

Example: Edge Detection using the Canny Method

```
import cv2

import matplotlib.pyplot as plt


# Load image

image = cv2.imread('input_image.jpg', 0)   # Load image in grayscale


# Apply Canny edge detection

edges = cv2.Canny(image, 100, 200)


# Display result

plt.imshow(edges, cmap='gray')

plt.title('Canny Edge Detection')

plt.show()
```

TensorFlow and Keras

Overview:

TensorFlow is an open-source deep learning framework developed by Google, while **Keras** is a high-level API built on top of TensorFlow (and other backends) that simplifies building and training neural networks. Together, they provide a robust ecosystem for developing computer vision models using deep learning techniques.

Key Features:

- **Deep Learning Models**: TensorFlow supports state-of-the-art architectures like CNNs, RNNs, and Transformer-based models.
- **Image Classification and Object Detection**: TensorFlow and Keras have pre-trained models (e.g., ResNet, YOLO, SSD) that can be fine-tuned for tasks like image classification, object detection, and segmentation.
- **TensorFlow Lite**: TensorFlow Lite allows developers to deploy models on mobile and embedded devices, enabling real-time computer vision tasks on edge devices.

Example: Image Classification with a Pre-Trained CNN (ResNet50) using Keras

```
import tensorflow as tf

from tensorflow.keras.applications import ResNet50

from tensorflow.keras.applications.resnet50 import preprocess_input, decode_predictions

from tensorflow.keras.preprocessing import image
```

```python
import numpy as np


# Load pre-trained ResNet50 model + higher level layers

model = ResNet50(weights='imagenet')


# Load and preprocess image

img = image.load_img('sample_image.jpg', target_size=(224, 224))

img_array = image.img_to_array(img)

img_array = np.expand_dims(img_array, axis=0)

img_array = preprocess_input(img_array)


# Predict the class of the image

predictions = model.predict(img_array)

decoded_predictions = decode_predictions(predictions, top=3)[0]


# Output predictions

for (imagenet_id, label, score) in decoded_predictions:

    print(f"{label}: {score:.4f}")
```

Applications:

- **Image Classification**: Keras simplifies the process of building image classifiers using CNNs.
- **Object Detection and Segmentation**: TensorFlow's Object Detection API enables the implementation of real-time object detection models.
- **Transfer Learning**: Pre-trained models can be fine-tuned on new datasets using TensorFlow, speeding up the development process for new tasks.

PyTorch for Computer Vision

Overview:

PyTorch is an open-source deep learning framework developed by Facebook that has gained popularity for its flexibility and dynamic computation graph. PyTorch is often used for research and rapid prototyping, as well as large-scale applications in computer vision.

Key Features:

- **Dynamic Computation Graph**: PyTorch's dynamic nature allows for easier debugging and modification of models, making it highly flexible.
- **Model Customization**: PyTorch is ideal for building custom neural network architectures for tasks like classification, detection, and segmentation.
- **Pre-trained Models**: The **torchvision** module in PyTorch provides access to pre-trained models such as ResNet, VGG, and MobileNet, as well as image datasets like CIFAR-10 and ImageNet.

Example: Training a CNN in PyTorch for Image Classification

```
import torch

import torch.nn as nn

import torch.optim as optim

from torchvision import datasets, transforms, models



# Define transformations for training and validation sets

transform = transforms.Compose([

    transforms.Resize((224, 224)),

    transforms.ToTensor(),

    transforms.Normalize(mean=[0.485, 0.456, 0.406], std=[0.229, 0.224, 0.225]),

])



# Load dataset

train_dataset = datasets.CIFAR10(root='./data', train=True, download=True, transform=transform)

train_loader = torch.utils.data.DataLoader(dataset=train_dataset, batch_size=32, shuffle=True)
```

```python
# Define a simple CNN model using PyTorch

class SimpleCNN(nn.Module):

    def __init__(self):

        super(SimpleCNN, self).__init__()

        self.conv1 = nn.Conv2d(3, 16, kernel_size=3)

        self.conv2 = nn.Conv2d(16, 32, kernel_size=3)

        self.fc1 = nn.Linear(32 * 6 * 6, 120)

        self.fc2 = nn.Linear(120, 10)


    def forward(self, x):

        x = torch.relu(self.conv1(x))

        x = torch.relu(self.conv2(x))

        x = torch.flatten(x, 1)

        x = torch.relu(self.fc1(x))

        return self.fc2(x)


# Instantiate the model, loss function, and optimizer

model = SimpleCNN()

criterion = nn.CrossEntropyLoss()

optimizer     =     optim.Adam(model.parameters(),
lr=0.001)
```

```
# Training loop

for epoch in range(2):  # Training for 2 epochs as an example

    for images, labels in train_loader:

        outputs = model(images)

        loss = criterion(outputs, labels)


        optimizer.zero_grad()

        loss.backward()

        optimizer.step()


    print(f'Epoch [{epoch+1}/2], Loss: {loss.item():.4f}')
```

Applications:

- **Image Classification**: PyTorch makes it easy to build and train custom CNNs for classifying images from datasets like CIFAR-10 or ImageNet.
- **Object Detection and Segmentation**: PyTorch offers state-of-the-art models like Faster R-CNN, Mask R-CNN, and YOLO, enabling robust object detection and instance segmentation.
- **Generative Models**: PyTorch is often used to build Generative Adversarial Networks (GANs) and Variational Autoencoders (VAEs) for tasks like image generation and style transfer.

Summary

- **OpenCV** is a powerful library for traditional computer vision tasks, including image processing, feature detection, and object tracking.
- **TensorFlow and Keras** are ideal for deep learning applications, providing access to high-level APIs and pre-trained models for tasks like image classification, object detection, and segmentation.
- **PyTorch** is highly flexible and is widely used for building custom deep learning models, especially in research and experimentation.

Each of these libraries has its strengths and use cases, making them essential tools in modern computer vision projects.

Datasets and Benchmarks

Datasets play a crucial role in the development and evaluation of computer vision models. They provide the necessary labeled data for training, validation, and testing, and benchmarks help standardize performance measurements across different models. Here are some of the most significant datasets in computer vision:

1. ImageNet

Overview:

ImageNet is one of the largest and most widely used datasets for image classification and object detection tasks. It contains over 14 million images labeled across more than 20,000 categories.

Key Features:

- **Hierarchy**: The dataset is structured according to the WordNet hierarchy, where each node corresponds to a synset (a set of synonymous words).
- **ImageNet Large Scale Visual Recognition Challenge (ILSVRC)**: An annual competition that focuses on classifying images into 1,000 categories, featuring a subset of about 1.2 million images for training and 50,000 for validation.

Applications:

- Used extensively for training and evaluating deep learning models, particularly CNNs.
- The dataset has been pivotal in advancing the field, leading to the development of notable architectures like AlexNet, VGG, and ResNet.

2. COCO (Common Objects in Context)

Overview:

COCO is a large-scale dataset designed for object detection, segmentation, and captioning tasks. It contains over 330,000 images, with more than 2.5 million labeled instances in 80 object categories.

Key Features:

- **Complex Scenes**: Images contain multiple objects, often with occlusion, variation in scale, and complex backgrounds, providing a challenging benchmark for object detection algorithms.
- **Annotations**: Includes object segmentation masks, bounding boxes, keypoints for human pose estimation, and image captions.

Applications:

- Widely used in tasks like object detection (via the COCO API), image segmentation, and image captioning.
- COCO has served as a benchmark for many state-of-the-art models like YOLO, SSD, and Mask R-CNN.

3. Pascal VOC (Visual Object Classes)

Overview:

Pascal VOC is a popular dataset for object detection and image segmentation tasks, containing a collection of images from various contexts and settings.

Key Features:

- **Categories**: The dataset includes 20 object classes, such as people, animals, and vehicles.
- **Challenge**: The PASCAL VOC Challenge is an annual competition that has contributed to the advancement of object detection algorithms. It provides evaluation metrics such as mean Average Precision (mAP).

Applications:

- Used for benchmarking object detection, segmentation, and classification tasks.
- Many classical algorithms were developed and evaluated using the Pascal VOC dataset.

4. KITTI (Autonomous Driving Dataset)

Overview:

KITTI is a dataset designed for various computer vision tasks in the context of autonomous driving, including stereo vision, optical flow, visual odometry, 3D object detection, and tracking.

Key Features:

- **Diverse Sensors**: The dataset is collected from a driving platform equipped with high-resolution cameras, LiDAR, GPS, and IMU sensors, providing rich contextual data.
- **Annotations**: Includes 3D bounding boxes for objects such as cars, pedestrians, and cyclists, along with ground truth data for various tasks.

Applications:

- Serves as a benchmark for algorithms focused on autonomous driving, including depth estimation, object detection, and scene flow.
- Widely used in research on visual perception for self-driving cars, enabling advancements in safety and navigation.

Summary

- **ImageNet**: A foundational dataset for image classification and object detection, crucial for training deep learning models.
- **COCO**: A complex dataset for object detection and segmentation with extensive annotations, widely used for benchmarking models.
- **Pascal VOC**: An established dataset for object detection and segmentation, associated with an annual challenge that drives innovation in the field.
- **KITTI**: A specialized dataset for autonomous driving applications, providing real-world data for developing and testing algorithms in the context of self-driving cars.

These datasets have significantly contributed to the advancement of computer vision techniques and continue to serve as benchmarks for evaluating new models and approaches.

Chapter 13: Future Trends and Research Directions

AI in Augmented Reality and Virtual Reality

Artificial Intelligence (AI) plays a transformative role in both Augmented Reality (AR) and Virtual Reality (VR), enhancing user experiences and enabling advanced functionalities. Here's an overview of how AI integrates with AR and VR technologies.

1. Augmented Reality (AR)

Overview:

AR overlays digital information, such as images, videos, or 3D models, onto the real-world environment, enhancing the user's perception of reality. AI enhances AR by enabling smarter interactions and more realistic experiences.

Key Applications:

- **Object Recognition and Tracking**: AI algorithms identify and track objects in the real world, allowing virtual elements to interact dynamically with physical surroundings. For instance, AR apps can recognize furniture and allow users to visualize how a new piece would look in their home.

- **Scene Understanding**: AI processes and interprets the environment, recognizing surfaces, objects, and spatial relationships. This capability enables the placement of virtual content in a contextually relevant manner.
- **User Interaction**: AI-driven natural language processing (NLP) allows users to interact with AR applications using voice commands. This creates a more intuitive experience in applications like virtual assistants.
- **Personalization**: AI algorithms analyze user behavior and preferences to customize AR experiences, such as personalized advertisements or tailored educational content.

Example:

- **IKEA Place**: An AR application that allows users to visualize furniture in their own space. AI helps in recognizing the dimensions and layout of the room to place virtual objects accurately.

2. Virtual Reality (VR)

Overview:

VR immerses users in a completely virtual environment, often using headsets and motion tracking. AI enhances VR experiences by making them more interactive, realistic, and adaptive.

Key Applications:

- **Intelligent NPCs (Non-Player Characters)**: AI algorithms control NPC behavior, allowing them to respond dynamically to user actions, creating more engaging gameplay in VR environments.

- **Adaptive Learning Environments**: In educational VR applications, AI personalizes learning experiences based on user performance and learning style, adjusting the difficulty and type of content accordingly.
- **Realistic Simulations**: AI models enhance the realism of virtual environments by simulating natural behaviors, such as weather patterns or crowd dynamics, providing users with more immersive experiences.
- **Gesture Recognition**: AI interprets user gestures through cameras and sensors, enabling natural interactions in VR environments, such as hand tracking for manipulating virtual objects.

Example:

- **Google Tilt Brush**: A VR painting application that uses AI to analyze brush strokes and provide users with intelligent feedback, helping them create more intricate designs.

3. Combining AI with AR and VR

Enhanced Experiences:

- **Mixed Reality (MR)**: AI enables seamless integration of AR and VR, creating mixed-reality experiences where users can interact with both physical and virtual elements in real-time.
- **Emotion Recognition**: AI can analyze user facial expressions and body language to adapt the virtual experience accordingly, creating more engaging and responsive environments.

- **Data Analytics**: AI analyzes user interactions and behaviors in AR/VR environments to provide insights for developers, helping improve future experiences.

Use Cases:

- **Training Simulations**: AI-powered AR/VR training applications are used in fields like healthcare and aviation to simulate real-world scenarios for training purposes, offering personalized feedback based on user performance.
- **Gaming**: AI enhances gaming experiences by creating adaptive difficulty levels and intelligent storylines that respond to player choices, increasing engagement.

Summary

AI significantly enhances both AR and VR by enabling smarter interactions, realistic simulations, and personalized experiences. As the technology continues to evolve, the integration of AI in AR and VR is expected to lead to even more immersive and engaging applications across various fields, including education, entertainment, healthcare, and training.

Quantum Computing for Computer Vision

Quantum computing, with its unique principles of superposition and entanglement, offers potential advantages for various computational tasks, including those in computer vision. While still in its early stages, the intersection of quantum computing and computer vision presents exciting opportunities for enhancing performance and tackling complex problems.

1. Overview of Quantum Computing

Key Concepts:

- **Superposition**: Quantum bits (qubits) can exist in multiple states simultaneously, allowing quantum computers to process a vast number of possibilities at once.
- **Entanglement**: Qubits can be entangled, meaning the state of one qubit is directly related to the state of another, regardless of the distance between them. This can enable complex correlations in data processing.
- **Quantum Parallelism**: The ability to perform multiple calculations simultaneously due to superposition can lead to faster processing times for certain tasks.

2. Applications of Quantum Computing in Computer Vision

1. Image Processing

- **Quantum Algorithms**: Quantum algorithms can potentially enhance traditional image processing techniques. For example, algorithms like the Quantum Fourier Transform can speed up tasks like filtering, edge detection, and image reconstruction.

2. Feature Extraction and Classification

- **Quantum Machine Learning**: Quantum computing can be applied to machine learning models that classify images or extract features, potentially speeding up training times and improving accuracy. Quantum support vector

377

machines and quantum neural networks are examples of approaches being explored.

3. Optimization Problems

- **Quantum Annealing**: Many computer vision tasks involve optimization, such as image segmentation and object detection. Quantum annealers can solve combinatorial optimization problems more efficiently than classical counterparts, potentially leading to better solutions in less time.

4. 3D Reconstruction

- **Point Cloud Processing**: Quantum algorithms may enable more efficient processing of 3D point clouds and the reconstruction of 3D scenes from multiple images. This can enhance applications in robotics and augmented reality.

5. Data Compression

- **Quantum Techniques**: Quantum computing could improve data compression methods for images and videos, allowing for faster storage and transmission of large datasets commonly used in computer vision.

3. Challenges and Considerations

1. Hardware Limitations

- **Current Quantum Technology**: Quantum computers are still in the experimental phase, and practical, scalable quantum hardware is needed before they can be effectively used for computer vision tasks.

2. Algorithm Development

- **Need for Quantum-Specific Algorithms**: Many existing computer vision algorithms need to be rethought and adapted for quantum computing, requiring significant research and development.

3. Integration with Classical Systems

- **Hybrid Approaches**: As quantum computing technology matures, hybrid systems that combine classical and quantum computing may provide practical solutions for computer vision challenges, leveraging the strengths of both paradigms.

4. Future Directions

- **Research and Collaboration**: Ongoing research is needed to explore the full potential of quantum computing in computer vision. Collaborations between computer vision experts and quantum computing researchers can lead to innovative applications and solutions.
- **Education and Awareness**: Increasing awareness of quantum computing's potential among computer vision practitioners will drive exploration and adoption of quantum methods.

Summary

Quantum computing holds promise for advancing computer vision by enabling faster processing, improved optimization, and novel algorithms for tasks like image classification and reconstruction. While there are significant challenges to overcome, the potential benefits could lead to groundbreaking advancements in the field, particularly as quantum technology continues to develop.

Continual Learning in Vision

Continual learning, also known as lifelong learning, refers to the ability of a model to learn continuously from new data over time without forgetting previously acquired knowledge. This approach is particularly important in computer vision, where models must adapt to new tasks, environments, or data distributions while maintaining performance on earlier tasks.

1. Overview of Continual Learning

Key Concepts:

- **Catastrophic Forgetting**: A significant challenge in continual learning where a model trained on new tasks tends to forget previously learned tasks. This issue arises from the model's tendency to overwrite its parameters during training.
- **Task-Specific and Task-Agnostic Learning**: Continual learning can be categorized into two approaches:
  - **Task-Specific**: The model is aware of different tasks and can allocate resources accordingly.
  - **Task-Agnostic**: The model learns from incoming data without explicit task distinctions, treating all data as part of a single continuous learning process.

2. Techniques for Continual Learning in Vision

1. Regularization-Based Methods

- **Elastic Weight Consolidation (EWC)**: This approach uses regularization to protect important weights for previously learned tasks, preventing them from changing significantly when training on new tasks.
- **L2 Regularization**: Penalizes changes to the model weights that are critical for past tasks, helping to preserve previous knowledge.

2. Memory-Based Methods

- **Replay Buffers**: Storing a subset of data from previous tasks and using it during training of new tasks to reinforce old knowledge. This helps mitigate catastrophic forgetting.
- **Generative Replay**: Using generative models (e.g., GANs) to create synthetic examples of previous tasks during training, allowing the model to "remember" without needing to store actual data.

3. Dynamic Architecture

- **Modular Networks**: Using different subnetworks for different tasks, allowing the model to allocate resources dynamically based on the task at hand.
- **Progressive Neural Networks**: New layers are added for new tasks while keeping old layers fixed, ensuring that the model retains knowledge from previous tasks.

4. Parameter Isolation

- **Pathway Isolation**: Allocating different subsets of parameters to different tasks, reducing interference between tasks and preserving knowledge.

3. Applications in Computer Vision

1. Object Recognition

- Continual learning enables models to recognize new objects or classes while maintaining recognition of previously learned objects, enhancing adaptability in dynamic environments.

2. Semantic Segmentation

- Models can learn to segment new classes of objects in images over time without forgetting how to segment earlier classes, useful in applications like autonomous driving and robotics.

3. Action Recognition

- In video analysis, models can continually learn new actions or behaviors while retaining the ability to recognize actions learned in earlier training phases.

4. Challenges and Future Directions

1. Scalability

- Developing models that can efficiently learn from large, diverse datasets over time without degradation in performance remains a challenge.

2. Evaluation Metrics

- Standard metrics for evaluating continual learning performance are still evolving. New benchmarks are needed to assess how well models retain old knowledge while acquiring new information.

3. Real-World Applications

- Continual learning is essential for applications like autonomous vehicles, drones, and interactive systems where the environment and tasks continually evolve.

4. Interdisciplinary Research

- Combining insights from neuroscience, cognitive science, and machine learning can lead to more robust models capable of true lifelong learning.

Summary

Continual learning is a crucial area of research in computer vision, addressing the need for models that can adapt to new tasks without forgetting previous knowledge. By employing various techniques, such as regularization, memory-based methods, and dynamic architectures, researchers aim to build models that exhibit human-like learning capabilities. As the field progresses, continual learning will play a vital role in developing more flexible, adaptable, and intelligent vision systems.

Vision for Autonomous Drones

Autonomous drones rely heavily on computer vision to navigate, perceive their environment, and perform tasks such as surveillance, mapping, and delivery. The integration of advanced vision technologies allows drones to operate safely and efficiently in dynamic environments.

1. Key Components of Vision Systems in Drones

1. Camera Sensors

- **Types of Cameras**: Drones typically use various types of cameras, including RGB cameras, stereo cameras, and thermal cameras, to capture visual data.

- **Field of View (FOV)**: Wide-angle lenses provide a broader perspective, enabling better situational awareness and obstacle detection.

2. Depth Sensors

- **LiDAR (Light Detection and Ranging)**: Provides accurate distance measurements by emitting laser pulses and measuring the time taken for the reflections to return. Useful for creating 3D maps of the environment.
- **Ultrasonic and Radar Sensors**: Complement visual data, especially in low-visibility conditions.

2. Computer Vision Techniques for Drones

1. Object Detection and Tracking

- **Algorithms**: Techniques such as YOLO (You Only Look Once), SSD (Single Shot MultiBox Detector), and Faster R-CNN are used to detect and track objects in real-time, allowing drones to avoid obstacles and identify targets.
- **Applications**: Critical for tasks like search and rescue, wildlife monitoring, and surveillance.

2. SLAM (Simultaneous Localization and Mapping)

- **Real-Time Mapping**: SLAM techniques enable drones to build a map of an unknown environment while simultaneously keeping track of their location within it. This is essential for autonomous navigation.
- **Visual SLAM**: Utilizes visual data from cameras to estimate the drone's position and create a 3D map, improving robustness in GPS-denied environments.

3. Image Processing and Analysis

- **Feature Extraction**: Techniques like SIFT (Scale-Invariant Feature Transform) and ORB (Oriented FAST and Rotated BRIEF) help identify and match features across images for navigation and recognition tasks.
- **Image Segmentation**: Used to identify and categorize different regions in an image, aiding in object detection and scene understanding.

4. Machine Learning and Deep Learning

- **Training Models**: Deep learning models are trained on large datasets to recognize patterns, objects, and actions in visual data. Transfer learning can be used to adapt models to specific tasks.
- **Reinforcement Learning**: Enables drones to learn from interactions with their environment, optimizing their navigation and decision-making processes.

3. Challenges in Drone Vision Systems

1. Environmental Conditions

- **Lighting Variations**: Drones must perform well in various lighting conditions (e.g., bright sunlight, shadows, low light).
- **Weather Conditions**: Rain, fog, and other adverse weather can impair vision systems, necessitating robust algorithms to handle such conditions.

2. Computational Constraints

- **Real-Time Processing**: Drones require fast processing capabilities for real-time decision-making, often limiting the complexity of algorithms used.

- **Power Consumption**: Energy-efficient algorithms and hardware are crucial to prolong flight times.

3. Safety and Regulation

- **Collision Avoidance**: Drones must navigate safely around obstacles and other air traffic, necessitating reliable vision systems for real-time detection and avoidance.
- **Regulatory Compliance**: Adhering to aviation regulations regarding drone operation and data collection is essential.

4. Future Directions

1. Advanced Sensor Fusion

- Combining data from multiple sensors (cameras, LiDAR, radar) to enhance situational awareness and improve accuracy in detection and navigation.

2. AI and Machine Learning Integration

- Continued advancements in AI will lead to more sophisticated algorithms capable of adapting to changing environments and learning from new experiences.

3. Swarm Intelligence

- Using vision systems to coordinate groups of drones (swarms) for collective tasks, enhancing efficiency in applications such as agriculture, search and rescue, and surveillance.

4. Robustness in Dynamic Environments

- Researching methods to improve performance in dynamic and unpredictable environments, such as urban areas with moving obstacles.

Summary

Computer vision is a critical technology for autonomous drones, enabling them to perceive, understand, and interact with their environment effectively. By leveraging advanced algorithms, sensor technologies, and machine learning, drones can perform a wide range of tasks, from surveillance to delivery. As technology advances, the capabilities of vision systems in drones will continue to evolve, leading to safer, more efficient, and intelligent autonomous aerial vehicles.

Drone Project Code Example:

Here's a simple drone project code example that demonstrates how to use Python with OpenCV and a drone control library like dronekit to capture video from a drone's camera and perform basic object detection using a pre-trained model (e.g., YOLO).

Requirements

1. **Python** installed on your system.
2. **OpenCV** for image processing.
3. **NumPy** for numerical operations.
4. **DroneKit** for communicating with the drone.
5. **YOLOv3 weights and config files** for object detection.

Installation

You can install the necessary libraries using pip:

pip install opencv-python numpy dronekit

387

Code Example

```python
import cv2

import numpy as np

from dronekit import connect, VehicleMode

import time


# Connect to the drone

vehicle         =          connect('udp:127.0.0.1:14550',
wait_ready=True)


# Load YOLO

net = cv2.dnn.readNet("yolov3.weights", "yolov3.cfg")

layer_names = net.getLayerNames()

output_layers    =    [layer_names[i   -   1]   for   i   in
net.getUnconnectedOutLayers()]


# Function to detect objects

def detect_objects(frame):

    height, width = frame.shape[:2]

    blob = cv2.dnn.blobFromImage(frame, 0.00392, (416,
416), (0, 0, 0), True, crop=False)

    net.setInput(blob)

    outputs = net.forward(output_layers)


    boxes = []

    confidences = []

    class_ids = []
```

```
    for output in outputs:
        for detection in output:
            scores = detection[5:]
            class_id = np.argmax(scores)
            confidence = scores[class_id]
            if confidence > 0.5:
                center_x = int(detection[0] * width)
                center_y = int(detection[1] * height)
                w = int(detection[2] * width)
                h = int(detection[3] * height)

                x = int(center_x - w / 2)
                y = int(center_y - h / 2)

                boxes.append([x, y, w, h])
                confidences.append(float(confidence))
                class_ids.append(class_id)

    indexes = cv2.dnn.NMSBoxes(boxes, confidences, 0.5, 0.4)
    return boxes, confidences, class_ids, indexes


# Main loop to capture video and detect objects
try:
    while True:
```

```
        # Assume drone is in the air

    if vehicle.mode.name == "GUIDED":

        # Capture frame from drone's camera

        # Replace this with actual camera frame capture
from the drone

        frame = cv2.imread('sample_frame.jpg')      #
Placeholder for actual frame


        boxes, confidences, class_ids, indexes =
detect_objects(frame)


        for i in indexes:

            x, y, w, h = boxes[i]

            label = str(classes[class_ids[i]])

            cv2.rectangle(frame, (x, y), (x + w, y + h), (0,
255, 0), 2)

            cv2.putText(frame, label, (x, y + 30),
cv2.FONT_HERSHEY_SIMPLEX, 1, (0, 255, 0), 2)


        cv2.imshow("Drone Camera Feed", frame)


        if cv2.waitKey(1) & 0xFF == ord('q'):

            break


except KeyboardInterrupt:

    print("Exiting...")

finally:
```

vehicle.close()

cv2.destroyAllWindows()

Notes

1. **Camera Input**: Replace the line that reads cv2.imread('sample_frame.jpg') with actual camera feed acquisition code from the drone. This can vary based on the specific drone hardware and SDK.
2. **YOLO Weights and Config**: Download the yolov3.weights and yolov3.cfg files from the YOLO website and place them in the same directory as your script.
3. **Run the Script**: Make sure your drone is connected and in a controlled environment before running the script.
4. **Safety Precautions**: Always follow local regulations and safety guidelines when operating drones.

This code is a basic starting point and can be extended with more features like advanced tracking, logging, or integration with other sensors.

The Future of Vision Transformers

Vision Transformers (ViTs) have emerged as a significant advancement in computer vision, leveraging the principles of transformer architectures initially developed for natural language processing. As research continues, the future of Vision Transformers looks promising, with several key trends and potential developments.

1. Enhanced Model Architectures

1. Hybrid Models

- **Combining CNNs and Transformers**: Future architectures may integrate convolutional neural networks (CNNs) with transformers to leverage the strengths of both, capturing local features with CNNs while utilizing the global context from transformers.

2. Efficient Transformers

- **Reducing Computational Costs**: Research into more efficient transformer architectures, such as Performer and Linformer, aims to reduce the quadratic complexity of self-attention mechanisms, making them more suitable for real-time applications and resource-constrained environments.

3. Adaptive Mechanisms

- **Dynamic Attention**: Future models may incorporate dynamic attention mechanisms that adaptively focus on important regions of an image, improving performance in tasks where specific features are more relevant.

2. Applications Across Domains

1. Multimodal Learning

- **Integrating Vision and Language**: The application of Vision Transformers in multimodal learning, where visual and textual data are processed simultaneously, is expected to expand, facilitating advancements in applications like image captioning and visual question answering.

2. 3D Vision and Spatial Awareness

- **Extending to 3D Data**: Future developments may focus on applying Vision Transformers to 3D data, improving performance in areas such as robotics, autonomous driving, and augmented reality.

3. Medical Imaging

- **Precision in Diagnosis**: Vision Transformers may play a crucial role in medical imaging, providing accurate analysis and classification in radiology, pathology, and other areas, enhancing diagnostic precision and supporting healthcare professionals.

3. Improvements in Training Techniques

1. Self-Supervised Learning

- **Learning from Unlabeled Data**: The adoption of self-supervised learning techniques in training Vision Transformers could enhance their ability to generalize from limited labeled data, making them more robust across various tasks and datasets.

2. Transfer Learning and Pretraining

- **Leveraging Large Datasets**: Future models may benefit from extensive pretraining on diverse datasets, followed by fine-tuning on specific tasks, improving efficiency and performance.

4. Addressing Challenges

1. Data Efficiency

- **Reducing Data Requirements**: Ongoing research is expected to focus on making Vision Transformers more data-efficient, reducing the need for large labeled datasets while maintaining high performance.

2. Interpretability and Explainability

- **Understanding Decisions**: As Vision Transformers become more prevalent, efforts to improve their interpretability will be essential, enabling practitioners to understand model decisions, particularly in critical applications like healthcare.

5. Integration with Edge Computing

1. Real-Time Applications

- **Deploying on Edge Devices**: The optimization of Vision Transformers for deployment on edge devices (e.g., drones, IoT devices) will enable real-time processing capabilities, allowing for applications in autonomous systems, smart cities, and more.

2. Reduced Latency

- **Efficiency Improvements**: Research into lightweight models and quantization techniques will facilitate faster inference times, making Vision Transformers viable for latency-sensitive applications.

6. Community and Ecosystem Growth

1. Open Source Collaborations

- **Growing Libraries and Frameworks**: The development of open-source libraries and frameworks for Vision Transformers (e.g., Hugging Face Transformers, TIMM) will foster community collaboration and accelerate advancements in research and application.

2. Benchmarking and Competitions

- **Standardized Evaluations**: Increased participation in benchmarking and competitions will drive improvements and encourage innovation, ensuring that the field continues to advance.

Summary

The future of Vision Transformers is bright, with significant potential for enhanced architectures, broader applications, and improved training techniques. As researchers continue to address existing challenges and optimize these models for real-world applications, Vision Transformers are likely to play a central role in the next generation of computer vision technologies, driving advancements across multiple domains.

www.ingramcontent.com/pod-product-compliance
Lightning Source LLC
LaVergne TN
LVHW022333060326
832902LV00022B/4008